PRINCE2™ A Practical Handbook

GU00982750

PRINCE2™
A Practical Handbook

Third edition

Colin Bentley

AMSTERDAM • BOSTON • HEIDELBERG • LONDON • NEW YORK • OXFORD
PARIS • SAN DIEGO • SAN FRANCISCO • SINGAPORE • SYDNEY • TOKYO
Butterworth-Heinemann is an imprint of Elsevier

Butterworth-Heinemann is an imprint of Elsevier
Linacre House, Jordan Hill, Oxford OX2 8DP, UK
30 Corporate Drive, Suite 400, Burlington, MA 01803, USA

First edition 1997
Reprinted 1998, 1999
Second edition 2002
Third edition 2010

Copyright © 2010 Colin Bentley. Published by Elsevier Ltd. All rights reserved

© Crown copyright material is reproduced with the permission of the Controller of
HMSO and Queen's Printer for Scotland.

The right of Colin Bentley to be identified as the author of this work has been asserted
in accordance with the Copyright, Designs and Patents Act 1988

PRINCE2™ is a Trade Mark of the Office of Government Commerce

No part of this publication may be reproduced, stored in a retrieval system or
transmitted in any form or by any means electronic, mechanical, photocopying,
recording or otherwise without the prior written permission of the publisher

Permissions may be sought directly from Elsevier's Science & Technology Rights
Department in Oxford, UK: phone (144) (0) 1865 843830; fax: (144) (0) 1865 853333;
email: permissions@elsevier.com. Alternatively you can submit your
request online by visiting the Elsevier web site at http://elsevier.com/locate/
permissions, and selecting Obtaining permission to use Elsevier material

Notice
No responsibility is assumed by the publisher for any injury and/or damage to
persons or property as a matter of products liability, negligence or otherwise,
or from any use or operation of any methods, products, instructions or ideas
contained in the material herein.

British Library Cataloguing in Publication Data
A catalogue record for this book is available from the British Library

Library of Congress Cataloging-in-Publication Data
A catalog record for this book is available from the Library of Congress

ISBN: 978-1-85617-822-8

For information on all Butterworth-Heinemann
publications visit our website at books.elsevier.com

Printed and bound in Great Britain

10 11   10 9 8 7 6 5 4 3

Working together to grow
libraries in developing countries

www.elsevier.com | www.bookaid.org | www.sabre.org

ELSEVIER   BOOK AID
            International   Sabre Foundation

Contents

Chapter 1

Introduction

PRINCE2™ is a Trade Mark of the Office of Government Commerce. Many of the process figures in this book are based on those in the official PRINCE2 manual.

This book is intended for those who have a basic understanding of the PRINCE2™ method and want to take this further, dig deeper into understanding the method and see examples of how to use the principles of PRINCE2 in various typical situations. For those without a basic understanding of PRINCE2, I would strongly recommend the companion book, *PRINCE2 Revealed.*

'Project management is just common sense.' Of course it is. So why do so many of us get it wrong? Even if we get one project right, we probably make a mess of the next. And why do we keep getting it wrong time after time? You need to be armed with a little more than common sense when diving into a project such as constructing a pyramid. It is no good getting half way through, then remembering you forgot to put in the damp course!

Why do so many professionals say they are project managing, when what they are actually doing is firefighting?

The answer is that, where project management is concerned, most of us do not learn from our mistakes. We do not think about the process, document it, structure it, repeat it and use experience to improve the model. Problems are likely to arise in every project we tackle, but planning ahead and controlling how things happen against that plan could have avoided many of the problems the firefighter tackles.

Those who are starting a project for the first time should not have to reinvent the wheel. They should be able to build on the experience of previous project managers. By the time we are doing our tenth project we should have a method that helps us avoid mistakes we made in the previous nine.

PRINCE2 is a structured project management method based on the experience of scores of other project managers who have contributed, some from their mistakes or omissions, others from their success. It can be applied to any kind or size of project, i.e. the basic philosophy is always the same. The method should be tailored to suit the size, importance and environment of the project.

My view of the tailoring flexibility within PRINCE2 says, 'Don't use a sledge-hammer to crack a walnut', but equally do not agree to important things informally where there is any chance of a disagreement later over what was agreed.

1.1 TYPICAL PROJECT PROBLEMS

So let us have a look at some typical problems from several different points of view.

Many years ago I was asked to implement PRINCE in the computer department of a large international company. They had drawn up a list of six typical complaints from their customers.

1. The end product was not what we originally asked for.
2. The system and the project changed direction without we realizing it.
3. The costs escalated without we realizing it, then it was too late to stop it.
4. We were told the system would be delivered late, but we were only told this when it was too late for us or the computer department to supply extra effort.
5. We were in the dark during most of the development, and even now we do not really understand how to make the system work.
6. The programs are not reliable, hence maintenance costs are more than we expected.

This was an embarrassing list for them, showing that the customers were ignored during most of the project. This was apart from poor planning and control problems during the project from their own perspective.

Speaking of control, the old Hoskyns Group did a survey of projects some years ago and listed symptoms that they found to indicate projects that were out of control. You might recognize some of the following symptoms:

- Unclear direction;
- Over- or under-worked staff;
- People and equipment not available when needed;
- Examples of rework or wasted effort;
- The final tasks were rushed;
- Poor quality work;
- Projects late and overspent;
- Small problems had a big impact.

But why do these problems occur? Their causes show the reasons why a formal project management method is needed:

- Lack of customer involvement;
- Lack of coordination;
- Lack of communication;
- Inadequate planning;

- Lack of progress control;
- Lack of quality control;
- Insufficient measurables.

So there we have it. Without good project management projects will:

- Take more time than expected;
- Cost more than expected;
- Deliver a product that is not exactly what the customer wants;
- Deliver a product of inadequate quality;
- Not reveal their exact status until they finish (If they ever do!).

These experiences show us why a good project management method such as PRINCE2 is needed if our projects are to be well managed and controlled.

1.2 BENEFITS OF A PROJECT MANAGEMENT METHOD

- The method is repeatable.
- It builds on experience.
- Everyone knows what to expect.
- If you take over a project in the middle, you know what documents to look for and where to find them.
- There is early warning of problems.
- It is proactive not reactive (but has to be prepared to be reactive to unexpected events – illness, pregnancy, accident, external event).

Organizations are becoming increasingly aware of the opportunities for adopting a 'project' approach to the way in which they address the creation and delivery of new business products or implement any change. They are also increasingly aware of the benefits which a single, common, structured approach to project management – as is provided through PRINCE2 – can bring.

Chapter 2

An Overview of PRINCE2

2.1 INTRODUCTION

All organizations need to change, and move on in order to survive. Standing still often means going backwards. But normal business operations have to go on, so an organization has to do two things:

1. Carry on with everyday business operations;
2. Change and upgrade those operations to match the direction and strategies needed for the future.

The changing and upgrading is done by projects.

1. PRINCE2 is a scalable, flexible project management method, suitable for use on any type of project. It has been derived from professional project managers' experiences and refined over years of use in a wide variety of contexts. It is owned by a stable public authority, the Office of Government Commerce (OGC), and is available free of charge for users. OGC has an ongoing commitment to maintaining the currency of the method, together with the manual and other books used to define the method.

PRINCE2 gives:

1. Controlled management of change by the business in terms of its investment and return on investment;
2. Active involvement of the users of the final product throughout its development to ensure the business product will meet the functional, environmental, service and management requirements of the users;
3. More efficient control of development resources.

A key approach of the method is that it firmly distinguishes the *management* of the development process from the *techniques* involved in the development process itself.

2.2 PROJECT CHARACTERISTICS

PRINCE2 believes that there are five characteristics of project work that make
a project different to regular business operations:

1. **Change:** We use projects to introduce change to a business.
2. **Uncertainty:** A project changes one or more things or develops something
   new. These are steps into the unknown, introducing uncertainty in what will
   be ahead of us in the project.
3. **Temporary:** A project team comes together, does a job and is then
   disbanded.
4. **Unique:** In some major or minor ways each project is unique. It may be
   completely unlike anything we have done before, or we may have repeated
   the same job several times, but at a different location or with different
   people.
5. **Cross-functional:** A project needs different people with different skills;
   some to define what is required, others to develop the required products.
   Another problem is that they probably work for several different line managers, maybe even different companies. So managing these resources is
   another problem for the Project Manager.

2.3 PROJECT PERFORMANCE VARIABLES

If a project is to be successful, there are six project performance variables to
control:

1. Cost;
2. Time;
3. Quality;
4. Scope;
5. Benefits;
6. Risk.

2.4 KEY PRINCIPLES

There are seven principles on which PRINCE2 is founded (Figure 2.1). This
set of principles is unique to the PRINCE2 method. As you read this book, you
will see how they are interwoven with the processes and themes to form a tre-
mendously strong structure.

The seven PRINCE2 principles are:

1. Continued business justification;
2. Learn from experience;
3. Defined roles and responsibilities;

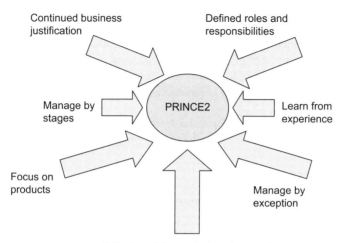

FIGURE 2.1   The seven PRINCE2 Principles.

- Manage by stages;
- Manage by exception;
- Focus on products;
- Tailor to suit the project environment.

The seven principles are explained below.

2.4.1 Continued Business Justification

PRINCE2 states that a project should be driven by its Business Case. Even projects to meet compulsory requirements should be justified. The existence of a viable Business Case should be proved before the project is allowed to start and its continued justification should be confirmed at all major decision points during the project. This principle can be summarized in the following points:

- Do not start a project unless there is a sound Business Case for it.
- Check that the project is still viable at regular intervals in the project.
- Stop the project if the justification has disappeared.
- The Business Case should be:
  - Documented and approved;
  - The basis for all decision-making.
- Ensure the project remains aligned to its business objectives and the expected benefits.

Justification may change, but must remain valid.

2.4.2 Learn from Experience

Project management should never be 'reinventing the wheel'. Those involved in the project may have previous experience, there will be earlier projects in the company from which lessons can be learned and there are other sources (e.g. the web, suppliers, sister companies) of valuable lessons that can be used by the project.

Lessons should be sought at the beginning of a project (in the process *Starting up a Project*), learned as the project progresses and passed on to other projects at the close.

2.4.3 Defined Roles and Responsibilities

Project management is different from line management.

Projects require a temporary organization for a finite timescale for a specific business purpose. Managing the project staff can be a headache for a Project Manager. A project is temporary and may include staff who report to different line managers or even work for other organizations. The project may require a mixture of full- and part-time resources. So how do we have everyone know who is responsible for what?

An explicit project management team structure is required. People must know what their and other people's responsibilities are. Good communication depends on this.

The roles and responsibilities are divided into three groups, the interests of which must be represented in any project (Figure 2.2). These are:

- Business;
- User;
- Supplier.

PRINCE2 provides an organization structure that engages everyone involved: the business, user and supplier stakeholder interests. Within the structure there are defined roles and responsibilities for every member of the project management team. The chosen people agree to a role description and sign their acceptance of that role. (Depending on the size of the project, roles can be split or combined.)

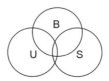

FIGURE 2.2   Business, user and supplier interests.

2.4.4 Manage by Stages

This comes from two different thoughts:

1. If the Project Board is, in PRINCE2 terms, ultimately accountable for the project and PRINCE2 does not like the idea of regular progress meetings, there must be some key points in a project when the Project Board needs to review progress and decide if it wants to continue with the project.
2. Very often a project will last longer and contain more detail than can be planned with any accuracy at the outset.

Based on these thoughts, PRINCE2 divides a project into management stages. PRINCE2 has a Project Plan, an overview of the whole project, which is often a 'best guess', but the Project Manager plans only the next stage in detail – only as much as can be accurately judged – and the Project Board keeps control by approving only one stage at a time, reviewing the status at stage end and deciding whether to continue or not.

The number of stages depends on the size, complexity and risk content of the project.

At the end of each stage, a plan is presented, together with an updated view of the Business Case, the Project Plan, the risks and suggested tolerances for the next stage. Thus senior management can review progress so far and decide from the information presented to them whether or not to authorize the next stage.

2.4.5 Manage by Exception

PRINCE2 recognizes four levels of authority in a project. Authority is delegated from one management level to the next. Each management level is allocated tolerances within which it can continue without the need to refer to the next higher level of management. There are six tolerance limits:

1. **Time:** $+/-$ an amount of time on the target completion dates.
2. **Cost:** $+/-$ amounts of planned budget.
3. **Quality:** $+/-$ degrees off a quality target, e.g. a product that weighs a target 10k (with an allowed $-50\,g$ to $+10\,g$ tolerance).
4. **Scope:** Permissible variation of the plan's products, e.g. mandatory requirements $+/-$ desirable requirements.
5. **Risk:** Limits on the plan's exposure to threats (e.g. the risk of not meeting the target date against the risk of overspending).
6. **Benefit:** $+/-$ degrees off an improvement goal (e.g. 30–40% staff saving).

To cut down on unnecessary meetings or problem referrals, PRINCE2 has the principle of allowing a management level to continue its work as long as there is no forecast that a tolerance will be exceeded. Only when there is a forecast of a tolerance being exceeded does the next higher level of authority need to be consulted.

2.4.6 Focus on Products

A PRINCE2 project focuses on the definition and delivery of products, in particular their quality requirements. Planning, controls and quality needs are all product based.

2.4.7 Tailor to Suit the Project Environment

PRINCE2 is tailored to suit the project's environment, size, risk, complexity, importance and capability of the people involved. Tailoring is considered before the project begins; roles may be split or combined, processes and documents may be combined, it may be agreed that some reports can be oral and some decisions made by phone or e-mail, rather than at meetings.

2.5 STRUCTURE OF THE PRINCE2 METHOD

There are three parts to the structure of the method itself:

- Principles;
- Themes;
- Processes.

PRINCE2 offers a set of *processes* that provide a controlled start, a controlled progress and a controlled close to any project. The processes explain what should happen and when it should be done.

PRINCE2 has a number of *themes* to explain its philosophy about various project aspects, why they are needed and how they can be used. This philosophy is implemented through the processes.

PRINCE2 offers only a few *techniques*. The use of most of them is optional. You may already have a technique which is covering that need satisfactorily. The exception is the product-based planning technique. This is a very important part of the PRINCE2 method. Its understanding and use bring major benefits and every effort should be made to use it.

PRINCE2 has a process-based approach to project management. The processes define the management activities to be carried out during the project. In addition, PRINCE2 describes a number of themes that are applied within the appropriate processes. Figure 2.3 shows the themes positioned around the central process model.

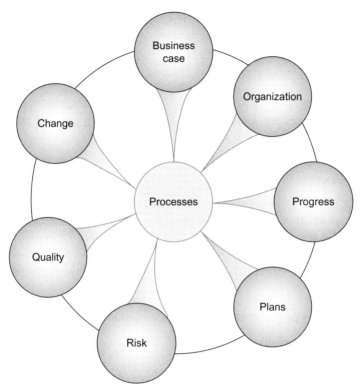

FIGURE 2.3 The PRINCE2 themes.

2.6 THE THEMES

The themes of PRINCE2 are discussed as follows.

2.6.1 Business Case

Every project should be driven by a business need. If it has no justification in terms of the business, it should not be undertaken. The Project Board should check the existence of a valid Business Case before the project begins and at every end stage assessment.

2.6.2 Organization

PRINCE2 provides the structure of a project management team, plus a definition of the roles, responsibilities and relationships of all staff involved in the project. PRINCE2 describes *roles*. According to the size and complexity of a project, these roles can be combined or shared.

2.6.3 Plans

PRINCE2 offers a series of plan levels that can be tailored to the size and needs of a project, and an approach to planning based on products rather than activities.

2.6.4 Progress

PRINCE2 has a set of controls which facilitate the provision of key decision-making information, allowing the organization to preempt problems and make decisions on problem resolution. For senior management. PRINCE2 controls are based on the concept of 'management by exception', i.e. if we agree a plan, let the Project Manager get on with it unless something is forecast to go wrong.

A project is split into stages as a way of defining the review and commit-ment points of a project in order to promote sound management control of risk and investment.

2.6.5 Risk

Risk is a major factor to be considered during the life of a project. PRINCE2 defines the key moments when risks should be reviewed, outlines an approach to the analysis and management of risk, and tracks these through all the processes.

2.6.6 Quality

PRINCE2 recognizes the importance of quality and incorporates a quality approach to the management and technical processes. It begins by establish-ing the customer's quality expectations and follows these up by laying down standards and quality inspection methods to be used, and checking that these are being used correctly throughout the project life cycle.

2.6.7 Change

The Change theme covers change control and configuration management, two tasks that go hand in hand.

PRINCE2 emphasizes the need for change control and this is enforced by a change control procedure plus identification of the processes that apply the change control.

Tracking the components of a final product and their versions for release is called 'Configuration Management'. There are many methods of configuration management available. PRINCE2 does not attempt to invent a new one, but defines the essential facilities and information requirements for a configuration management method and how it should link with other PRINCE2 themes and techniques.

2.7 THE PROCESSES

The steps of project management are described in seven processes, which are summarized in Figure 2.4.

Any project run under PRINCE2 will need to address each of these processes *in some form*. However, the key to successful use of the process model is in tailoring it to the needs of the individual project. Each process should be approached with the question 'How extensively should this process be applied on this project?'

2.7.1 Directing a Project (DP)

This process is aimed at the Project Board, the management team representing the sponsor, the users of the final product and the suppliers of the product. These people are responsible for the project, the key decision-makers. They are usually very busy people and should be involved in only the decision-making process of a project. PRINCE2 helps them achieve this by adopting the philosophy of 'management by exception'. The DP process covers the steps to be taken by this Project Board throughout the project from start-up to project closure and has five major steps:

1. Authorizing the preparation of a Project Plan and Business Case for the project;
2. Approving the project go-ahead;
3. Checking that the project remains justifiable at key points in the project life cycle;
4. Monitoring progress and giving advice as required;
5. Ensuring that the project comes to a controlled close.

2.7.2 Starting up a Project (SU)

This is intended to be a very short pre-project process with six objectives:

1. Design and appoint the project management team.
2. Ensure that the objectives and scope of the project are known.
3. Decide on the approach which will be taken within the project to provide a solution.

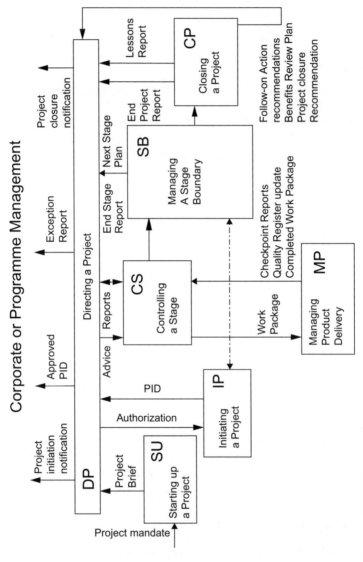

FIGURE 2.4   The seven PRINCE2 processes.

4. Identify the customer's quality expectations.
5. Ensure that there is business justification for initiating the project.
6. Plan the work needed to draw up the PRINCE2 'contract' between customer and supplier.

2.7.3 Initiating a Project (IP)

This process identifies how the required quality will be achieved and creates a Project Plan to give a guide on how long the project will take and what the cost is likely to be. It then prepares the information on whether there is sufficient justification to proceed with the project, establishes a sound management basis for the project and creates a detailed plan for the next stage – as much of the project as management wish to authorize. The management product created is the Project Initiation Document (PID), the baseline against which progress and success will be measured.

2.7.4 Controlling a Stage (CS)

This process describes the monitoring and control activities of the Project Manager involved in ensuring that a stage stays on course and reacts to unexpected events. The process forms the core of the Project Manager's effort on the project, being the process that handles day-to-day management of the project development activity.

Throughout a stage there will be many cycles of:

- Authorizing work to be done;
- Gathering progress information about that work;
- Watching for changes;
- Watching for changes in risks;
- Reviewing the stage status;
- Reporting;
- Taking any necessary corrective action.

The process covers these activities, together with the ongoing work of risk management and change control.

2.7.5 Managing Product Delivery (MP)

This process provides a control mechanism so that the Project Manager and specialist teams can agree on the details of the work required. This is particularly important where one or more teams are from third-party suppliers not using PRINCE2. The work agreed upon between the Project Manager and the Team Manager, including target dates, quality and reporting requirements, is called a Work Package.

The process covers:

- Making sure that work allocated to the team is authorized and agreed upon;
- Planning the team work;
- Ensuring that the work is done;
- Ensuring that products meet the agreed quality criteria;
- Reporting on progress and quality to the Project Manager;
- Obtaining acceptance of the finished products.

2.7.6 Managing a Stage Boundary (SB)

The objectives of this process are to:

- Check that all work from the current stage is finished;
- Plan the next stage;
- Update the Project Plan;
- Update the Business Case;
- Update the risk assessment;
- Report on the outcome and performance of the stage which has just ended;
- Obtain Project Board approval to move into the next stage.

If the Project Board requests the Project Manager to produce an Exception Plan (see 'Progress' for an explanation), this process also covers the steps needed for that.

2.7.7 Closing a Project (CP)

The process covers the Project Manager's work to request Project Board permission to close the project either at its natural end or at a premature close decided by the Project Board. The objectives are to:

- Note the extent to which the objectives set out at the start of the project have been met;
- Confirm the customer's satisfaction with the products;
- Confirm that maintenance and support arrangements are in place (where appropriate);
- Make any recommendations for follow-on actions;
- Ensure that all lessons learned during the project are annotated for the benefit of future projects;
- Report on whether the project management activity itself has been a success;
- Prepare a plan to check on achievement of the final product's claimed benefits.

2.8 STRUCTURE OF THIS BOOK

Having gone through an introduction and overview of the method, the book will explore the processes and themes. This will provide a project skeleton and a general project time frame. Where appropriate there will be links from processes to the themes. The book also includes sample descriptions of the PRINCE2 roles and standard product descriptions.

Chapter 3

Starting up a Project (SU)

3.1 WHAT DOES THE PROCESS DO?

How does a project start? 'Project mandate' is the term used in PRINCE2 to describe the trigger for a project. The project mandate handed down to the Project Manager may be a full specification of the problem, a brief, written request to 'look into' something or 'do something about ....', or even a verbal request (Figure 3.1). This activity will turn this request (over whose format there may have been no control by the Project Manager) into a Project Brief, a complete set of terms of reference (Cartoon 3.1).

The process carries out the following tasks:

- Appoints (at least most of) the project management team;
- Completes (or confirms the existence of) terms of reference for the project (Project Brief);
- Ascertains the customer's quality expectations;
- Checks for lessons from earlier projects from which the project can learn;
- Checks that there is sufficient justification for requesting the resources to initiate a project (outline Business Case);

CARTOON 3.1 Project mandate.

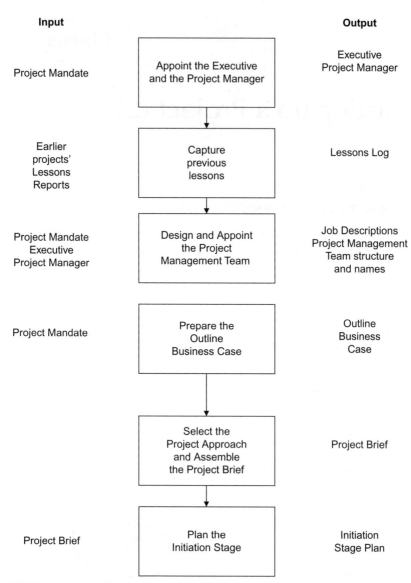

FIGURE 3.1 Starting up a project.

- Defines the Acceptance Criteria;
- Identifies the type of solution to be provided (the project approach);
- Plans the initiation stage.

3.2 WHY?

The purpose of this process is to gather basic information about what the project's scope is, what level of quality is required from the finished product, what measurements the customer will apply to check that the 'finished' product is acceptable and what the approach will be to providing a solution. At least one decision-maker (the Executive) must be appointed in order to look at the information gathered and decide if there is enough to justify proceeding to initiate a project. All of this work must be managed, so we also need a Project Manager to be appointed.

The process has to establish:

- What is to be done?
- Who will make the decisions?
- Who is funding the project?
- Who will say what is needed?
- What quality is required?
- Who will provide the resources to do the work?

3.3 APPOINT THE EXECUTIVE AND PROJECT MANAGER

3.3.1 What Does the Activity Do?

- Corporate/programme management appoint the Executive and Project Manager, prepare job descriptions for them (Figure 3.2).

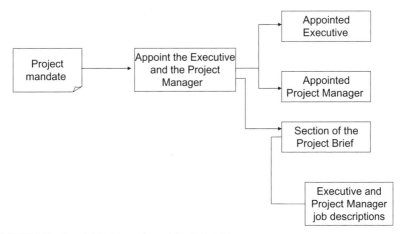

FIGURE 3.2   Appoint the Executive and the Project Manager.

3.3.2 Why?

Every project needs a sponsor, the key decision-maker. But normally this person is too busy to manage the project on a day-to-day basis. So we also need a Project Manager to do the planning and control. We need to identify these two people before anything can happen (in a controlled manner) in a project.

3.3.3 Responsibility

Corporate/programme management appoint the Executive. The Executive appoints the Project Manager, but may need agreement from corporate or programme management. .

3.3.4 How?	Links to other parts of the book
Corporate/programme management identify the Executive to be responsible for the project.	Organization theme and B.2
Either corporate/programme management or the Executive or both identify a suitable Project Manager.	Organization theme and B.5
The standard PRINCE2 role descriptions for their jobs are tailored by discussion between corporate/programme management and the Executive and Project Manager.	Appendix B
The tailored roles are typed up; both people sign two copies of their job descriptions. The individual keeps one; the other is kept in the project file once the project filing system has been set up.	
The Project Manager sets up a Daily Log for the project.	13.7.4.9

3.3.5 In Practice

The Executive:

- Holds the purse strings for the project;
- Has to ensure that the project meets company strategies;
- Has to ensure that there is always a valid Business Case in existence.

The Executive should have strong links with the senior management group responsible for this appointment. Ideally the person nominated should be one of that group, e.g. a member of the programme management team. It is necessary to have a strong bond of confidence between corporate/programme management and the Executive. This person will be making key decisions on their behalf. If the higher level of management wants to check every decision made by the Executive, this will slow down the entire project process. The relationship between the Executive and corporate/programme management should be similar to that between the Project Board and the Project Manager, i.e. 'As long as work is progressing within laid down constraints, then get on with it. We will back you up.'

3.3.6 For Small Projects

A small project is more likely to be stand-alone. There may be no corporate/ programme management involved with the project. In this case the sponsor becomes the Executive by default and would appoint the Project Manager personally. Some of the Project Board roles can be combined, such as the Executive and Senior User roles. There may be no need for any Team Managers, their work reverting to the Project Manager. There may be no Project Support needed to assist the Project Manager. One of the project team may be appointed as Configuration Librarian.

3.4 CAPTURE PREVIOUS LESSONS

3.4.1 What Does the Activity Do?

- Looks at Lessons Reports from other projects to see if any lessons can be learned and applied to the current project (Figure 3.3).

3.4.2 Why?

It would be foolish to repeat the mistakes of earlier projects or to fail to benefit from their successes.

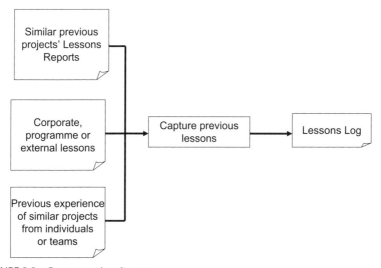

FIGURE 3.3   Capture previous lessons.

3.4.3 Responsibility

The Project Manager.

3.4.4 How?	Links to other parts of the book
Create a Lessons Log for the project.	A.14
Review Lessons Reports from earlier projects, especially ones with similarities to the current one. Talk to those with previous experience on similar projects. Document any useful lessons in this project's Lessons Log.	A.15

3.4.5 In Practice

This depends on a number of factors; how experienced you are, how many Lessons Reports you can call on (probably not many if you are not working in a PRINCE2 environment), are lessons recorded by the Project Assurance group or center of expertise, how experienced are your team members and so on.

3.4.6 For Small Projects

Do not be afraid to ask around. People who have run completely dissimilar projects may remember lessons that will be useful to you, such as 'build enough time in the plan for you to do your project management work as well as any technical work you have to do'.

3.5 DESIGN AND APPOINT THE PROJECT MANAGEMENT TEAM

3.5.1 What Does the Activity Do?

- Proposes the other Project Board members.
- Discusses with the Project Board members whether they will need help to carry out their Project Assurance responsibilities.
- Designs any separate Project Assurance roles.
- Identifies candidates for any separate Project Assurance roles.
- Identifies any required Team Managers.
- Appoints the other Project Board members, any required Project Assurance and Project Support roles. There may also be Team Managers appointed, particularly for the early stages.
- Identifies any Project Support requirements (Figure 3.4).

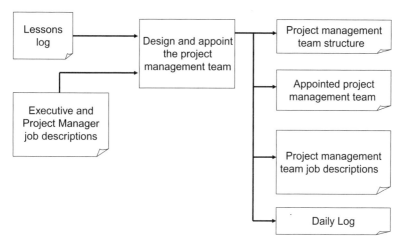

FIGURE 3.4   Design and appoint the project management team.

3.5.2 Why?

You need to know who the users of the final product will be and who makes decisions for them. Who controls the resources? Who will create the required products? Is the project big enough to need Team Managers? Is there a central service that will supply Configuration Librarian support to the project? A job description for each member of the project management team needs to be agreed with the individual.

The complete project management team needs to reflect the interests, and have the approval of:

• Corporate/programme management;
• The users of the final product, those who will specify details of the required product;
• The supplier(s) of that product.

After the project management team has been designed, the appointments need to be confirmed by corporate/programme management.

Project Board members must decide whether they want independent checks on their particular interests in the project as the project progresses (the Project Assurance part of the role), or whether they can do this verification themselves.

The Project Manager has to decide if any administrative support is needed, such as planning and control tool expertise, configuration management, filing or help with specialist techniques.

3.5.3 Responsibility

The Executive is responsible for the work of the process, but is likely to delegate much of the work to the Project Manager.

3.5.4 How?	Links to other parts of the book
Are there any lessons about setting up a project management team to be learned from previous Lessons Reports?	A.15
Identify customer areas that will use or control the end product, the commitment required and the level of authority and decision-making which is suitable for the criticality and size of the project (Senior User).	Organization theme
Identify who will provide the end product(s) (Supplier) and the level of commitment and authority required from them. • Identify candidates for the roles. • Check out their availability and provisional agreement.	B.4
Check whether the Project Board members will carry out their own Project Assurance responsibilities.	B.1 and B.7
Try to find out what volume of change requests might come in during the project. If it is high, discuss with the proposed Project Board if it wants to appoint a Change Authority to handle change request decisions.	Change theme
Identify candidates for any Project Assurance functions which are to be delegated.	B.7
Check out their availability.	
Decide if any Project Support will be required.	B.8
Identify resources for any required support.	
The project management team design is presented to corporate/programme management for approval.	
The Executive informs each project management team member of their appointment.	
The Project Manager discusses and agrees each member's job description with them.	Appendix B
Capture any identified risks in the Daily Log.	A.7

3.5.5 In Practice

Corporate/programme management may have already defined some or all of the composition of the Project Board, particularly where the project is part of a programme.

If the project is part of a programme, the use of the programme's assurance and support functions may be imposed.

If the management of many different user areas is looking for Project Board representation, it may be more effective to form a user committee, whose chair represents all user area interests on the Project Board. An alternative approach to having lots of suppliers sharing the Senior Supplier role is to appoint the user's Purchasing Manager as Senior Supplier. This person then controls the suppliers and commits their resources via a series of contracts.

In theory the Project Board should decide on what action to take about project issues. If the volume is likely to be high, the board may choose to appoint a Change Authority to assess all issues on their behalf. This Change Authority might be the same body as those charged with Project Assurance, or may be a small group of representative user managers. If appointed, the Project Board should give a Change Budget to such a body. This is usually accompanied by a couple of constraints, such as 'No more than X on any one change, no more than Y spent in any stage without reference to the Project Board.'

3.5.6 For Small Projects

There may be no need to get approval from any higher level of authority than the Executive. There may be no Project Support functions. If Project Board roles are to be amalgamated, it may be sufficient to use the standard role descriptions listed in this book.

It would be normal for Project Board members to carry out their own Project Assurance. In very small projects the Executive and Senior User roles will often be combined. If a department is developing a product for its own use and all the project's resources are from that department, the Senior Supplier and Senior User may also be the same person as the Executive.

3.6 PREPARE THE OUTLINE BUSINESS CASE

3.6.1 What Does the Activity Do?

- The activity prepares a high-level view of the justification for the project – at least enough to justify the expenditure needed to initiate a project. At this point it may only be a set of reasons why the project is needed. The project mandate may contain a suitable outline; otherwise it has to be developed. The outline will be expanded into a full Business Case in the *Initiating a Project* process (Figure 3.5).

3.6.2 Why?

It is very easy to spend all the time in a project on the design and creation of products. This is the interesting stuff, and there is often a lot of senior management pressure to 'just get it done'. With this attitude it is easy to overlook why

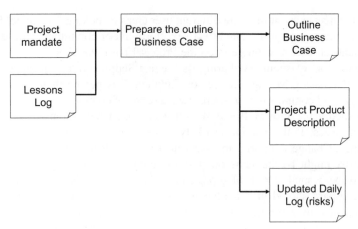

FIGURE 3.5   Prepare the outline Business Case.

the project is being done and whether the benefits will outweigh the cost of the project.

3.6.3 Responsibility

The responsibility lies with the Executive, but often the Project Manager will be asked to do a lot of research and presentation.

3.6.4 How?	Links to other parts of the book
The Executive prepares the outline Business Case: • Understand the background of the project request; • Understand the objectives of, and the reasons for, the project as, hopefully, defined in the project mandate. Otherwise obtain this information from interviews, any feasibility study or other documents; • Check the objectives against corporate/programme objectives and strategies; • Identify from where the funding will come; • Review the Lessons Log for any lessons that might affect the business justification.	B.2
Ensure that corporate/programme management agree with the prepared outline Business Case.	

The Project Manager creates the Project Product Description:	Quality theme and A.25
• Identify the customer's quality expectations; • Identify and agree the final product's acceptance criteria; • Check the feasibility of achieving any mentioned timescale for the project; • Add any new risks to the Daily Log.	
Summarize any key risks to viability in the outline Business Case.	B.2

3.6.5 In Practice

At this early point only the reasons for wanting the project may be known. You may be lucky and find that there was an earlier feasibility study that estimated some of the benefits, but beware; these are notoriously optimistic.

The Project Manager should remember that it is a responsibility of the Project Board, particularly the Executive, to produce the Business Case, not the Project Manager.

3.6.6 For Small Projects

There is always the temptation in small projects to assume that a Business Case is not necessary, its creation a waste of time, holding you back from getting on with the job. An outline Business Case normally takes only a few lines in a small project, but it is always worthwhile finding out the reasons for the project and doing a little common sense check on the validity of these reasons. It stops you from being embarrassed when corporate management ask 'Why are you doing this project?'

A long time ago when online computing was just beginning, a large computer company had an off-line system that would break down data on future sales into inventory demands on a number of factories. This was to avoid under- and over-production of expensive components. A small team of programmers was assembled and produced an online version of this. When the programmes were done, the sales chief was invited in, seated down in front of a terminal and asked to input a set of sales figures. This took almost an hour. The sales chief then asked how long it would be before the results would appear on the screen. The answer was about four hours. When the figures were eventually ready, the sales chief had to scroll through about 200 screens full of the data, which was not as quick as sifting through a printout. The project, although only small in terms of manpower, was a complete waste of time and effort, and could have been easily avoided by checking the benefits in an outline Business Case.

3.7 SELECT THE PROJECT APPROACH AND ASSEMBLE THE PROJECT BRIEF

3.7.1 What Does the Activity Do?

- Decides what kind of a solution (project approach) will be provided and the general method of providing that solution;
- Identifies the skills required by the project approach;
- Identifies any timing implications of the project approach (Figure 3.6).
- Fills in any gaps in the project mandate handed down.

The main project approaches to be considered are:

- Build a solution from scratch.
- Take an existing product and modify it.
- Give the job to another organization to do for you.
- Buy a ready-made solution off the shelf.

3.7.2 Why?

The project approach will affect the timescale and costs of the project, plus possibly its scope and quality. This information should be made available to the Project Board in deciding whether to initiate the project.

A check should be made that the proposed project approach is in line with the customer's (or programme) strategy.

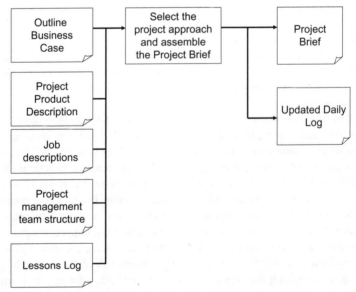

FIGURE 3.6 Select the project approach and assemble the Project Brief. © Crown copyright material (source Managing Successful Projects with PRINCE2 as produced by OGC).

The Project Brief is to ensure that sufficient information is available for the Project Board to decide if it wishes to proceed into initiation.

3.7.3 Responsibility

The Project Manager is responsible for examining the project mandate and collecting any missing details, and also for preparing the project approach. The outline Business Case is the responsibility of the Executive.

3.7.4 How?	Links to other parts of the book
Identify any time, money, resource, support or extension constraints.	
Check for any direction or guidance on project approach from earlier documents such as the project mandate or corporate/programme strategies.	A.24
Check the Lessons Log, current industry thinking and any new techniques or tools available for any help about project approach. • Identify any security constraints. • Check for any corporate/programme statement of direction which might constrain the choice of project approach. • Produce a range of alternative project approaches. • Identify the training needs of the alternatives. • Compare the alternatives against the gathered information and constraints. • Consider how the product might be brought into use and whether there are any problems which would impact the choice of project approach. • Prepare a recommendation.	A.14
Compare the information available about the required project against the information required by the Project Board in order to approve project initiation. Gather any missing information.	
Assemble the Project Brief.	A.22
Add to the Daily Log any risks shown in the Project Brief.	A.7

3.7.5 In Practice

Be careful about how you go about this. Although the activity title suggests that you can sort out the project approach before doing the Project Brief, you need to do it the other way round. The Project Brief contains the objectives, scope, constraints, and you cannot say how you will approach the provision of a solution before you know what the problem and objectives are.

The customer needs to think very carefully about the project approach. Preparation of the above information can avoid the customer being pushed into a project approach which is favoured by a supplier, but which turns out to have later problems for the customer, such as lack of flexibility or maintenance difficulties.

There may have been an earlier feasibility study that looked at a number of different options for achieving the end objective and selected one that will be the basis for your project. If the project is part of a programme, a Project Brief may have already been provided, thus rendering this process unnecessary.

The Project Manager should informally check out the Project Brief with Project Board members to ensure there are no problems before formal presentation.

3.7.6 For Small Projects

There may be pressure on the Project Manager to 'get on with the job' and start with incomplete terms of reference. This should be resisted as it opens up the possibility of disagreement later on what the project was supposed to do (scope). The Project Manager also needs to know how much the solution is worth in order to make appropriate judgments if changes occur later.

3.8 PLAN THE INITIATION STAGE

3.8.1 What Does the Activity Do?

● Produces a plan for the initiation stage of the project (Figure 3.7).

3.8.2 Why?

Preparing a document to get approval to start the project is important work. It needs planning, and since initiation will consume some resources, the Project Board should approve the plan for it.

3.8.3 Responsibility

The Project Manager.

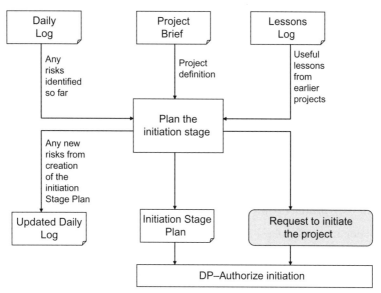

FIGURE 3.7 Plan the initiation stage. © Crown copyright material (source Managing Successful Projects with PRINCE2 as produced by OGC).

3.8.4 How?	Links to other parts of the book
Examine the Project Brief and decide how much work is needed in order to produce the Project Initiation Document.	A.23
Evaluate the time needed to create the Project Plan.	Plans theme
Evaluate the time needed to create the next Stage Plan after initiation.	Plans theme
Evaluate the time needed to create or refine the Business Case.	Business Case theme
Review risks in the Daily Log to see if any might affect the initiation stage. Evaluate the time needed to perform risk analysis.	A.7
Define the reporting and control arrangements for initiation.	Progress theme
Create a plan for the initiation stage.	Plans theme
Update the Daily Log with any changed or new risks.	Risk
Get Project Board approval for the plan.	DP process

3.8.5 In Practice

The initiation stage should normally be short and inexpensive compared to the cost and time of the whole project, say 2% or 3% of the whole.

The Project Initiation Document is an extension of the Project Brief to include details of the project management team and risk analysis, plus a refinement of the Business Case and the Project Plan. The initiation Stage Plan should show the effort and resources to generate the extra information and the plan for the next stage.

If informal communication with members of the Project Board is to be frequent during initiation, this can reduce the need for formal reporting.

3.8.6 For Small Projects

Initiation may only take a matter of an hour or two and therefore may not need a formal plan.

Chapter 4

Initiating a Project (IP)

4.1 WHAT DOES THE PROCESS DO?

- Defines the quality standards, responsibilities, quality methods and tools to be used;
- Plans the whole project;
- Lays the foundation for a well-planned and controlled project;
- Confirms the existence of a viable Business Case;
- Re-assesses the risks facing the project;
- Gets all the decision-makers signed up to the project (Figure 4.1).

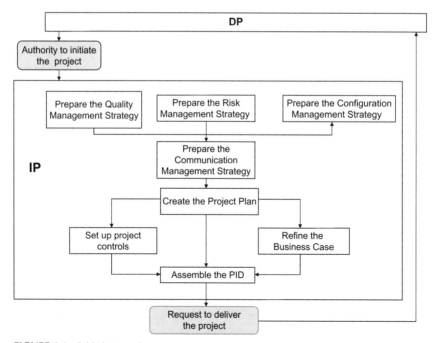

FIGURE 4.1 Initiating a project.

CARTOON 4.1 Project Board.

4.2 WHY?

All stakeholders with interest in the project should reach agreement before major expenditure starts on what is to be done; how, when and why it is being done; the expected benefits and how the required quality will be achieved (Cartoon 4.1).

4.3 PREPARE THE QUALITY MANAGEMENT STRATEGY

4.3.1 What Does the Activity Do?

- Takes the quality expectations of the customer, the quality standards of both customer and supplier and the project approach, and defines how the quality expected by the customer will be achieved (Figure 4.2).

4.3.2 Why?

To be successful, the project must deliver a quality product, as well as meeting time and cost constraints. The means of achieving quality must be specified and agreed before work begins.

Quality work cannot be planned until the quality expectations of the customer are known.

The time and cost of the project will be affected by the amount of quality work that has to be done; therefore, quality planning must be done before a realistic Project Plan can be produced.

4.3.3 Responsibility

The Project Manager and those with Project Assurance responsibilities are responsible for quality planning.

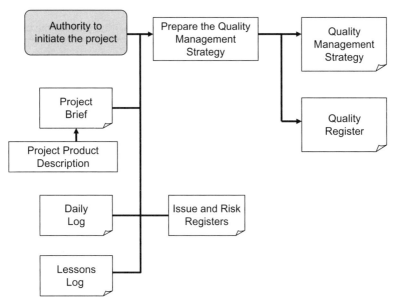

FIGURE 4.2 Prepare the Quality Management Strategy.

4.3.4 How?	Links to other parts of the book
Review the Project Product Description to understand the customer's quality expectations. • Establish links to any corporate/programme quality assurance function. • Establish what the customer's quality standards are. • Establish what the supplier quality standards are.	Quality theme and A.25
Review the Lessons Log for any lessons from earlier projects that might affect quality.	SU and A.14
Check the Daily Log for anything that affects product quality (unless the Risk and Issue Registers have been created already).	A.7
Decide if there is a need for an independent quality assurance function to have representation on the project management team.	Quality theme
Identify quality responsibility for project products of both the customer and supplier in their job descriptions.	Role Descriptions (Appendix B)

(Continued)

4.3.4 How?	Links to other parts of the book
Define the Quality Management Strategy, including: • The procedures to be used for quality planning, quality control and quality assurance; • Any tools and techniques to be used in achieving or checking quality; • Quality records to be kept; • Quality responsibilities (see the two entries above before 'Define the QMS').	A.26
Create a Quality Register.	Quality theme

4.3.5 In Practice

For in-house projects there may be no doubt about the quality standards to be used, but where customer and supplier are from different companies it is necessary to agree and document which standards will be used. In such circumstances it is important that the Project Manager specifies how the quality of the products from the supplier will be checked. Sensibly, this would be done by customer involvement in the supplier's quality testing (Cartoon 4.2).

4.3.6 For Small Projects

Even if the customer leaves the quality checking to the developer, there should be customer involvement in specifying the testing environment and the test situations with which the products should successfully cope.

But it's better than we've ever had before!!

Let me see your Quality Management Strategy. – Hmmm, 'Don't make mistakes' – Seems a little abrupt?

CARTOON 4.2 Quality Management Strategy.

4.4 PREPARE THE RISK MANAGEMENT STRATEGY

4.4.1 What Does the Activity Do?

- The Risk Management Strategy describes the procedures to be used for risk identification and management, when these procedures should be carried out and risk responsibilities (Figure 4.3).

4.4.2 Why?

As projects deal with change, the potential for risks will be ever-present. A project needs to prepare in advance how it will deal with risks.

4.4.3 Responsibility

The Project Manager will handle risk management. The Project Board has responsibilities to make the Project Manager aware of external risks, any coming from possible changes to corporate strategies or changes in the composition of the Project Board. The Project Board is also required to make decisions on risk responses recommended by the Project Manager.

4.4.4 How?	Links to other parts of the book
Create a Risk Register.	A.29
Transfer any risks so far noted in the Daily Log.	A.7
Check for any corporate/programme risk strategies that should be used.	
Check the Lessons Log for any lessons on risk from earlier projects that might be useful.	A.14
Define the project's Risk Management Strategy, including: • Procedures to identify and assess risks, plan and implement responses and communicate actions; • Any risk tools, software and techniques to be used; • Records to be kept; • Definition of risk categories; • Guidance on grading probability, impact and proximity; • Any early warning indicators to be used; • Risk tolerances for the project; • Any risk budget to be used; • Risk responsibilities.	A.28
Check the draft Risk Management Strategy with Project Assurance to see if it satisfies the project's needs.	

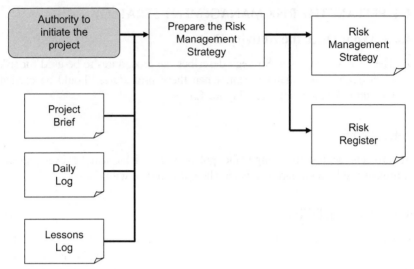

FIGURE 4.3   Prepare the Risk Management Strategy.

4.4.5 In Practice

There will always be risks in projects, and it is useful to have a checklist of typical risks to run through when planning and monitoring.

4.4.6 For Small Projects

Risks will be encountered in even the smallest of projects. You may be happy to make a note of them in your Daily Log, rather than create a separate Risk Register, but you do need a reminder to check plans and other management products for potential risks. You may decide to act as risk owner for all risks, but you should make a note in the Daily Log to check on the status of each risk at an appropriate time.

4.5 PREPARE THE CONFIGURATION MANAGEMENT STRATEGY

4.5.1 What Does the Activity Do?

- A strategy is needed to define where and how project management and specialist products will be stored, how they will be identified and how access to them will be controlled.

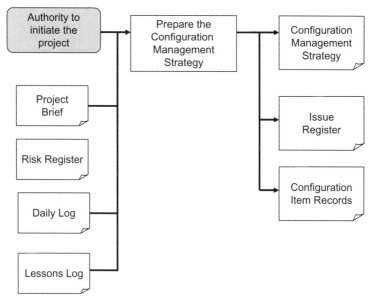

FIGURE 4.4   Prepare the Configuration Management Strategy.

- Because of the close link between change control and configuration management, the strategy also defines how changes will be controlled (Figure 4.4).

4.5.2 Why?

Changes are inevitable in any project, and can destroy plans, the scope of the project, quality, benefits, the ability of one product to interface with another, etc., unless carefully controlled.

A project must maintain control over the management and specialist products created and used. There should only be one version of a product in circulation at any one time. All products should be protected against unauthorized changes. Time and money can be wasted if people work from old copies that should have been withdrawn.

4.5.3 Responsibility

The Project Manager is responsible for creation of this strategy. Care must be taken to confirm the strategy with any Project Assurance, centre of expertise or company standards.

4.5.4 How?	Links to other parts of the book
Create an Issue Register and transfer to it any issues previously noted in the Daily Log.	A.13
Check for any existing strategies, standards or practices relating to configuration management at corporate/programme or supplier level.	
Check the Lessons Log for any lessons on the subject of change control and configuration management.	A.14
Review the Risk and Issue Registers for anything on the subject of change control or configuration management.	A.13 and A.28
Define the Configuration Management Strategy with: • The configuration management procedure to be used; • The issue and change control procedure to be used; • Roles and responsibilities for both of these.	11. Change theme
Discuss with the Project Board whether a Change Authority and change budget should be set up.	11.4.5.1
Create Configuration Item Records for any management products already created or preexisting, such as a feasibility study.	A.5
Check the proposed strategy with Project Assurance.	
Record any new risks or issues in the relevant register.	

4.5.5 In Practice

There is a saying that if a project has more than one product or more than one person working in it, the project is already using configuration management. It is then just a question of how well it is being done.

A company may have good, working procedures and possibly software in use in all its projects and in all operational products. In such a case the Project Manager may have to acknowledge and use the same procedures.

4.5.6 For Small Projects

You may not need – or be able to afford – a separate configuration librarian. You may allocate the job to one of the project team, but everyone on the project needs to understand about version control, how version numbers will be used and where old versions will be stored.

In a small project that I knew, to create a design for a product, one of the systems analysts was appointed configuration librarian in addition to their normal duties. Master copies and archived versions were stored in a filing cabinet. The other analysts were supposed to hand over a copy of their documents whenever they reached a point where they could be 'frozen'. If further work was needed later, a copy would be taken with a new version number and the fact recorded by the librarian. Once a week the librarian went round the team, checking that the 'master' documents held in the filing cabinet were the same versions as those that were being worked on. If not, the records were brought up-to-date.

4.6 PREPARE THE COMMUNICATION MANAGEMENT STRATEGY

4.6.1 What Does the Activity Do?

- Prepares a strategy of how the project management team will send information to and receive information from stakeholders, including media to be used and frequency (Figure 4.5).

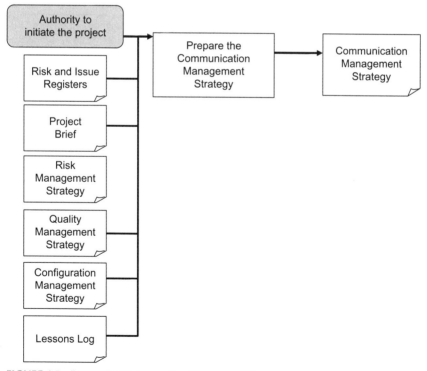

FIGURE 4.5   Prepare the Communication Management Strategy.

4.6.2 Why?

It is important to keep stakeholders informed of project status, especially if the project is part of a programme. In this case the strategy must include details of all communications to and from the programme.

4.6.3 Responsibility

The Project Manager is responsible for creation of this strategy. Care must be taken to confirm the strategy with any Project Assurance, centre of expertise or company standards.

4.6.4 How?	Links to other parts of the book
Review the Project Brief to understand if any corporate/ programme strategies, standards or practices relating to communication need to be used by the project.	A.22
Check the Lessons Log for any communications lessons.	A.14
Check the Risk and Issue Registers for any risks or issues concerning communications.	A.12 and A.29
Identify the information flow needed by the Quality, Risk and Configuration Management Strategies.	A.6, A.26, A.28
Identify with the help of the Project Board all stakeholders and find out their project information needs.	
Define the Communication Management Strategy, including: • Procedures; • Tools and techniques; • Stakeholder analysis; • Roles and responsibilities.	A.4
Review the strategy with Project Assurance.	
Record any new or changed risks or issues in the relevant register.	

4.6.5 In Practice

There are many people who will identify themselves as stakeholders when in fact they are not, but want as much information as they can get to form part of their 'power base' as they attempt to climb the management ladder. There are also stakeholders who want to be decision-makers, or at least opinion-givers. Always check the list with the Project Board and confirm that what the stakeholders want is genuinely needed.

Be careful of line management oriented companies. Often a senior line manager only reluctantly gives decision-making power to a subordinate and will insist on receiving copies of End Stage Reports and want to be part of the decision on whether to approve a Stage Plan – or try to make that decision personally. This happens in the armed forces in particular, and can delay decisions for days, weeks or even months.

4.6.6 For Small Projects

The list of stakeholders may be very small, in which case you can probably keep a list in the Daily Log. It is easiest if you can agree that any stakeholder other than the Project Board will just get a copy of reports that you send to the Project Board.

4.7 CREATE THE PROJECT PLAN

4.7.1 What Does the Activity Do?

- Produces the Project Plan;
- Invokes the activity to produce the next Stage Plan (Figure 4.6).

4.7.2 Why?

As part of its decision on whether to proceed with the project, the Project Board needs to know how much it will cost and how long it will take. Details of the Project Plan also feed into the Business Case to indicate the viability of the project.

If the Project Board makes a general decision to proceed with the project, it needs to have more detailed information about the cost and time of the next stage before committing the required resources.

4.7.3 Responsibility

The Project Manager is responsible for the products of the activity. There may be help from any Project Support appointed, especially if any planning tool expertise is offered, and drafts of the plan should be checked with those carrying out Project Assurance functions, particularly in terms of the quality work.

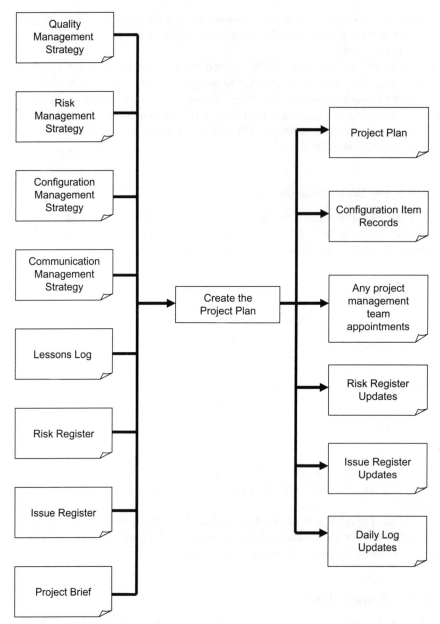

FIGURE 4.6 Create the Project Plan.

4.7.4 How?	Links to other parts of the book
Review the Project Brief to understand what it is that the project has to deliver and any prerequisites, constraints, external dependencies and assumptions.	A.22
Understand the selected project approach.	
Check the Lessons Log for any appropriate lessons.	A.14
Check the Risk and Issue Registers for anything that might affect the Project Plan.	A.12 and A.28
Identify any planning and control tools to be used.	
Decide on the method of estimation to be used.	
Review the four strategy documents to assess what allowances in planning should be made to meet the time and resources needed for their work.	
Use Product-based Planning to create the Project Plan.	Appendix C
Confirm the availability of the required resources.	
Create or update Configuration Item Records for the products in the plan.	A.5
Analyze project risks. Modify the plan accordingly.	Risk theme
Decide on a suitable breakdown of the project into stages.	Progress theme
Review the Project Product Description to see if it needs updating.	A.25
Invoke the *Plan the next stage* activity to produce the next Stage Plan.	
Check that both plans meet the requirements of the Quality Management Strategy.	Quality theme and A.26
Check the plans with Project Assurance.	

4.7.5 In Practice

A Project Plan is always needed. The breakdown into stages may be encouraged by other considerations than just the project size. Examples might be risk assessment, major cash flow moments (invoice payment, invoice submission) and Project Board membership changes.

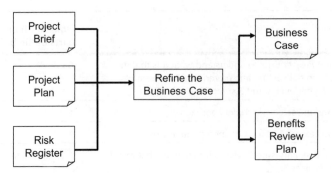

FIGURE 4.7   Refine the Business Case.

4.7.6 For Small Projects

It may not be necessary to produce Stage Plans if the Project Plan can hold sufficient detail to allow day-to-day control. The Project Manager should decide at what point the inclusion of sufficient detail makes the plan too large to grasp in totality.

4.8 REFINE THE BUSINESS CASE

4.8.1 What Does the Activity Do?

- Takes whatever outline Business Case exists for the project, plus the Project Plan, and creates a full Business Case for inclusion in the Project Initiation Document (PID);
- Creates a Benefits Review Plan (Figure 4.7).

4.8.2 Why?

Before commitment to the project it is important to ensure that there is sufficient justification for the resource expenditure. It is also important to plan in advance how and when measurement of the expected benefits can be done.

4.8.3 Responsibility

The responsibility for the Business Case rests with the Executive, probably with input of reasons from the user(s). Much of the work will probably be delegated to the Project Manager.

4.8.4 How?	Links to other parts of the book
Check the Project Brief for any requirements from corporate/ programme management for the format and content of the Business Case.	A.2 and A.22
Check the Lessons Log for any lessons about Business Case preparation.	A.14
Take the outline Business Case and enhance it to be a complete Business Case with: • Costs and timescale from the Project Plan; • Any identified major risks; • Expected benefits; • Tolerance margins for each benefit.	A.12
Create the Benefits Review Plan, including: • How each benefit is to be measured; • A baseline measurement of the current situation for each benefit against which improvements or achievements can be measured; • When each benefit should be measured.	A.1
Update the Risk and Issue Registers (or Daily Log) with any new or changed risks and issues.	A.12 and A.28
Check the draft Business Case and Benefits Review Plan with Project Assurance, particularly the Executive's Project Assurance.	

4.8.5 In Practice

The Project Manager will normally have the work of pulling together the various inputs to the Business Case.

If the project is part of a programme, the programme will provide the overall Business Case. In such cases it may be sufficient in the PID to point to the programme's Business Case (Cartoon 4.3).

4.8.6 For Small Projects

It is easy to start small projects without confirming that there are good business reasons for doing it. It is important, however small the project, to go through the exercise of justification. Otherwise, late in the budget year, it may be found

Don't let the user exaggerate the business benefits

'This product will conquer the world, cure AIDS, cancer and the common cold! The ingredients are readily available at little or no cost, production costs are negligible and we can charge the earth for it!!'

CARTOON 4.3   Business benefits.

that several unjustified projects have consumed the budget now needed for an important larger project.

4.9 SET UP THE PROJECT CONTROLS

4.9.1 What Does the Activity Do?

- Establishes control points and reporting arrangements for the project, based on the project's size, criticality, risk situation, the customer's and supplier's control standards, and the diversity of interested parties (Figure 4.8).

4.9.2 Why?

In order to keep the project under control it is important to ensure that:

- The right decisions are made by the right people at the right time;
- The right information is given to the right people at the right frequency and timing.

4.9.3 Responsibility

The Project Manager is responsible for establishing the monitoring and reporting necessary for day-to-day control, and agreeing the correct level of reporting and decision points for the Project Board to ensure management by exception.

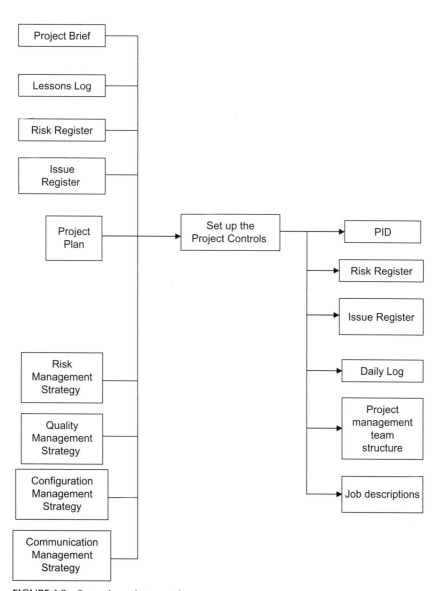

FIGURE 4.8 Set up the project controls.

4.9.4 How?	Links to other parts of the book
Read the Project Brief to understand if there are corporate/ programme standards for controls to be used by the project.	A.22
Review the project's strategy documents to identify their control requirements.	
Check the Lessons Log for any lessons relating to project control.	
Check the Risk Register to see if the number and seriousness of risks identified so far should affect the timing and level of control activities.	A.28
Agree the stage breakdown with the Project Board.	13.2 Stages
Confirm project tolerances have been set by corporate/ programme management.	
Ensure escalation procedures cross all project management levels.	Configuration Management Strategy
Agree the format of reports to the Project Board.	A.10 and A.11
Agree the frequency of Project Board reports.	Progress theme
Summarize the controls in the PID.	A.23
Check the proposed controls with Project Assurance.	
Update the Risk and Issue Registers or Daily Log with any new or changed risks and issues.	

4.9.5 In Practice

If there are comprehensive control standards in existence, it may be sufficient to point to the manual containing them, mention any that will not apply or detail any extra ones. This may require some tailoring of PRINCE2 reports and procedures. The frequency of reports and controls should still be agreed for the project.

4.9.6 For Small Projects

It may be acceptable to the Project Board that many of the reports are given orally. But there should always be a formal initiation and a formal close.

4.10 ASSEMBLE THE PROJECT INITIATION DOCUMENT

4.10.1 What Does the Activity Do?

• Gathers together the information from the other IP activities and assembles the PID (Figure 4.9).

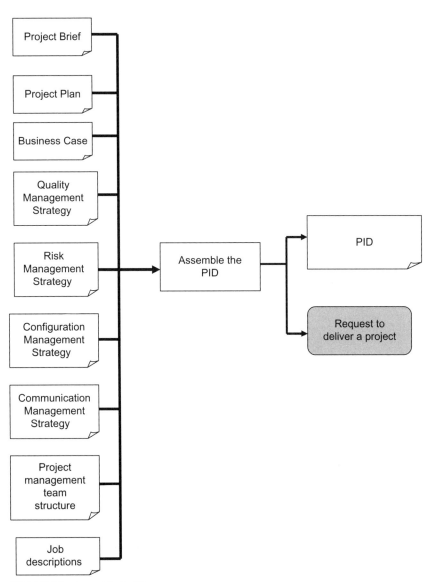

FIGURE 4.9   Assemble the PID.

CARTOON 4.4(A) AND (B)   PID.

4.10.2 Why?

The PID encapsulates all the information needed for the Project Board to make the decision on whether to go ahead with the project or not. It also forms a formal record of the information on which this decision was based, and can be used after the project finishes to judge how successful the project was (Cartoon 4.4(a) and (b)).

4.10.3 Responsibility

The Project Manager is responsible for the assembly with the help of any appointed Project Support and the advice of those with Project Assurance responsibility.

4.10.4 How?	Links to other parts of the book
Transfer information from the Project Brief (Background, objectives, constraints, project approach, etc.), checking if any of it needs expansion or change.	A.22
Incorporate into the PID all the information gathered during the IP process.	A.23
Check for those who should receive a copy of the PID. Distribute the PID to the Project Board and relevant stakeholders.	Communication Management Strategy A.4

4.10.5 In Practice

Discuss with the Project Board whether it wants the PID to present all the information in full, or whether certain sections, such as Product Descriptions and job descriptions should be referred to but not included.

4.10.6 For Small Projects

The PID should be a small document. Most of the material can be referred to with just the major points included.

Chapter 5

Directing a Project (DP)

5.1 WHAT DOES THE PROCESS DO?

- Authorizes project initiation;
- Provides liaison with corporate/programme management;
- Advises the Project Manager of any external business events which might impact the project;
- Approves Stage Plans;
- Approves stage closure;
- Decides on any changes to approved products;
- Approves any Exception Plans;
- Gives ad hoc advice and direction throughout the project;
- Safeguards the interests of the customer and the supplier;
- Approves project closure (Figure 5.1).

5.2 WHY?

Day-to-day management is left to the Project Manager, but the Project Board must exercise overall control and make the key decisions.

5.3 AUTHORIZE INITIATION

5.3.1 What Does the Activity Do?

- Checks that adequate terms of reference exist;
- Checks and approves the initiation Stage Plan;
- Commits the resources required to carry out the initiation stage work (Figure 5.2).

5.3.2 Why?

The initiation stage confirms that a viable project exists and that everybody concerned agrees what is to be done. Like all project work, the effort to do this needs the approval of the Project Board.

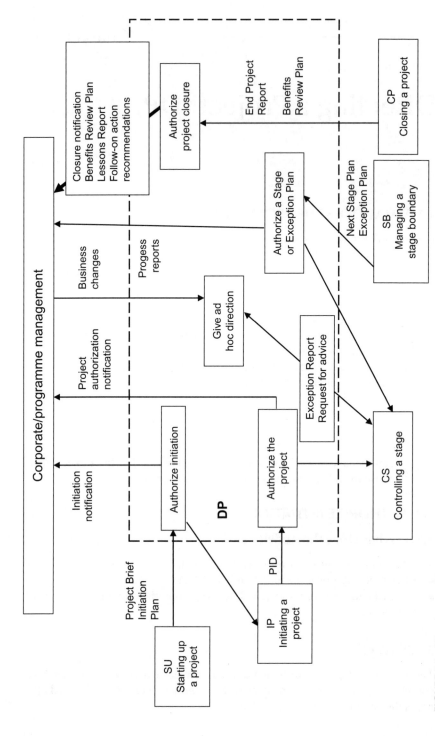

FIGURE 5.1 Directing a project.

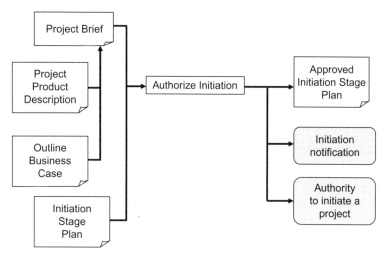

FIGURE 5.2   Authorize initiation.

5.3.3 Responsibility

The Project Board is responsible, based on information provided by the Project Manager and those with Project Assurance responsibility.

5.3.4 How?

- Confirm the terms of reference in the Project Brief, checking if necessary with corporate/programme management.
- Review and approve the Project Product Description.
- Confirm the customer's quality expectations and acceptance criteria.
- Check that the outline Business Case shows that there are valid reasons to authorize initiation at least.
- Confirm that the recommended project approach is suitable.
- Formally approve appointments to the project management team and confirm that everyone has an agreed role description.
- Check the initiation Stage Plan and approve it if satisfied.
- Agree tolerance margins for the initiation stage.
- Agree control and reporting arrangements for the initiation stage.
- Inform all stakeholders that initiation has been authorized, and request any support required from them for initiation.
- Commit the resources required by the plan.

5.3.5 In Practice

The Project Board is expected to be heavily involved in the initiation stage's work, and therefore should check on and advise the Project Manager of its own availability during the stage.

5.3.6 For Small Projects

This activity can be done informally if the Project Board feels that is suitable. The stage may be so short that no reporting during the stage is required.

5.4 AUTHORIZE A PROJECT

5.4.1 What Does the Activity Do?

- Decides whether to proceed with the project;
- Approves the next Stage Plan (Figure 5.3).

5.4.2 Why?

The activity allows the Project Board to check before major resource commitment that:

- A reasonable Business Case for the project exists;
- The project's objectives are in line with corporate/programme strategies and objectives;
- The project's estimated duration and cost are within acceptable limits;
- The risks facing the project are acceptable;
- Adequate controls are in place.

5.4.3 Responsibility

The Project Board with advice from those with Project Assurance responsibility.

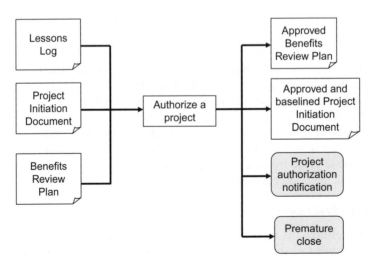

FIGURE 5.3   Authorize a project.

5.4.4 How?	Links to other parts of the book
Confirm that the project's objectives and scope are clearly defined and understood by all.	IP
Confirm that the objectives are in line with corporate/ programme objectives.	
Confirm that all authorities and responsibilities are agreed.	Organization theme
Confirm that the Business Case is adequate, clear and, wherever possible, measurable and confirms the viability of the project.	Business Case theme
Confirm that any useful lessons from previous projects have been incorporated.	SU
Confirm the existence of a credible Project Plan which is within the project constraints.	Plans theme
Check that the proposed project controls are prepared and are suitable for the type and size of the project.	Progress theme
Check that the plan for the next stage is reasonable and matches that portion of the Project Plan.	
Review and approve the Product Descriptions created so far.	A.19
Have any desired changes made to the draft Project Initiation Document.	A.23
Confirm that the Quality, Risk, Configuration and Communication Strategies are prepared and provide adequate management and control over their areas.	A.4, A.6, A.26 and A.28
Check that the Benefits Review Plan is established, covers all the expected benefits and provides details of how and when each benefit will be measured.	Business Case theme
Confirm deviation limits for the project and the next stage.	Progress theme
Give written approval for the next stage (or not, if unhappy with any of the details) and commit the necessary resources.	
Arrange a date for the next stage's end stage assessment.	Progress theme
Notify all stakeholders that the project has been authorized.	

5.4.5 In Practice

The Project Manager should have been in regular informal contact with the Project Board to ensure that there will be no surprises when the Project Initiation Document is presented. If this contact has been maintained, the above list should be a quick confirmation.

If some minor item in the Project Initiation Document needs further work, but in general the Project Board is happy, approval to proceed can be given with the proviso that the corrective work be done – usually with a target date.

Very often the Project Board members are so busy with day-to-day duties that it is not easy to arrange an end stage assessment at short notice. It is better to plan the next end stage assessment date at the end of the previous stage.

5.4.6 For Small Projects

The Project Initiation Document details may have been discussed and agreed to informally over a (short) period of time. It may be sufficient for the Project Board to give the go-ahead when the last piece of information is presented without a formal full presentation. Approval to proceed should still be confirmed in writing as an important management document.

5.5 AUTHORIZE A STAGE OR EXCEPTION PLAN

5.5.1 What Does the Activity Do?

● The activity authorizes each stage (except initiation) and any Exception Plans that are needed (Figure 5.4).

5.5.2 Why?

An important control for the Project Board is to approve only one stage at a time. At the end of one stage the Project Manager has to justify both progress so far and the plan for the next stage before being allowed to continue.

5.5.3 Responsibility

The Project Board carries responsibility for this process, based on information provided by the Project Manager and with advice from any separate Project Assurance responsibility.

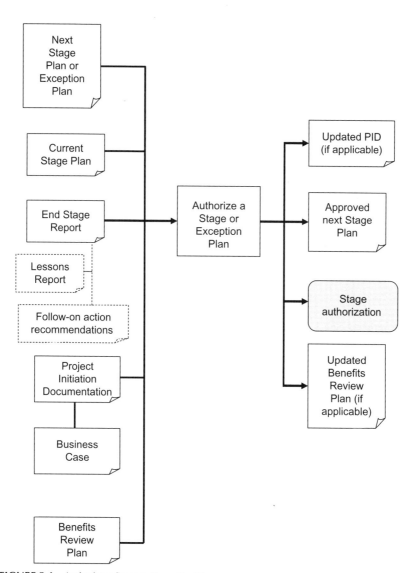

FIGURE 5.4 Authorize a Stage or Exception Plan.

5.5.4 How?	Links to other parts of the book
Review and approve the End Stage Report.	A.9
Compare the results of the current stage against the approved Stage Plan.	
Assess progress against the updated Project Plan.	
Ask the Project Manager to explain any deviations from the Stage and Project Plans that were approved before the start of the current stage.	
Assess the acceptability of the next Stage Plan against the Project Plan.	
Review and approve any new or revised Product Descriptions.	
Review the prospects of achieving the Business Case.	A.2
Review and approve any changes to the Benefits Review Plan.	A.1
Review the risks facing the project.	Risk theme
Get direction from corporate/programme management if the project is forecast to exceed tolerances or there is a change to the Business Case.	13.3 Progress theme
Review any Lessons Report that may have been created and direct it to the group that should take action on it.	A.15
Review tolerances and reporting arrangements for the next stage.	13.3
For any phased handover of products during the current stage: • Check that the handover was done in accordance with the procedures laid down in the Configuration Management Strategy; • Check that users and operational and maintenance staff were happy to accept the products.	
If any follow-on action recommendations were made in the End Stage Report, ensure that they are passed to the appropriate group for action.	A.9
Give approval to move into the next stage (if satisfied) and commit the required resources.	
If the Project Plan and/or Business Case show that the project is no longer viable, instruct the Project Manager to prematurely close the project.	
Communicate the decision to all interested parties as shown in the Communication Management Strategy.	A.4

5.5.5 In Practice

The Project Board can stop the project for any reason, e.g. if the Business Case becomes invalid, project tolerances are going to be exceeded, product quality is unacceptable or the risks become unacceptably high.

If the end stage assessment date was arranged some time ago and occurs before the actual end of the stage, the Project Board can give provisional approval to proceed based on one or more target dates being met to complete the current stage.

If the stage finishes before the planned assessment date, interim approval can be given to do some of the next stage work before formal approval is given. In such a case, the Project Board would clarify what work was to be done before the assessment, rather than give carte blanche to the Project Manager.

5.5.6 For Small Projects

The decisions can be made informally, but the Project Board should still carry out the above activities and keep a record of the decisions.

5.6 GIVE AD HOC DIRECTION

5.6.1 What Does the Activity Do?

- Advises the Project Manager about any external events which impact the project;
- Gives direction to the Project Manager when asked for advice or a decision about an issue;
- Advises on or approves any changes to the project management team;
- Makes decisions on the actions to take on receipt of any Exception Reports (Figure 5.5).

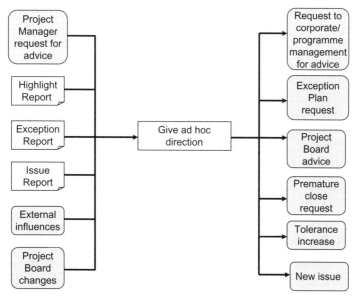

FIGURE 5.5 Give ad hoc direction.

5.6.2 Why?

There may be a need for occasional Project Board direction outside end stage assessments.

5.6.3 Responsibility

The Project Board.

5.6.4 How?	Links to other parts of the book
Check for external events, such as business changes, which might affect the project's Business Case or risk exposure and inform the Project Manager.	Business Case theme
Monitor any allocated risk situations.	Risk theme
Make decisions on any Exception Reports, such as:	A.10
• Increase the threatened tolerance if this is possible within project tolerances; • Ask the Project Manager to produce an Exception Plan; • Instruct the Project Manager to bring about a premature close to the project; • Defer the decision on the situation until more information is available; • Defer the requested change until a subsequent update project; • Grant a concession for any off-specification.	
Ensure that the project remains focused on its objectives and achievement of its Business Case.	A.2
Keep corporate/programme management informed of project progress.	
Make decisions about any necessary changes to the project management team.	11.2 Organization
Make decisions on informal requests for advice, seeking advice, where necessary, from corporate/programme management.	Change theme
Review Highlight Reports and respond to any action or advice requests in the report.	A.11

5.6.5 In Practice

The key activity in this process is deciding what action should be taken on issues, including requests for change and off-specifications. The procedure to be followed should have been agreed and documented in the Project Initiation Document.

This process does not encourage general interference with the work of the Project Manager. The need for Project Board direction will be triggered by either a problem reported in a Highlight Report or an Exception Report, or an external event that it is monitoring on behalf of the project.

5.6.6 For Small Projects

It may be sufficient for the Project Board and Project Manager to agree informally how to action an issue as soon as it is documented.

There may be agreement that any Highlight or Exception Reports can be delivered orally to the Project Board.

5.7 AUTHORIZE PROJECT CLOSURE

5.7.1 What Does the Activity Do?

- Checks that the objectives of the project have been met;
- Reviews any deviations of the project from the original aims and plans;
- Checks that there are no loose ends;
- Advises senior management of the project's termination;
- Recommends a plan for checking on achievement of the expected benefits (Figure 5.6).

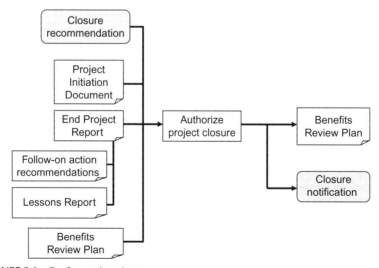

FIGURE 5.6 Confirm project closure.

5.7.2 Why?

There must be a defined end point in a project in order to judge its success. The Project Board must assure itself that the project's products have been handed over and are acceptable. Where contracts (and money) are involved, there must be agreement between customer and supplier that the work contracted has been completed.

5.7.3 Responsibility

The Project Board is responsible, advised by the Project Manager and any Project Assurance responsibility.

5.7.4 How?	Links to other parts of the book
Review the original and current versions of the Project Initiation Document to understand the project's original objectives and Business Case, any changes made to these during the project and the reasons for the changes.	A.23
Review the End Project Report against the Project Initiation Document and assess the performance of the project.	A.8
Check that there has been acceptance from the customer that all the required products have been delivered and the acceptance criteria have been met. Check that there has been a satisfactory handover of the finished product(s) to those responsible for its use and support.	A.6 Configuration Management Strategy
Check that there are no outstanding issues.	
Approve the follow-on action recommendations and pass them to the appropriate group.	
Approve the Lessons Report and pass it to the appropriate body.	A.15
Release the resources allocated to the project.	
Advise corporate/programme management of the project's closure.	
The Project Board disbands the project management team.	

5.7.5 In Practice

It is sensible for the Project Manager to obtain written confirmation from the users and those who will support the final product that they have accepted the outcome of the project, and present this confirmation to the Project Board.

5.7.6 For Small Projects

Not all the reports may be needed, but there should still be a formal sign-off by the Project Board to close the project.

Chapter 6

Controlling a Stage (CS)

6.1 WHAT DOES THE PROCESS DO?

- Manages the stage-from stage approval to completion;
- Assigns work to be done;
- Monitors work progress and quality;
- Deals with issues and risks;
- Reports progress to the Project Board;
- Keeps the Business Case under review;
- Takes any corrective action to ensure that the stage stays within its tolerances (Figure 6.1).

6.2 WHY?

The production of the stage's products within budget and schedule and to the required quality must be driven by the Project Manager and also requires careful monitoring and control.

6.3 AUTHORIZE WORK PACKAGE

6.3.1 What Does the Activity Do?

- Allocates work to be done to a team or individual, based on the needs of the current Stage Plan;
- Ensures that any work handed out is accompanied by measurements such as target dates, quality expectations, delivery and reporting dates;
- Ensures that agreement has been reached on the reasonableness of the work demands with the recipient (Figure 6.2).

6.3.2 Why?

No work in a stage should start without the permission and authority of the Project Manager; otherwise it would be very difficult to keep control. The

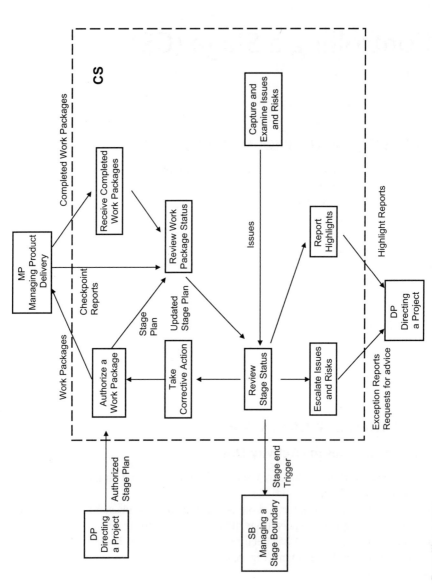

FIGURE 6.1   Controlling a stage.

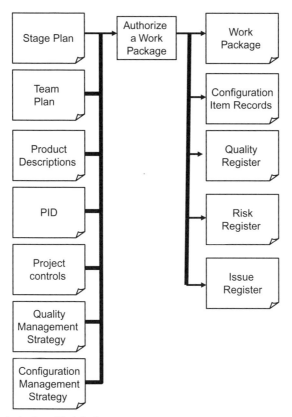

FIGURE 6.2 Authorize a Work Package.

Project Manager must control the sequence of at least the major activities of a stage and when they begin. This ensures that the Project Manager knows what those working on the project are doing and that the Stage Plan correctly reflects the work and progress. The Work Package is the means of authorizing work.

6.3.3 Responsibility

The Project Manager is responsible for the authorization of Work Packages. The recipient of the Work Package must agree with the targets and constraints before the authorization can be considered complete. The process '*Managing Product Delivery*' (MP) covers the steps of a Team Manager receiving a Work Package on behalf of a team.

6.3.4 How?	Links to other parts of the book
Review the Stage Plan to understand the products required, the time, budget and tolerances available.	A.16
Understand from the strategies in the Project Initiation Document the controls to be employed, the quality standards to be met and, if appropriate, how any products are to be handed over.	A.23
Ensure that there are Product Descriptions for the work to be done and that these are complete. Identify specific quality checking needs.	A.19
Make up the Work Package. Discuss the Work Package with the Team Manager or team member if there is only one team.	Work Package Product Description
Jointly assess any risks or problems and modify the Work Package and Risk Register as necessary.	A.28
Review the Team Plan for the work and ensure that sufficient resources and time have been allocated for the work.	
Record the agreement of the Team Manager in the Work Package.	
Update the status of the relevant products' Configuration Item Records.	A.5
Update the Stage Plan with any adjustments made as part of the agreement.	
Update the Quality Register with details of any planned quality management activities.	A.27
If necessary, update the Risk and/or Issue Registers.	A.12 and A.28

6.3.5 In Practice

If the Team Manager represents a different company, this activity should be used formally with appropriate documentation of both the Work Package and the Team Manager's agreement to its targets. In such cases it is sensible to specifically refer to the manner of work allocation in the contract.

If the Stage Plan were to be merely a summary of the start and finish times of major deliverables from a number of teams, there would be a Work Package for each of these major deliverables. There should be definitions in the section of the relevant Product Description on quality method and quality skills required of who will check the product on behalf of the Project Manager (and/or Project Board) and at which points in the product's development.

If a Team Manager uses contractors to deliver any parts of a Work Package, it is recommended that this is also handled in the same way, i.e. as a Work Package between the Team Manager and the third party.

6.3.6 For Small Projects

The same process can be used if the work is being allocated to an individual, rather than to a team, but it can be done less formally. The Project Manager should, however, consider if a record is needed for any later appraisal of an individual's performance. Where the Project Manager is also personally performing the work, the process should not be needed.

6.4 REVIEW THE WORK PACKAGE STATUS

6.4.1 What Does the Activity Do?

- Gathers information from Checkpoint Reports on the status of Work Packages to update the Stage Plan to reflect actual progress, effort expended and quality work carried out;
- Assesses the remaining effort and forecast completion dates of any incomplete work;
- Reviews the Team Plan with the Team Manager to see if work will be completed according to the plan;
- Reviews any Quality Register entries for the work to ascertain the quality status of products;
- Checks that Configuration Item Records reflect the correct status of their products (Figure 6.3).

6.4.2 Why?

In order to control the stage and make sensible decisions on what, if any, adjustments need to be made, it is necessary to gather information on what has actually happened and be able to compare this against what was planned.

6.4.3 Responsibility

The Project Manager is responsible, but may delegate the actual collection of data to Project Support.

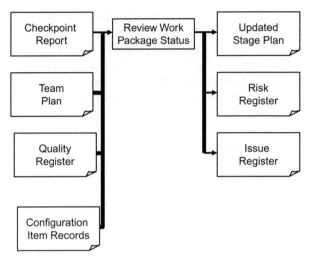

FIGURE 6.3   Review Work Package Status.

6.4.4 How?	Links to other parts of the book
Collect Checkpoint Reports.	A.3
Update the Stage Plan with the information.	
Obtain estimates on time, cost and effort needed to complete work which is in progress or has not yet started.	
Check whether sufficient resources are available to complete the work as now estimated.	
Check the feedback on quality activities.	Quality Register A.27
Note any potential or real problems.	

6.4.5 In Practice

According to the size and environment of the project, the Checkpoint Reports may be written or verbal.

In fixed-price contracts the Project Manager may not be interested in the gathering of costs or the remaining effort of team work, just any changes to estimated completion dates and any risks and issues.

6.4.6 For Small Projects

The Checkpoint Reports may be verbal.

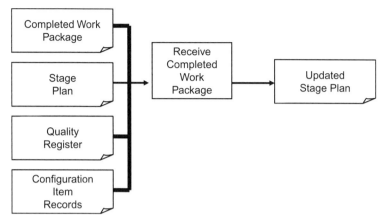

FIGURE 6.4   Receive Completed Work Package.

6.5 RECEIVE COMPLETED WORK PACKAGE

6.5.1 What Does the Activity Do?

- This activity balances with the MP activity, '*Deliver a Work Package*'. It records the completion and return of approved Work Packages. The information is passed to the CS activity, '*Review the Work Package Status*' (Figure 6.4).

6.5.2 Why?

Where work has been recorded as approved to a team or individual, there should be a matching process to record the return of the completed product(s) and its/their acceptance (or otherwise).

6.5.3 Responsibility

The Project Manager is responsible, assisted by any appointed Project Support staff.

6.5.4 How?	Links to other parts of the book
Check the delivery against the requirements of the Work Package.	A.30
Obtain confirmation from the Quality Register that the planned quality checks have been carried out.	A.27
Check that the recipients have accepted the products.	
	(Continued)

6.5.4 How?	Links to other parts of the book
Ensure that the delivered products have been passed to the configuration library and baselined.	
Document any relevant team member appraisal information.	
Pass information about completion to update the Stage Plan.	

6.5.5 In Practice

This activity is ongoing throughout the stage.

6.5.6 For Small Projects

The formality of this activity will relate to the formality of the activity, *'Authorize a Work Package'* (See 6.3). Both will often be informal and brief.

6.6 REVIEW STAGE STATUS

6.6.1 What Does the Activity Do?

- Provides a regular reassessment of the status of the stage;
- Triggers new work;
- Triggers corrective action for any problems;
- Provides the information for progress reporting (Figure 6.5).

6.6.2 Why?

It is better to check the status of a stage on a regular basis and take action to avoid potential problems than have problems come as a surprise and then have to react to them. The objective is therefore to maintain an accurate, up-to-date picture of stage work and resource utilization.

6.6.3 Responsibility

The Project Manager, who may seek guidance from the Project Board (*'Escalate Issues and Risks'* See 6.9) for any problems that appear to be beyond his/her authority.

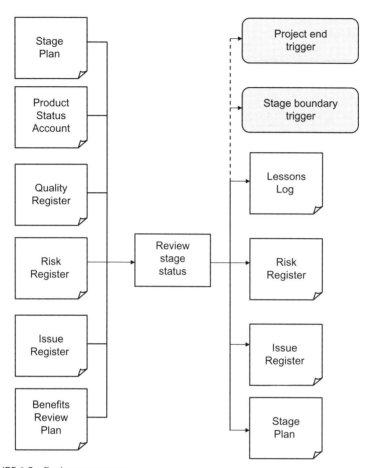

FIGURE 6.5 Review stage status.

6.6.4 How?	Links to other parts of the book
Review progress and forecasts against the Stage Plan.	Controls theme
Review resource and money expenditure.	
Request, if appropriate, a Product Status Account to view the status of products planned in the stage.	A.21
Decide on and implement any actions on problems noted in the Quality Register.	A.27
Review the impact of any implemented issues on Stage and Project Plans.	
	(Continued)

6.6.4 How?	Links to other parts of the book
Assess if the stage and project will remain within tolerances.	
Check the continuing validity of the Business Case.	A.2
Check for changes in the status of any risks.	
Check for any changes external to the project which may impact it.	
If any products are to be handed over at this point, ensure that the necessary procedures have been followed.	
Review the Lessons Log and decide whether a Lessons Report should be generated at this time.	A.14 and A.15
If the end of the stage is approaching, trigger production of the next Stage Plan.	Manage a Stage Boundary
If the end of the project is approaching, trigger the process to close the project.	Closing a Project

6.6.5 In Practice

The activity should be viewed as one that is happening continuously through-out a stage, rather than one that is done, say, every two weeks. Each activity may not need to be done each day, but the Project Manager should ensure that there are sufficient monitoring points (and people allocated to do them) to keep a continuous check. This does not mean that there should always be an instant change of plan in reaction to each slight deviation, but rather an extra monitor-ing point, a forecast of the potential impact if the situation were to get worse and a tolerance setting at which to trigger remedial work.

A change that affects the Business Case or the risk situation may come at any time. As well as trying to identify such a change as it occurs, it is useful to review the assumptions on which the Business Case and risks are based on a formal, regular basis.

The Project Manager may seek guidance on any issue from the Project Board, and should always do so if there is a threat to the stage or project tolerances.

6.6.6 For Small Projects

These activities are still required. The Project Manager should make a decision about their frequency according to the project situation and environment.

6.7 REPORT HIGHLIGHTS

6.7.1 What Does the Activity Do?

● Produces Highlight Reports for the Project Board (Figure 6.6).

6.7.2 Why?

The Project Board needs to be kept informed of project progress if it is to exercise proper control over the project, rather than have regular progress meetings,

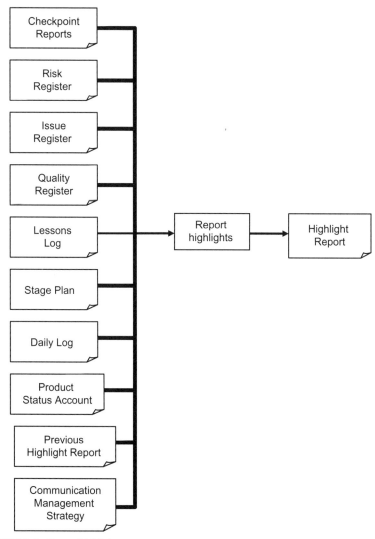

FIGURE 6.6   Report highlights.

reports at regular intervals are recommended between assessments at the end of each stage. The Project Board decides the frequency of the reports at project initiation.

6.7.3 Responsibility

The Project Manager is responsible. This process covers the moments when the Project Manager has to stand back and take stock of the situation.

6.7.4 How?	Links to other parts of the book
Collate the information from any Checkpoint Reports made since the last Highlight Report.	7.4 'Execute a Work Package'
Review the previous Highlight Report for details of open items that were to be followed up and products that were to be completed in the period that has just finished.	A.11
Identify any significant Stage Plan revisions made since the last report.	6.4 'Review the Work Package Status'
Identify current or potential risks to the Business Case. Identify any change to other risks.	
Assess the Issue Register for any potential problems which require Project Board attention.	A.13
Report a summary of this information to the Project Board.	A.11
Check the Communication Management Strategy for other recipients of the report.	A.4

6.7.5 In Practice

Input should come from the CS activity 'Review the Work Package Status' (See 6.4).

The Highlight Report is a formal means of giving a progress update from the Project Manager to the Project Board. It can be used to bring to Project Board attention any failing in resources not under the direct control of the Project Manager and to give early warning of any potential problems that, with Project Board attention, can be avoided.

The report should be kept brief in order to hold the attention of busy senior management.

It does not prevent informal contact between Project Manager and Project Board if there is an urgent need for information to be passed or advice sought.

6.7.6 For Small Projects

The Highlight Report need not be in writing if the Project Board agrees to an oral report.

6.8 CAPTURE AND EXAMINE ISSUES AND RISKS

6.8.1 What Does the Activity Do?

● Capture, log and categorize new issues. (Figure 6.7).

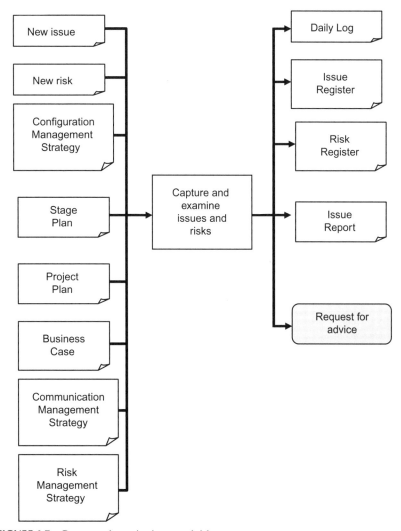

FIGURE 6.7 Capture and examine issues and risks.

6.8.2 Why?

At any time during the project a problem may occur, a change may be requested or the answer to a question may be sought. If these are missed, it may mean that the project fails to deliver what is required. Alternatively the project may run into some other trouble that could have been foreseen, had the issue been noted at the time it arose. There must be a process to capture these so that they can be presented for the appropriate decision and answer.

6.8.3 Responsibility

The Project Manager is responsible. If the project warrants it, help may be given by a Project Support function.

6.8.4 How?	Links to other parts of the book
The Project Manager ensures that all possible sources of issues and risks are being monitored.	Change theme
Issues that can be dealt with informally are noted in the Daily Log.	A.7
For issues that need to be managed formally: • Follow the issue and change control procedure in the Configuration Management Strategy; • Enter the issue in the Issue Register; • Raise an Issue Report; • Assess the category, severity and priority of the issue; • Assess the impact on the Stage Plan, Project Plan and Business Case.	A.13
For risks: • Follow the risk management procedure defined in the Risk Management Strategy; • Enter the risk event and cause in the Risk Register; • Assess the effect of the risk on the Stage Plan, Project Plan and Business Case; • Select the most suitable response and plan its implementation; • Check the Risk and Communication Management Strategies to see who should be informed of the risk.	Risk theme A.29 A.28 and A.4

6.8.5 In Practice

The Project Manager may ask a Team Manager or team member to carry out the analysis, depending on the expertise required. It will be necessary to analyze the financial impact as well as the technical impact. It is part of the Project Assurance role of the Executive to review this. Thought should be given to the time required to do this analysis when designing the project management team, or at least the Executive's Project Assurance role. When producing Stage or Team Plans, an allowance should always be made for the time that the senior specialist people are likely to spend in performing impact analysis on project issues. Thought should be given to the likely volume of issues.

Possible responses to issues or risks are to '*Take Corrective Action*' (See 6.10), seek advice from the Project Board or raise an Exception Report (CS activity '*Escalate Issues and Risks*' See 6.9). Before taking any of these actions, the Project Manager should run through the CS activity '*Review Stage Status*' (See 6.6) in order to understand the full situation.

A check should be made to ensure that the procedure covers not only requests to change the specification, but also potential failure to meet the specification; potential deviations from objectives or plans; and questions about some aspect of the project which require an answer.

6.8.6 For Small Projects

Requests for change or failures on the part of the supplier still need to be documented as part of the audit trail of the project.

The Project Manager may be able to carry out impact analysis as soon as the issue or risk is presented and get a decision on the action to take. Thus, in practice, it may be possible to combine the capture and examination processes with the taking of corrective action or the escalation of the Issue Report to the Project Board for decision.

6.9 ESCALATE ISSUES AND RISKS

6.9.1 What Does the Activity Do?

- Analyze each new issue and risk and recommend a course of action;
- Review each open issue and risk for any change to its circumstances or impact and potentially make a new recommendation;
- Review all open issues for any impact on the project risks or the Business Case (Figure 6.8).

6.9.2 Why?

Part of the concept of management by exception is that the Project Manager will bring to the immediate attention of the Project Board anything that can be *forecast* to drive the plan beyond the tolerance limits agreed with the Project Board. This is part of the Project Board staying in overall control.

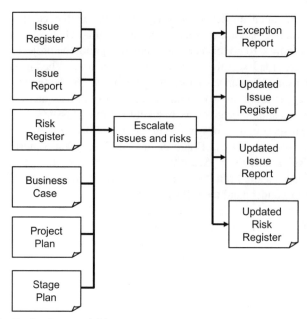

FIGURE 6.8   Escalate issues and risks.

Where an issue threatens to go beyond tolerances and the Project Manager feels that he/she cannot take corrective action within the authority limits imposed by the Project Board, the situation must be brought to the attention of the Project Board for advice.

Having captured all issues in the CS activity '*Capture and Examine Issues and Risks*' (See 6.8), these should be examined for impact and the appropriate body for any extra information and decisions identified.

Escalating issues and risks that threaten tolerances should not be seen as a failure. Project Boards welcome warnings of potential problems far more than advice of a situation when the event has already occurred.

6.9.3 Responsibility

The Project Manager together with any staff allocated Project Assurance responsibility.

6.9.4 How?	Links to other parts of the book
Check the recommended response for its impact on the Stage and Project Plans and Business Case. Revise the recommendation if any problems are found in it.	6.8 'Capture and Examine Issues and Risks'

Describe the situation, options and recommendation to the Project Board in an Exception Report.	A.10
Check the Communication Management Strategy for any stakeholders who should also receive a copy of the report.	A.4
Direct the Project Board's decision to the relevant activity.	

6.9.5 In Practice

If it is likely to take some time to gather all the information required for an Exception Report, it is sensible to alert the Project Board to the situation immediately, following up with the Exception Report when all data has been gathered.

There are many reasons why the tolerances set for a plan might come under threat. The plan could have been too optimistic, resources may not be performing at expected levels, unexpected activities or events such as illness may have arisen. The opposite may also be true, that the work will finish earlier than the plan's time tolerance or cost less than the budget tolerance.

The most likely cause of a deviation beyond tolerance margins is the work involved in implementing one or more Issue Reports. Let us be clear about where a Project Manager stands here. Tolerances are not there to allow the Project Manager (or Team Manager) to 'fit in' change requests. They are there because planning is not an exact science. If the customer wants to add new facilities or change those that were specified, this should lead to the provision of more cash and time from the Project Board. So the Exception Report would say, "Hey, you've changed your mind. This is what it will cost you. Do you want to provide the extra cash and time?"

Another reason for a forecast deviation may be an off-specification, some failing of the current solution to meet part of the specification. The onus here is on the Project Manager to find a remedy within the current tolerances. Only if this cannot be done should the Project Manager resort to an Exception Report.

A Team Manager should act in the same way as the Project Manager when dealing with issues, i.e. the tolerances for the Work Package are not there to pay for any extra work that the Project Manager may request, and the Team Manager should try to find a remedy for any off-specifications in the team's work within the Work Package tolerances before reporting the problem to the Project Manager.

6.9.6 For Small Projects

The formality of this process will relate to the formality of the CS activity, *'Report Highlights'*. Both will often be informal and brief.

Any event that gives the possibility of exceeding stage or project tolerances should be escalated to the Project Board as soon as possible. There may be an agreement with the Project Board to do this orally, rather than in a document, but the Project Manager should consider whether it is better to document the matter for possible later reference.

6.10 TAKE CORRECTIVE ACTION

6.10.1 What Does the Activity Do?

- Within the limits of the tolerance margins established by the Project Board, the Project Manager takes action to remedy any problems that arise (Figure 6.9).

6.10.2 Why?

Failing to take action when the project is drifting away from the Stage Plan invites loss of control.

6.10.3 Responsibility

The Project Manager assisted by any Project Support and Project Assurance staff appointed. If the corrective action is to issue a new Work Package or revise an existing one, then the relevant Team Manager will be involved (see 'Authorize a Work Package' 6.3).

6.10.4 How?	Links to other parts of the book
Ensure that all necessary information about the problem is available.	
Identify action options.	
Evaluate the effort and cost of the options and the impact of the options on the Stage and Project Plans, Business Case and risks.	
Where necessary, ask for Project Board advice. Select the most appropriate option. Check that it will keep the plans within tolerances.	5.6 'Give ad hoc Direction'
Implement the corrective actions via a new or revised Work Package and update the Stage Plan, if the work is within tolerances.	6.3
Have any necessary changes made to the affected Configuration Item Records, such as change in producer, cross-references.	A.5

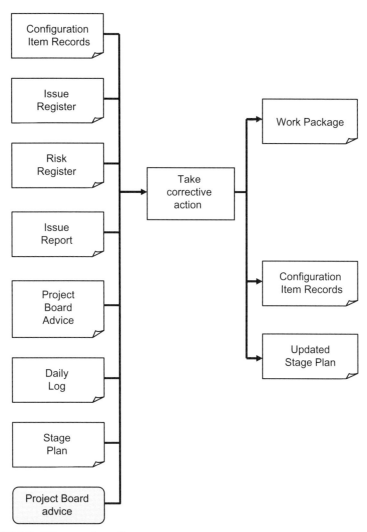

FIGURE 6.9 Take corrective action.

6.10.5 In Practice

This activity is normally triggered by the CS activity '*Review Stage Status*' (See 6.6), and typically deals with seeking advice from the Project Board and acting on that advice. The situation leading to the need to take corrective action should be formally recorded as part of the project audit trail, and the Issue Register is the easiest and most available means of doing this. Many of the reasons for corrective action will be issues raised by other people.

6.10.6 For Small Projects

It is still important to put in the Daily Log why plans were changed. Much of the corrective action can be taken without changing plans, such as having a word with the team member or Team Manager who is causing the problem.

Chapter 7

Managing Product Delivery (MP)

7.1 WHAT DOES THE PROCESS DO?

- Agrees work requirements with the Project Manager;
- Does the work;
- Keeps the Project Manager informed on progress, quality and any problems;
- Gets approval for the finished work;
- Notifies the Project Manager that the work is finished (Figure 7.1).

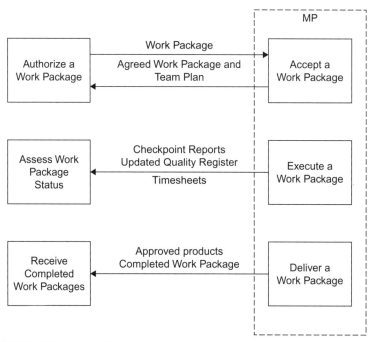

FIGURE 7.1 Managing product delivery.

7.2 WHY?

Where work is delegated by the Project Manager, there must be appropriate steps by the team or person to whom the work is delegated to indicate understanding and acceptance of the work. While the work is being done, there may be a need to report progress and confirm quality checking. When the work is complete there should be an agreed way of confirming the satisfactory completion.

7.3 ACCEPT A WORK PACKAGE

7.3.1 What Does the Activity Do?

- Agrees the details of a Work Package with the Project Manager;
- Plans the work necessary to complete the Work Package;
- Performs the management of risk against the Work Package plan;
- Negotiates the time and resource requirements or the target date;
- Agrees the quality requirements of the product(s) in the Work Package, the reporting requirements and any tolerance margins or constraints;
- Confirms how approval and handover of the finished product(s) is to be done (Figure 7.2).

7.3.2 Why?

There must be understanding and agreement between a Team Manager (or an individual) and the Project Manager on any delegated work, constraints, interfaces, reporting requirements and tolerances. The Team Manager has to be satisfied that the Work Package requirements are reasonable and achievable.

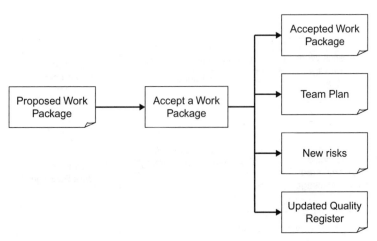

FIGURE 7.2   Accept a Work Package.

7.3.3 Responsibility

Normally the responsibility will lie with a Team Manager to agree a Work Package with the Project Manager. If there are no Team Managers, the person who will do the work reports directly to the Project Manager, and this person would be responsible.

7.3.4 How?	Links to other parts of the book
Agree with the Project Manager on what is to be delivered.	
Obtain any referenced documents.	
Ensure that the quality requirements are clear.	Quality theme
Identify in conjunction with Project Assurance any independent people who must be involved in quality checking.	Appendix D
Identify any target dates and/or constraints for the work. Identify any reporting requirements.	A. 30
Understand how the products of the Work Package are to be handed over when complete.	A.30
Make a Team Plan to do the work (often this will be done as part of the SB activity, *Plan a Stage*, in order to have an accurate Stage Plan).	
Check the plan against the Work Package.	
Advise the Project Manager of any changed or new risks caused as a result of the Team Plan	
Ensure that the Quality Register is updated with any additional participants identified and target dates from the Team Plan.	A.27
Adjust the plan or negotiate a change to the Work Package so that the Work Package is achievable.	
Agree suitable tolerance margins for the Work Package.	

7.3.5 In Practice

Where the Team Manager works for an external contractor, care should be taken to ensure that all work requirements, as defined above, are understood. A Team Plan for the work will have to be created before the Team Manager can confirm the ability to meet target dates. A Team Manager should avoid pressure from the Project Manager or management within his/her own company to agree to a commitment before checking that the targets can be achieved. This may include confirmation with the Senior Supplier that the necessary resources will be made available.

7.3.6 For Small Projects

If it is just a single team working directly under the Project Manager, then the CS–MP activities of agreeing work that the Project Manager wants to have done will simply be an agreement between the Project Manager and the individual team member. This can either be done formally or informally. The same points need to be covered, but common sense will indicate how much should be documented. The Project Manager should consider whether a record of the work needs to be kept for any future performance appraisal of the individual. It is easy to think that a formal Work Package is not required, and for simple tasks, this may be so. But following the structure and information requirements of the Work Package, even if it is given out orally, can often avoid the omission of vital information.

7.4 EXECUTE A WORK PACKAGE

7.4.1 What Does the Activity Do?

- Manages the development/supply of the products/services defined in the Work Package;
- Obtain approval of the products developed/supplied;
- Handover the products to whoever is responsible for Configuration Management (Figure 7.3).

7.4.2 Why?

Having agreed and committed to work in the activity 'Accept a Work Package', this activity covers the management of that work until its completion.

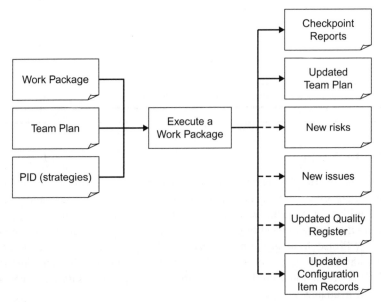

FIGURE 7.3 Execute a Work Package.

7.4.3 Responsibility

The process is the responsibility of the Team Manager.

7.4.4 How?	Links to other parts of the book
Allocate work to team members.	
Ensure that work is conducted according to the procedures and techniques defined in the Work Package.	A. 30
Capture and record the effort expended.	
Monitor progress against the tolerances agreed for the work.	Progress theme
Monitor and control the risks, advising the Project Manager of any new risks.	Risk theme
Evaluate progress and the amount of effort still required to complete the product(s) of the Work Package.	
Feed progress reports back to the Project Manager at the frequency agreed in the Work Package.	Checkpoint Reports
Ensure that the required quality checks are carried out.	
Ensure that any personnel identified in the Work Package or Quality Register is/are involved in the quality checking.	A.27 and A.30
Ensure that the Quality Register is updated with results of all quality checks, following the procedure specified in the Work Package.	Quality theme
Obtain approval for the completed products according to the direction given in the Work Package.	
Transfer the products and control their release to the project's Configuration Librarian.	
Ensure that the relevant Configuration Item Records are kept up-to-date.	A.5
Update the Team Plan to reflect progress.	
Raise issues to advise the Project Manager of any problems.	

7.4.5 In Practice

Depending on the size of the Work Package, this is a continuous, cyclic process. The emphasis is on being aware of the status of team members' work and keeping the Project Manager up-to-date on that status.

As long as the work is forecast to stay within the tolerance limits defined in the Team Manager, the Team Manager manages the activity, including taking any necessary corrective action. If it is forecast to exceed a tolerance, the Team Manager must send an issue to the Project Manager detailing the forecast deviation.

7.4.6 For Small Projects

Where the project is too small to have Team Managers, the Project Manager or a member of his team will carry out this activity.

7.5 DELIVER A WORK PACKAGE

7.5.1 What Does the Activity Do?

● Advise the Project Manager of the completion of the work (Figure 7.4).

7.5.2 Why?

There has to be a process to deliver the requested product(s) and document the agreement that the work has been done satisfactorily.

7.5.3 Responsibility

Team Manager. If there is no Team Manager, then the responsibility lies with either an individual team member or the Project Manager, depending on to whom the Work Package was allocated.

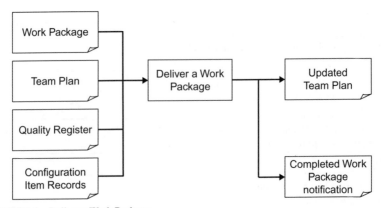

FIGURE 7.4　Deliver a Work Package.

7.5.4 How?	Links to other parts of the book
Confirm that the Quality Register has been updated with details of a successful check on the quality of the product(s).	A.27
Update the Team Plan to show completion of the Work Package.	
Follow the procedure in delivering completed products to the destination defined in the Work Package.	
Advise the Project Manager that the Work Package is complete.	

7.5.5 In Practice

This can be done formally or informally. The original Work Package should say how it is to be done. The formality usually depends on the criticality of the product and the state of the relationships between the customer and the supplier.

7.5.6 For Small Projects

This is usually a very simple, informal process of passing the work back to the correct recipient and telling the Project Manager that the work is done. If you expect the work to form part of a later appraisal of your work, you should ensure that the Project Manager documents how well you did. You should be shown or given a copy of the appraisal.

Chapter 8

Managing a Stage Boundary (SB)

8.1 WHAT DOES THE PROCESS DO?

- Confirms to the Project Board which products planned to be produced in the current Stage Plan have been delivered;
- Gives reasons for the non-delivery of any products which were planned (in the case of deviation forecasts);
- Verifies that any useful lessons learned during the current stage have been recorded in the Lessons Log;
- Provides information to the Project Board to allow it to assess the continued viability of the project;
- Obtains approval for the next Stage Plan or the Exception Plan;
- Ascertains the tolerance margins to be applied to the new plan (Figure 8.1).

8.2 WHY?

The ability to authorize a project to move forward a stage at a time is a major control for the Project Board. There is also a need for a process to create a plan to react to a forecast deviation beyond tolerances. This process aims to provide the information needed by the Project Board about the current status of the Project Plan, Business Case and risks to enable them to judge the continuing worth of the project and commitment to a new plan.

8.3 PLAN A STAGE

8.3.1 What Does the Activity Do?

- Prepares a plan for the next stage (Figure 8.2).

8.3.2 Why?

In order to adequately control a stage, the Project Manager needs a plan in which the detailed activities go down to the level of a handful of days.

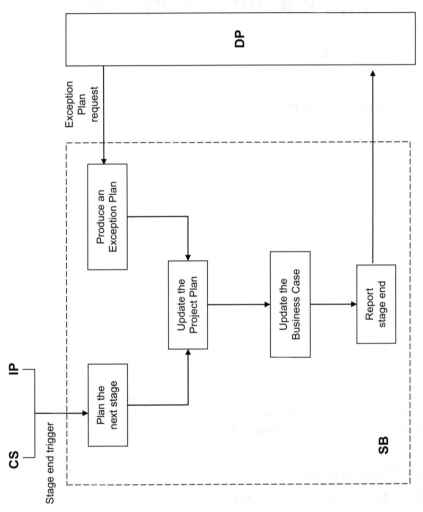

FIGURE 8.1 Managing a stage boundary.

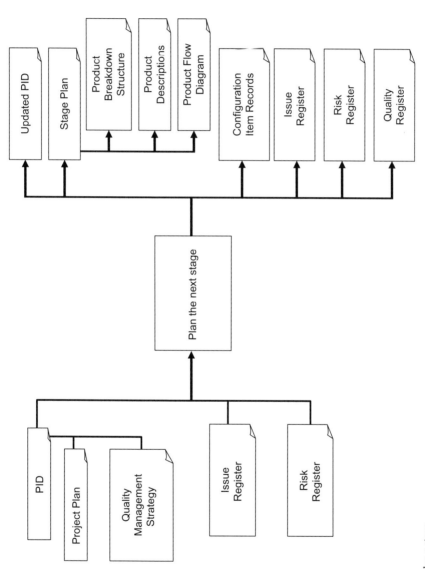

FIGURE 8.2 Plan a stage.

8.3.3 Responsibility

The Project Manager is responsible, but will need help from Project Support, the Project Board and Team Managers. Any Project Assurance functions should review the plan to ensure products have suitable and timely quality checks with appropriate resources assigned.

8.3.4 How?	Links to other parts of the book
Check for any changes to the customer's quality expectations and acceptance criteria.	A.25
Check the project approach for any guidance on how the products of the next stage are to be produced.	A.23
Check the Issue Register for any issues which will affect the next Stage Plan.	A.12
Review the Project Plan for the products to be produced in the next stage.	
Review the Risk and Issue Registers for entries that may affect the next stage.	A.12 and A.28
Use the Product-based Planning technique to create the draft Stage Plan.	Appendix C
Document any changes to the personnel of the project management team.	Organization theme
Discuss the draft plan with those who have Project Assurance responsibilities for the Senior User and Senior Supplier in order to include quality checking activities.	11.2.7
Review the Quality Management Strategy for the quality standards and procedures to be used.	A.26
Add any formal quality reviews and any other quality checks required for Project Assurance purposes. Identify (as a minimum) the chair of each formal quality review. Identify with those with Project Assurance responsibility the required reviewers for each formal quality check.	Appendix D
Enter details of quality checks and involved personnel in the Quality Register.	A.27
Ensure that the plan includes all required management products.	
Create or update Configuration Item Records for the products of the next stage.	A.5
Check the plan for any new or changed risks and update the Risk Register.	A.29
Modify the plan, if necessary, in the light of the risk analysis.	

8.3.5 In Practice

Although Team Plans are described as being created in the MP process, it may be necessary to have them produced in parallel with the Stage Plan in order to get an accurate picture of target dates and resource requirements. If the company has a centre of expertise, this may include expertise in use of the standard planning tools, and this may be available through the role of Project Support.

8.3.6 For Small Projects

It is dangerous to believe that a project is so small that it does not need to be planned. It does not need to be a big effort, and a planning tool may not be needed, but you should think through what products are needed and in what sequence. This often shows up products or steps that you had overlooked.

8.4 UPDATE A PROJECT PLAN

8.4.1 What Does the Activity Do?

- The Project Plan is updated with the actual costs and schedule from the stage that is just finishing, plus the estimated cost and schedule of the next Stage Plan (Figure 8.3).

8.4.2 Why?

As one stage is completed and the next one planned, the Project Plan must be updated so that the Project Board has the most up-to-date information on likely project costs and a schedule on which to partially base its decision on whether the project is still a viable business proposition.

8.4.3 Responsibility

The Project Manager is responsible, but may have help from Project Support.

8.4.4 How?	Links to other parts of the book
Ensure that the current Stage Plan has been updated with final costs and dates.	
Create a new version of the Project Plan ready to be updated. Update the Project Plan with the actual costs and dates of the current stage. Update the Project Plan with the estimated costs, resource requirements and dates of the next stage or Exception Plan.	A.16

(Continued)

8.4.4 How?	Links to other parts of the book
Update any later stages of the Project Plan on the basis of any relevant information made available since the last update.	
Check to see if events mean that the project approach has to be modified.	
Check to see if events require any changes to the Quality Management Strategy.	A.26
Check the latest version of the Project Initiation Document for any change to strategies or the project management team that might affect the Project Plan.	A.23
Update the Risk and Issue Registers if new or changed issues or risks have been identified.	A.12 and A.29

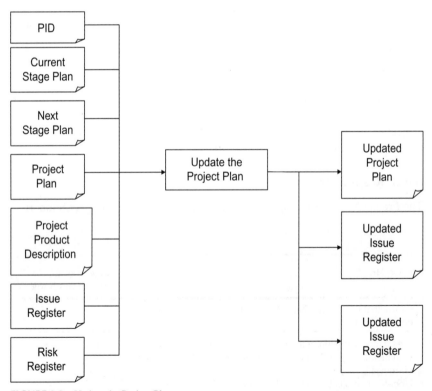

FIGURE 8.3 Update the Project Plan.

8.4.5 In Practice

Text should be added to the new version, explaining why any changes have occurred. This is an important part of the Project Manager's audit trail of documents covering the management of the project.

8.4.6 For Small Projects

All the activity detail may be in the Project Plan with no separate Stage Plans. The Project Plan should be updated with the information described above.

8.5 UPDATE THE BUSINESS CASE

8.5.1 What Does the Activity Do?

- Modifies the Business Case, where appropriate, on the basis of information from the updated Project Plan;
- Checks the known risks to project success for any change to their circumstances and looks for any new risks;
- Updates the Benefits Review Plan with the results of any benefit reviews carried out in the stage (Figure 8.4).

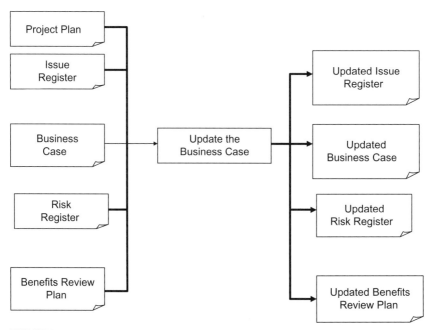

FIGURE 8.4　Update the Business Case.

8.5.2 Why?

The whole project should be business-driven, so the Project Board should review a revised Business Case as a major part of the check on the continued viability of the project.

Part of the assessment of the project's viability is an examination of the likelihood and impact of potential risks.

8.5.3 Responsibility

The Project Manager and whoever has responsibility for the Executive's Project Assurance for the project.

The Project Manager collates the information on risks, but each known risk should have been allocated to an 'owner', the person best placed to monitor that risk (not necessarily the person who will have to make a decision if the risk occurs, but the best placed to keep an eye on the risk).

8.5.4 How?	Links to other parts of the book
Create a new version of the Business Case ready to be updated.	A.2
Review the impact of any approved changes on the expected benefits.	
Review the expected costs in the investment appraisal against the new forecast in the updated Project Plan.	
Review the financial benefits in the investment appraisal against any new forecasts.	
Review the reasons in the Business Case and check that there has been no change or that no new reasons have come to light.	
Modify the new version of the Business Case in the light of any changes to forecast benefits.	
Update the Benefits Review Plan with the results of any benefit reviews carried out in the current stage.	A.1
Check that the project's risk exposure remains within risk tolerances.	
Check if the project's risk appetite has changed.	
Ensure that the Risk Register is up-to-date with the latest information on the identified risks. Ensure that any new risks identified in creating the next Stage Plan have been entered on the Risk Register. Assess all open risks to the project, as defined in the Risk Register.	A.29

Decide if the next Stage Plan needs to be modified to avoid,
reduce or monitor risks.

Create contingency plans for any serious risks which cannot be
avoided or reduced to manageable proportions.

Update the Issue and Risk Registers if required.

8.5.5 In Practice

The Business Case should be reviewed *minimally* at each stage end, but more
frequently if the stages are long or the Business Case is at all at risk.

An assessment of the risks should be part of the End Stage Report. In practice, the Project Manager should informally discuss any serious risks with the
Project Board so that the risk situation and any extra costs incurred in reacting
to those risks do not come as a surprise at the end stage assessment.

8.5.6 For Small Projects

It should not be assumed that the Business Case is unimportant for a small
project. Many of the above list of actions will only take minutes to do.

Continuous risk assessment and management are important to all levels of
project.

8.6 REPORT THE STAGE END

8.6.1 What Does the Activity Do?

- Reports on the results of the current stage;
- Forecasts the time and resource requirements of the next stage, if
  applicable;
- Gives a view on the continuing viability of the project to meet the Project
  Plan and Business Case;
- Assesses the overall risk situation;
- Looks for a Project Board decision on the future of the project (Figure 8.5).

8.6.2 Why?

Normally the Project Board manages by exception and therefore only needs
to meet if things are forecast to deviate beyond tolerance levels. But as part
of its control the Project Board only gives approval to the Project Manager to

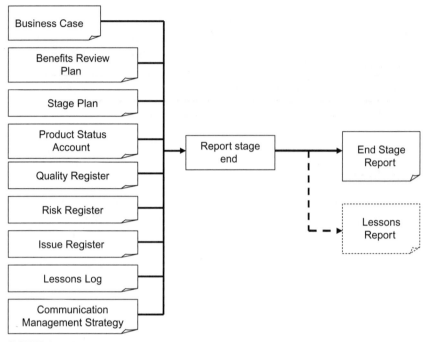

FIGURE 8.5   Report stage end.

undertake one stage at a time, at the end of which it reviews the anticipated benefits, costs, timescale and risks and makes a decision whether to continue with the project or not.

8.6.3 Responsibility

The Project Manager is responsible.

8.6.4 How?	Links to other parts of the book
Report on the actual costs and time of the current stage and measure these against the plan which was approved by the Project Board.	A.9
Report on the impact on the Project Plan of the current stage's costs and time taken.	A.9
Report on any impact from the current stage's results on the Business Case.	A.2
Report on the status of the Issue Register.	A.12

Report on the extent and results of the quality work done in the current stage.

Provide details of the next Stage Plan (if applicable).

Identify any necessary revisions to the Project Plan caused by the next Stage Plan.

Identify any changes to the Business Case caused by the next Stage Plan.

Report on any benefit reviews carried out in the stage.

Report on the risk situation.

Recommend the next action (e.g. approval of the next Stage Plan).

8.6.5 In Practice

The activity should take place as close to the end of a stage as possible without causing delay to the Project Board decision.

The Project Board should be aware of what will be in the End Stage Report before it formally receives it. The Project Board should be kept informed of progress and any problems discussed and advice sought via the DP activity, '*Give ad hoc Direction*', before presentation of the Stage Plan.

It is normally sensible to undertake an End Stage Report even if the current stage is to be replaced by an Exception Plan.

8.6.6 For Small Projects

In a very small project, there may be only one specialist stage, so this activity may not be needed.

The project may be small enough that the Project Plan contains sufficient detail to manage each stage, thus separate Stage Plans are not needed. The report may be verbal, if this has the agreement of the Project Board.

It is unlikely, although not impossible, that benefit reviews will be carried out within the stage.

8.7 PRODUCE AN EXCEPTION PLAN

8.7.1 What Does the Activity Do?

- At the request of the Project Board, the Project Manager prepares a new plan to replace the remainder of the current plan in response to an Exception Report (Figure 8.6).

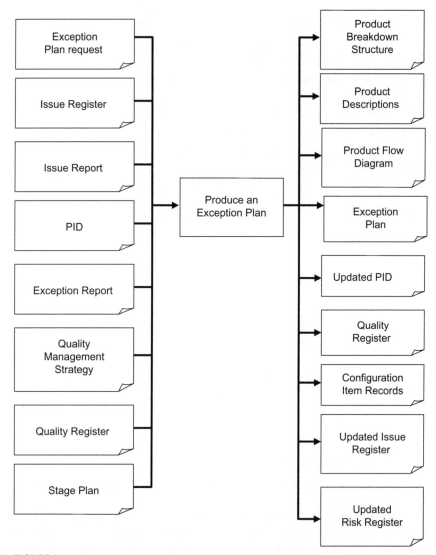

FIGURE 8.6   Produce an Exception Plan.

8.7.2 Why?

The Project Board approves a Stage Plan on the understanding that it stays within its defined tolerance margins. When an Exception Report indicates that the current tolerances are likely to be exceeded, the Stage Plan no longer has that approval. The Project Board may ask for a new plan to reflect the changed situation, which can be controlled within newly specified tolerance margins.

8.7.3 Responsibility

The Project Manager is responsible in consultation with the Project Assurance function.

8.7.4 How?	Links to other parts of the book
Record the Project Board request for an Exception Plan on the Issue Register and Issue Report.	A.12 and A.13
Consult with the Project Board on any changes required to the Project Initiation Document, such as: • Are changes to the customer's quality expectations needed? • Are changes to the project approach needed? • Do any of the strategies need to be amended? • Are changes needed to the project management team, such as suppliers or Project Assurance, or simply resource needs?	A.23
Extract from the current Stage Plan the incomplete products.	
Examine the Exception Report for any newly identified products or changes to existing ones.	A.10
Create a Product Breakdown Structure, any new or revised Product Descriptions and a Product Flow Diagram for the Exception Plan.	Appendix C
Review the Quality Management Strategy to understand the quality requirements, standards and activities that need to be added to the Exception Plan.	A.26
Complete the Exception Plan with activities, resources and scheduling.	Plans theme
Update the Quality Register with details of the planned checks and personnel.	A.27
Create any new Configuration Item Records and check existing ones that are included in the Exception Plan for any required updates.	A.5
Review the Exception Plan for new or changed risks or issues.	

8.7.5 In Practice

An Exception Plan for a stage has exactly the same format as a Stage Plan. An Exception Plan covers the time from the present moment to the end of the current stage.

Although not a planned stage boundary, the production of an Exception Plan for a stage is treated in the same way as a normal stage end.

In extreme cases the Exception Plan may be for the Project Plan. In such cases the Stage Plan will need to be replaced as well. The Project Board must consider whether this can be done within the project tolerances or whether the project should be stopped and restarted with revised constraints and tolerances from corporate/programme management.

Reasons for the deviation forecast can be many, such as:

- Work on approved requests for change cannot be done within current tolerances;
- The supplier has discovered that it cannot supply part of the solution;
- The stage cannot deliver all its products within the current tolerances.

It should be remembered that a request for an Exception Plan is not the only possible outcome from the DP activity, '*Give ad hoc Direction*', when an Exception Report is presented. Other possible results are premature closure of the project, a concession from the Project Board to accept whatever the current lack or fault may be or a decision to delay the requested change until after the current project finishes.

8.7.6 For Small Projects

There is the temptation not to re-plan, but only to 'remember' that changes have occurred. It is, however, important to advise the Project Board of any potential deviation beyond tolerances, to have a record that the Stage Plan was changed to accommodate the change *and that the Project Board approved* the new targets.

The same concept can be applied by the Project Manager to Team Plans if they are forecast to deviate beyond tolerances.

Chapter 9

Closing a Project (CP)

9.1 WHAT DOES THE PROCESS DO?

- Checks that all required products have been delivered and accepted;
- Checks that support and maintenance teams are prepared to take over the running of the project outcome;
- Checks that all issues have been dealt with;
- Records any recommendations for subsequent work on the product;
- Passes on any useful lessons learned during the project;
- Reviews project performance against the Project Initiation Document;
- Recommends closure of the project to the Project Board;
- Confirms plans to measure the achievement of the project's Business Case (Figure 9.1).

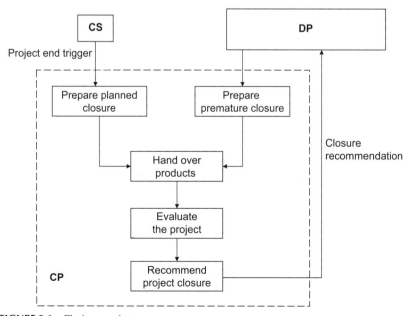

FIGURE 9.1   Closing a project.

9.2 WHY?

Every project should come to a controlled completion.

In order to have its success measured, a project must be brought to a close when the Project Manager believes that it has met the objectives set out in the Project Initiation Document.

There should be an agreed plan to judge achievement of the claimed benefits when it is appropriate to do so.

9.3 PREPARE PLANNED CLOSURE

9.3.1 What Does the Activity Do?

- Updates the Project Plan with the final costs and times from the final Stage Plan;
- Gets agreement from the customer that the acceptance criteria have been met;
- Confirms acceptance of the project's product from the customer and those who will support the product during its operational life;
- Checks that all issues are closed;
- Obtains agreement from the Project Board that project resources can be released (Figure 9.2).

9.3.2 Why?

The customer, Project Manager and supplier must agree that a project has met its objectives before it can close.

There must be a check that there are no outstanding problems or requests.

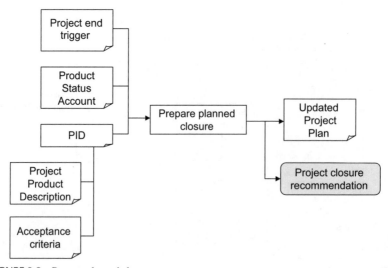

FIGURE 9.2   Prepare planned closure.

The project documentation, particularly agreements and approvals, should be preserved for any later audits.

9.3.3 Responsibility

The Project Manager and any Project Support staff assigned to the project.

9.3.4 How?	Links to other parts of the book
Update the Project Plan with actuals from the final stage.	
Obtain a Product Status Account and review the Project Product Description to: • Ensure that all products have been completed and accepted by the customer; • Get the customer's agreement that the acceptance criteria have been met.	A.21
Check that all issues have been closed and any incomplete ones transferred as follow-on action recommendations.	
Check that any open risks that might affect the products in their operational environment have been transferred as follow-on action recommendations.	
Ensure that, where applicable, those who will be responsible for maintenance and support of the products are ready to accept the product.	
Prepare a request to the Project Board to release project staff and set a date for receipt of final invoices from suppliers.	

9.3.5 In Practice

There will need to be a carefully managed handover of the products between the project and operational and/or support staff unless one central group handles configuration management methods for both parts of the product's life cycle.

If any acceptance criteria have not been fully met, the customer and the supplier may agree to record this as an issue (off-specification) to be dealt with in a later project.

The final product may be handed over to a new third party to operate and maintain, and there may be contractual arrangements involved in the acceptance of the product.

9.3.6 For Small Projects

Notification of the release of resources may be very informal, if required at all.

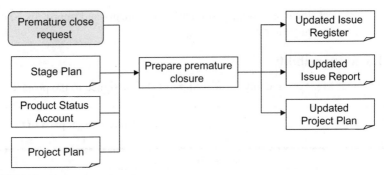

FIGURE 9.3   Prepare premature closure.

9.4 PREPARE PREMATURE CLOSURE

9.4.1 What Does the Activity Do?

- Identifies any finished or unfinished products that can be used;
- Passes any problems caused by the premature termination of the project via the Project Board to corporate/programme management (Figure 9.3).

9.4.2 Why?

The project and its products should not simply be abandoned. Every effort should be made to salvage anything useful from the terminated project.

9.4.3 Responsibility

The Project Manager is responsible. Input should be sought from any Project Assurance roles used.

9.4.4 How?	Links to other parts of the book
Update the Exception Report (if there is one), the Issue Report and Issue Register to note the instruction to prematurely close the project.	A.10, A.12 and A.13
Update the Project Plan with final details of costs and times from the Stage Plan.	
Obtain a Product Status Account to identify which products: • Have already been approved; • Are under development, especially those that will still require work, e.g. buildings to be made safe and secure; • May be useful to other projects.	A.21

Agree with the Project Board any work required from examination of the Product Status Account. This work may require an Exception Plan and approval from the Project Board.	A.21
Check that all issues have been closed and any incomplete ones transferred as follow-on action recommendations.w	A.8
Check that any open risks that might affect the operational environment have been transferred as follow-on action recommendations.	A.8
Ensure that, where applicable, those who will be responsible for maintenance and support of the products are ready to accept those products that were completed or are in a state where use can be made of them.	
Ensure that the reason for premature close is recorded in the Lessons Log.	A.14
Prepare a request to the Project Board to release project staff and set a date for receipt of final invoices from suppliers.	

9.4.5 In Practice

How much work is entailed will depend on where in the project life cycle the project is terminated.

Where the project is part of a programme, any recommendations for follow-on actions should be passed via the Project Board to the programme.

9.4.6 For Small Projects

There may be so few products in the project that a Product Status Account may not be needed or may be dealt with by a discussion with the team members.

9.5 HAND OVER PRODUCTS

9.5.1 What Does the Activity Do?

- Passes the project's products to the relevant operational and maintenance environment;
- Updates the Benefits Review Plan to show how and when those benefits that will only be achieved after an amount of operational use are to be calculated (Figure 9.4).

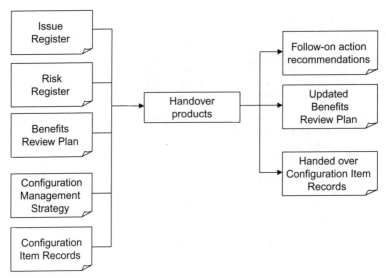

FIGURE 9.4 Handover products.

9.5.2 Why?

There must be a controlled handover of the project's products to those who will operate and maintain the finished product.

9.5.3 Responsibility

The Project Manager is responsible but must liaise with the customer and the supplier to ensure a smooth and complete handover.

9.5.4 How?	Links to other parts of the book
Ensure there are follow-on action recommendations for any incomplete issues or risks that might affect operational use of the products.	A.8
Checks the Benefits Review Plan contains measurements for all claimed benefits that cannot be checked until after a period of operational use of the products.	A.1
Check the Configuration Management Strategy to confirm how products are to be handed over to the customer.	A.6

Check that a suitable operational and maintenance
environment is ready and prepared to accept the
handover.

Transfer the products to the customer.

Update the Configuration Item Records.   A.5
Check if the configuration library is to be moved
to a new site.

9.5.5 In Practice

If the project is part of a programme, any post-project benefit reviews will be
planned and done by the programme.

It may be sensible to set a number of phases for the measurement of benefits to reflect, e.g., the learning curve in using the new products and the spread
of their use. For example, with an IT product, there may be a period of tun-
ing the computer environment to best suit the new system; spreading training
across a multi-location company may take a long time with benefits measured
as each new area comes on board. The speed of a channel tunnel journey may
have one measurement at the outset, but need measuring again when Railtrack
opens the fast link to St. Pancras.

Where the project has been an internal one, the Configuration Item Records
may not physically move.

9.5.6 For Small Projects

There may be no need to move the configuration library, but it should be kept
and archived with the rest of the project documentation.

9.6 EVALUATE THE PROJECT

9.6.1 What Does the Activity Do?

- Assesses the project's results against its objectives;
- Provides statistics on the performance of the project;
- Records useful lessons that were learned (Figure 9.5).

9.6.2 Why?

One way in which to improve the quality of project management is to learn
from the lessons of past projects.

As part of closing the project, the Project Board needs to assess the performance of the project and the Project Manager. This may also form part of

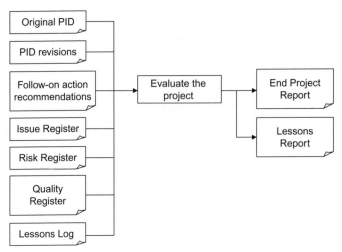

FIGURE 9.5   Evaluate the project.

the customer's appraisal of a supplier, to see if the contract has been completed or to see if that supplier should be used again.

9.6.3 Responsibility

The Project Manager, Project Support and any quality assurance or centre of expertise personnel used.

9.6.4 How?	Links to other parts of the book
Review the original Project Initiation Document and the changes to it to understand what the project was supposed to achieve.	A.23
Write the End Project Report: • Evaluate the project performance against the expectations described in the Project Initiation Document, including the Project Plan and tolerances; • Evaluate the management, quality and technical methods, tools and processes used; • Examine the Risk Register and actions taken and record any useful comments; • Examine the Issue Register and actions taken and record any useful comments; • Examine the Quality Register and record any useful comments.	A.8
Assemble the items in the Lessons Log into the Lessons Report.	A.15

9.6.5 In Practice

The Lessons Log should have been updated throughout the project.

If there are suggestions that the Quality Management Strategy used by the project needed modification, this should be made clear and such comments directed to the appropriate quality assurance or centre of expertise function.

9.6.6 For Small Projects

The Project Board may not require an extensive End Project Report.

9.7 RECOMMEND PROJECT CLOSURE

9.7.1 What Does the Activity Do?

- A recommendation for closure of the project should be sent to the Project Board;
- All the project's registers and logs should be closed;
- All project documentation should be archived (Figure 9.6).

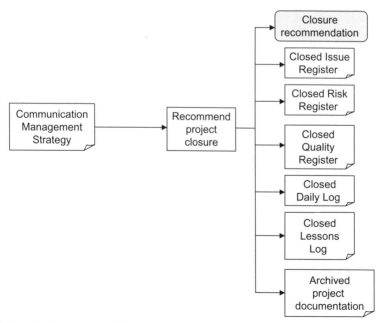

FIGURE 9.6 Recommend project closure.

9.7.2 Why?

9.7.3 Responsibility

The Project Manager, Project Support and any quality assurance or centre of expertise personnel used.

9.7.4 How?	Links to other parts of the book
Review the Communication Management Strategy to identify who needs to be informed of the project closure.	A.4
Close all the project's registers and logs.	
Archive the project documentation in such a way that the documents can be easily retrieved.	

9.7.5 In Practice

Although officially the Project Manager sends only a recommendation for closure, the Project Board will expect copies for all relevant stakeholders to have been prepared for when it endorses the closure to corporate/programme management (Cartoon 9.1).

CARTOON 9.1 Archiving.

9.7.6 For Small Projects

There may be no Communication Management Strategy as the circle of those who need to know is small and well known to the Project Manager and Project Board.

The Project Manager may have contained all the registers within the Daily Log.

Chapter 10

Business Case

10.1 PHILOSOPHY

PRINCE2's philosophy is that the driving force of a project is its Business Case. No project should start without a valid Business Case; a project should be terminated if its Business Case becomes invalid.

A project's Business Case must include all the business changes, costs and impacts of the final product. Examples of this might include retraining staff, the provision of new premises and equipment and the costs of changeover to the new product.

The Executive is the owner of the Business Case. It is the Executive's responsibility to ensure that the Business Case remains aligned with the company's business strategy. Having said this, the Senior User is responsible for specifying the benefits, which is reasonable, because the Senior User will be responsible for realizing the benefits when the finished product is delivered. The Executive must check that the claimed benefits are realistic and represent good value for the project's investment.

10.2 BUSINESS CASE OVERVIEW

In an ideal world there would be a Business Case within the project mandate. Certainly the Project Brief must contain at least the reasons why the project should be done as part of its outline Business Case. This would be checked by the Project Board as part of its decision on whether to enter the initiation stage.

During initiation the Business Case is fleshed out and completed. Costs are given to it from the Project Plan; a summary of risks is added, together with an overview of the options considered for meeting the business problem and reasons for the selection of the chosen option. An investment appraisal is created to show the benefits and savings that the new product is expected to achieve. Appendix A contains a Business Case Product Description, showing the recommended contents of a Business Case.

10.2.1 Business Case Options

The options mentioned here are not those considered when creating the project approach. The Business Case options are the different ways that were considered to solve the business problem. For example, if the business problem is that sales are dropping, options might be:

- Do nothing;
- A TV advertising campaign;
- Newspaper advertisements;
- Buying out a competitor;
- Lowering prices;
- Making a calendar advertising the company's products.

If the last one is the chosen option, the project approach would look at how to provide the calendar.

'Do nothing' should always be the first business option. It provides a basis for quantifying the other options. What would happen to the business problem if nothing was done? What would be the potential losses? What are the costs of continuing as we are today? This can be compared against the costs and potential savings and benefits of each other option. After the 'Business Case' for each option has been considered, the recommended option should also be documented in the Business Case, together with the reasons for choosing it.

Benefits and savings should be defined in measurable form wherever possible. Careful measurements of the current situation should be taken in order to later discover whether use of the new product has achieved the benefits and savings.

The expected benefits will influence the products to be provided by the project. Mapping benefits to outcomes to required products helps decision-making in the planning and control of the project. No products should be there that do not directly or indirectly enable the expected benefits to be achieved.

10.2.2 Expected Disbenefits

The PRINCE2 2009 manual uses this term in the Business Case to describe negative outcomes or consequences of the project. I hate this non-word and prefer to use the term 'negative outcomes', 'negative effects' or even 'negative benefits'. Whichever phrase you use, it describes the bad results expected either during the project or when using the project outcome. For example, a project that turns a motorway into a toll road would have a negative outcome of a number of drivers leaving the motorway and driving through already-congested towns rather than paying the toll.

10.2.3 Benefits Tolerance

Stating benefits in measurable terms helps the setting of benefit tolerance, e.g., a sales increase of 15–25%, or a reduction in road casualties by 5–10% for a project to provide a pedestrian crossing.

10.2.4 Investment Appraisal

This compares the development and operational costs against the expected savings and benefits. It normally evaluates these over a period of years or the life of the product. The customer will define the range to be used and may have accounting rules on how the investment appraisal is to be calculated (Cartoon 10.1).

10.2.5 Use of the Business Case

The Business Case forms part of the Project Initiation Document. The Project Board must be sure that the Business Case is valid before authorizing the project.

A review of the Business Case is part of every Project Board decision, such as each end stage assessment, consideration of an Exception Report and confirmation of project closure. This means that the Business Case must be maintained throughout the project. For example, it is updated in *Managing a Stage Boundary*, taking the latest information from the revised Project Plan.

CARTOON 10.1   Discounted Cash Flow.

10.2.6 Benefits Review Plan

The Business Case feeds the claimed benefits into the Benefits Review Plan. This plan defines how, when and with what resources measurement of benefit achievement should be done. It may not be possible to realize most or all benefits until the products have been in operational use for some time, maybe months. This is one reason why benefits have to be stated in measurable terms and why measurements should be taken at the beginning of the project, so that progress in achieving them can be seen.

The Benefits Review Plan is created in IP (*Refine the Business Case*), and updated at the end of each stage (SB *Update the Business Case*) and when closing the project (CP *Handover Products*).

If part of a programme, the Benefits Review Plan may be held and managed by the programme.

Some benefits may be achieved within the life of the project. In such cases this is reported by the Project Manager in the End Stage Report (SB *Report the Stage End*). The Executive is responsible for ensuring that any benefits reviews done within the project are planned and executed.

For post-project benefit reviews the responsibility passes from the Executive to corporate/programme management. This is because the project management team will have been disbanded and the benefit review(s) will have to be funded and resourced. Corporate/programme management will expect those who were the Senior User(s) to provide evidence of benefit achievement.

Post-project reviews should also consider whether there are any side effects or bottlenecks caused and a review of user opinions of the outcome.

10.3 LINKS

10.3.1 Organization

As already stated, the Executive 'owns' the Business Case and needs to confirm this with senior or programme management as part of the DP activity, *Authorize the Project*.

Many of the expected benefits will come from the users, and this is why it is the responsibility of the Senior User role to provide these. This will often require the Project Manager help to identify sensible measurements.

In a project that uses external suppliers to provide some of the products, each external supplier will have its own Business Case, quite different from that of the customer. If the external suppliers participate in the Senior Supplier role, it will be the Senior Supplier's responsibility to monitor their own Business Case.

The Executive might delegate the monitoring of the customer's Business Case to a Project Assurance role. Monitoring would mainly be done when looking at the impact of a major project Issue Report (CS activity, *Capture and Examine Issues and Risks*) and as part of the SB activity, *Update the Business Case*.

If the project is part of a programme, the programme will often provide the Business Case and the project simply contributes to it.

In large or very important projects there may be a need to have the participation of a specialized business analyst to prepare the investment appraisal. This may come from a central Project Support office or a centre of expertise.

10.3.2 Types of Business Case

Whilst most project Business Cases will be based on their return on investment, there are other types of project that will need different measurements. Types of project are:

- Customer/supplier;
- Multiorganization;
- Compulsory;
- Not-for-profit.

10.3.3 Plans

The Project Plan provides the Business Case with the project costs. Thus, whenever the Project Plan is updated (SB activity, *Update the Project Plan*) the Business Case may need to be updated. Stage Plans and any required Exception Plans may cause the Project Plan to be updated, but both of these would lead to updating the Project Plan in the SB process, and so any changes at that level would be captured.

10.3.4 Controls

Much of this has already been mentioned in the overview. The Business Case is a major Project Board control throughout the project. A valid outline Business Case must be present before the Project Board authorizes the initiation stage. A valid and complete Business Case is required before the Project Board will authorize the project at the end of initiation. The Business Case must still be valid when updated and presented to the Project Board in the DP activity '*Authorize a Stage or Exception Plan*', before the next stage can be authorized.

Part of the Executive's role is to establish benefit tolerances; that is, what margins are there in benefits and savings within which the Business Case can be regarded as valid.

The Project Manager must present the Benefits Review Plan to show the Project Board when and how achievement of the benefits and savings can be measured before the Project Board will confirm project closure in the DP activity, *Authorize Project Closure*.

So to summarize the times of Business Case creation or review:

Action	Process
When creating the outline Business Case	SU
Before authorizing initiation	DP
As input to creating the Benefits Review Plan	IP
As input to requesting authorization of the project	IP
Before authorizing the project	DP
As part of any impact assessment of risks and issues	CS
Before submission of a Stage or Exception Plan to the Project Board	SB
Before authorizing an Exception Plan	DP
Before authorizing a Stage Plan	DP
When evaluating project performance and final review of the Benefits Review Plan	CP
As part of benefits review to measure their achievement	Post project

10.3.5 Risk

The Business Case often needs to be balanced against risk tolerance when considering a costly or risky addition to the specification in return for the potential of greater benefits.

An assessment of the impact of a proposed change on the Business Case is part of the CS activity, *Capture and Examine Issues and Risks*. It is just like any other gamble. Do you go for the risky big winner or do you stick to a conservative no-risk policy and settle for smaller, but more secure benefits?

10.3.6 Quality

There is a link between the quality of a product, the cost of achieving that quality and the price that can be charged for that product in the marketplace. Part of the decisions leading up to the production of the Business Case is the balance between cost and quality.

10.3.7 Configuration Management

Because the Business Case may be updated on a number of occasions, it must come under configuration management. It is likely that there will be several versions during the project and it is important to know which the latest version is.

10.3.8 Change Control

There are two links between the Business Case and change control. First, the impact on the Business Case is part of the analysis of an issue or risk. Secondly, an issue may be raised to request a change in the Business Case. An example here might be where someone notices an error in the Business Case, an incorrect calculation or an over-optimistic benefit claim, but also an external event may cause a change to the Business Case. A competitor bringing a better product to the market place may reduce or destroy the expected benefits from the project. Government legislation may make the final product unusable or require major modification to it.

10.4 DO'S AND DON'TS

Do beware of exaggerated claims for the new product. Do ensure that the current situation has been accurately recorded in terms that will allow the expected benefits and savings of the new product to be checked. Do review the Business Case as part of a decision on whether to start the next stage.

Do not believe that your project does not need a Business Case. Do not believe that one or two reasons constitute an adequate Business Case. Do not keep making changes without checking on their impact on the Business Case, or you may find that the final product will never recoup its cost. Do not be afraid to close a project if the Business Case ceases to be valid.

10.5 IF IT IS A LARGE PROJECT

Creation of the Business Case will take some time. Be wary of dashing into a large project with a Business Case through which some auditor can later drive a coach and horses.

If the project is part of a larger programme, the project may simply be contributing to the programme's Business Case.

10.6 IF IT IS A SMALL PROJECT

You will probably not require a full-blown Business Case, but there should be an assessment of the cost and time against the expected benefits.

Chapter 11

Organization

11.1 PHILOSOPHY

The PRINCE2 organization for any project is based on a customer/supplier relationship. The customer is the person or group who wants the end product, specifies what it should be and, usually, pays for the development of that product. The supplier is whoever provides the resources to build or procure the end product. This is true even if the customer and supplier work for the same company. If this is the case they may still report to different lines of management, have different budgets and therefore have a different view of the finances of the project. The customer will be asking, 'Will the end product save me money or bring in a profit?' The supplier will be asking if the providing of appropriate resources will earn a profit.

Establishing an effective organizational structure for the project is crucial to its success. Every project needs direction, management, control and communication. Before you start any project you should establish what the project organization is to be. You need to ask the questions *even if it is a very small project*. Answers to these questions will separate the real decision-makers from those who have opinions, identify responsibility and accountability and establish a structure for communication. Examples of the questions to ask are:

- Who is providing the funds?
- Who has the authority to say what is needed?
- Who is providing the development resources?
- Who will manage the project on a day-to-day basis?
- How many different sets of specialist skills are needed?
- Who will establish and maintain the required standards?
- Who will safeguard the developed products?
- Who will know where all the documents are?
- What are the limits to the Project Manager's authority and who sets those limits?

A project needs a different organization structure to line management. It needs to be more flexible and is likely to require a broad base of skills for a

CARTOON 11.1   Responsibility.

comparatively short period of time. A project is often cross-functional and may need to combine people working full time on the project with others who have to divide their time between the project and other duties. The Project Manager may have direct management control over some of the project staff, but may also have to direct staff that report to another management structure (Cartoon 11.1).

The management structure of the customer will very often be different to that of the supplier. They will have different priorities, different interests to protect, but in some way they must be united in the common aims of the project.

11.2 PROJECT MANAGEMENT TEAM STRUCTURE

To fulfill the philosophy described at the start of this chapter, PRINCE2 has a project management team structure (Figure 11.1).

It would be good if we could create a generic project management structure that could be tailored to any project. Without knowing anything about a project's size or complexity we could understand the same organizational terms and by fitting names to these understand quickly who does what. But if we were to have one structure for all sizes of project, it would be important that we made it flexible, a structure that would be adequate for large as well as small projects. The only way in which we can do this is to talk about *roles* that need to be filled, rather than jobs that need to be allocated on a one-to-one basis to individuals. In order to be flexible and meet the needs of different environments and different project sizes, our structure will define roles that might be allocated to one person, shared with others or combined according to a project's needs. Examples are given later in the chapter.

The structure allows for the *possible* inclusion of the four layers of management (see 11.2.9). Whether they are all needed depends on the specific project.

Corporate/programme management hand the decision-making for a project to the Project Board. The Project Board members are busy in their own right

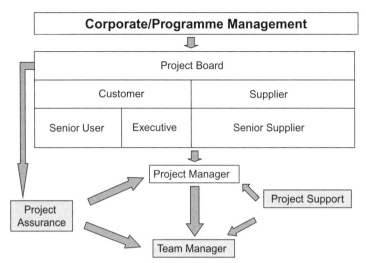

FIGURE 11.1 Project management team structure.

and have not the time to look after the project on a day-to-day basis. They delegate this to the Project Manager, reserving to themselves the key stop/go decisions. If they are too busy or do not have the current expertise, they can appoint someone to a Project Assurance role to monitor an aspect of the project on their behalf. A typical example here would be the participation of a company's quality assurance function on behalf of the Senior User or the Senior Supplier. Another example of the assurance role would be a role for internal audit.

Depending on the project environment or the Project Manager's expertise, he or she might need some support. This might be purely administration, such jobs as filing or note-taking, but it also includes specialist jobs such as configuration management or expertise in the planning and control software tool that is to be used on the project.

Below is a description for each role in the project management structure. These can be used as the basis for discussion of an individual's job and tailored to suit the project's circumstances. The tailored role description becomes that person's job description for the project. Two copies of an agreed job description should be signed by the individual, one for retention by the individual, the other to be filed in the project file.

11.2.1 Project Board

11.2.1.1 General

The Project Board is appointed to provide overall direction and management of the project. The Project Board is accountable for the success of the project, and has responsibility and authority for the project within the limits set by corporate/programme management. It follows that members of the Project Board have to be managers with adequate authority for the resources that have to be committed.

The Project Board is the project's 'voice' to the outside world and is responsible for any publicity or other dissemination of information about the project.

11.2.1.2 Specific Responsibilities

The Project Board approves all major plans and authorizes any major deviation from agreed Stage Plans. It is the authority that signs off the completion of each stage as well as authorizes the start of the next stage. It ensures that required resources are committed and arbitrates on any conflicts within the project or negotiates a solution to any problems between the project and external bodies. In addition, it approves the appointment and responsibilities of the Project Manager and any delegation of its assurance responsibilities.

The Project Board has the following responsibilities. It is a general list and will need tailoring for a specific project.

At the beginning of the project:

- Assurance that the Project Initiation Document (PID) complies with relevant customer standards and policies, plus any associated contract with the supplier;
- Agreement with the Project Manager on that person's responsibilities and objectives;
- Confirmation with corporate/programme management of project tolerances;
- Specification of external constraints on the project such as quality assurance;
- Approval of an accurate and satisfactory PID;
- Delegation of any Project Assurance roles;
- Commitment of project resources required by the next Stage Plan.

As the project progresses:

- Provision of overall guidance and direction to the project, ensuring it remains within any specified constraints;
- Review of each completed stage and approval of progress to the next;
- Review and approval of Stage Plans and any Exception Plans;
- 'Ownership' of one or more of the identified project risks as allocated at plan approval time, i.e. the responsibility to monitor the risk and advise the Project Manager of any change in its status and to take action, if appropriate, to ameliorate the risk;
- Approval of changes;
- Compliance with corporate/programme management directives.

At the end of the project:

- Assurance that all products have been delivered satisfactorily;
- Assurance that all acceptance criteria have been met;

- Approval of the End Project Report;
- Approval of the Lessons Report and the passage of this to the appropriate standards group to ensure action;
- Decisions on the recommendations for follow-on actions and the passage of these to the appropriate authorities;
- Arrangements, where appropriate, for a post-project review;
- Project closure notification to corporate/programme management.

The Project Board is ultimately responsible for the assurance of the project, that it remains on course to deliver the desired outcome of the required quality to meet the Business Case defined in the project contract. According to the size, complexity and risk of the project, the Project Board may decide to delegate some of this Project Assurance responsibility. Later in this chapter assurance is defined in more detail.

One Project Board responsibility that should receive careful consideration is that of approving and funding changes. The Change theme should be read before finalizing this responsibility of approving and funding changes.

Responsibilities of specific members of the Project Board are described in the respective sections below.

11.2.2 Executive

11.2.2.1 General

The Executive is ultimately responsible for the project, supported by the Senior User and Senior Supplier. The Executive has to ensure that the project is value for money, ensuring a cost-conscious approach to the project, balancing the demands of business, user and supplier. The Executive is responsible for the appointment of the other members of the Project Board and the Project Manager.

Throughout the project the Executive 'owns' the Business Case (Cartoon 11.2).

11.2.2.2 Specific Responsibilities

- Appoint the Project Manager;
- Appoint people to the Senior User and Senior Supplier roles;
- Ensure that a tolerance is set for the project by corporate/programme management in the project mandate;
- Authorize customer expenditure and set stage tolerances;
- Approve the End Project Report and Lessons Report;
- Brief corporate/programme management about project progress;
- Organize and chair Project Board meetings;
- Recommend future action on the project to corporate/programme management if the project tolerance is exceeded;
- Approve the sending of the notification of project closure to corporate/programme management.

CARTOON 11.2   Executive.

The Executive is responsible for overall business assurance of the project, i.e. it remains on target to deliver products that will achieve the expected business benefits, and the project will complete within its agreed tolerances for budget and schedule. Business assurance covers:

- Validation and monitoring of the Business Case against external events and against project progress;
- Keeping the project in line with customer strategies;
- Monitoring project finance on behalf of the customer;
- Monitoring the business risks to ensure that these are kept under control;
- Monitoring any supplier and contractor payments;
- Monitoring changes to the Project Plan to see if there is any impact on the needs of the business or the project Business Case;
- Assessing the impact of potential changes on the Business Case and Project Plan;
- Constraining user and supplier excesses;
- Informing the project of any changes caused by a programme of which the project is part (this responsibility may be transferred if there is other programme representation on the project management team);
- Monitoring stage and project progress against the agreed tolerance.

If the project warrants it, the Executive may delegate some responsibility for the above business assurance functions.

11.2.3 Senior User

11.2.3.1 General

The Senior User is responsible for the specification of the needs of all those who will use the final product(s), user liaison with the project team and for monitoring that the solution will meet those needs within the constraints of the Business Case.

The role represents the interests of all those who will use the final product(s) of the project, those for whom the product will achieve an objective, or those who will use the product to deliver benefits. The Senior User role commits user resources and monitors products against requirements. This role may require more than one person to cover all user interests. For the sake of effectiveness, the role should not be split between too many people (Cartoon 11.3).

11.2.3.2 Specific Responsibilities

- Ensure the desired outcome of the project is specified;
- Make sure that progress toward the outcome required by the users remains consistent from the user perspective;
- Promote and maintain focus on the desired project outcome;
- Ensure that any user resources required for the project are made available;
- Approve Product Descriptions for those products which act as inputs or outputs (interim or final) from the supplier function, or will affect them directly and that the products are signed off once completed;
- Prioritize and contribute user opinions on Project Board decisions on whether to implement recommendations on proposed changes;
- Resolve user requirements and priority conflicts;
- Provide the user view on recommended follow-on actions;
- Brief and advise user management on all matters concerning the project.

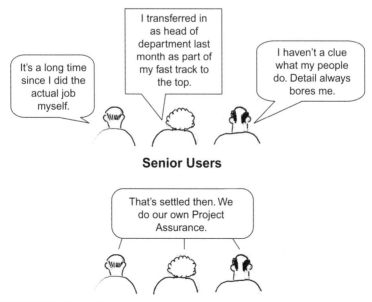

CARTOON 11.3 Senior Users.

The assurance responsibilities of the Senior User are that:

- Specification of the user's needs is accurate, complete and unambiguous;
- Development of the solution at all stages is monitored to ensure that it will meet the user's needs and is progressing toward that target;
- Impact of potential changes is evaluated from the user point of view;
- Risks to the users are constantly monitored;
- Testing of the product at all stages has the appropriate user representation;
- Quality control procedures are used correctly to ensure products meet user requirements;
- User liaison is functioning effectively.

Where the project's size, complexity or importance warrants it, the Senior User may delegate the responsibility and authority for some of the assurance responsibilities.

11.2.4 Senior Supplier

11.2.4.1 General

Represent the interests of those designing, developing, facilitating, procuring, implementing, operating and maintaining the project products. The Senior Supplier role must have the authority to commit or acquire any supplier resources required.

If necessary, more than one person may be required to represent the suppliers.

11.2.4.2 Specific Responsibilities

- Agree objectives for specialist activities;
- Make sure that progress toward the outcome remains consistent from the supplier perspective;
- Promote and maintain focus on the desired project outcome from the point of view of supplier management;
- Ensure that the supplier resources required for the project are made available;
- Approve Product Descriptions for specialist products;
- Contribute supplier opinions on Project Board decisions on whether to implement recommendations on proposed changes;
- Resolve supplier requirements and priority conflicts;
- Arbitrate on, and ensure resolution of any specialist priority or resource conflicts;
- Brief nontechnical management on specialist aspects of the project.

The Senior Supplier is responsible for the specialist assurance of the project. The specialist assurance role responsibilities are to:

- Advise on the selection of technical strategy, design and methods;
- Ensure that any specialist and operating standards defined for the project are met and used to good effect;

- Monitor potential changes and their impact on the correctness, completeness and assurance of products against their Product Description from a technical perspective;
- Monitor any risks in the specialist and production aspects of the project;
- Ensure quality control procedures are used correctly so that products adhere to technical requirements.

If warranted, some of this assurance responsibility may be delegated. Depending on the particular customer/supplier environment of a project, the customer may also wish to appoint people to specialist assurance roles.

11.2.5 Project Manager

11.2.5.1 General

The Project Manager has the authority to run the project on a day-to-day basis on behalf of the Project Board within the constraints laid down by the board. In a customer/supplier environment the Project Manager will normally come from the customer organization.

The Project Manager's prime responsibility is to ensure that the project produces the required products, to the required standard of quality and within the specified constraints of time and cost. The Project Manager is also responsible for the project producing a result that is capable of achieving the benefits defined in the Business Case.

11.2.5.2 Specific Responsibilities

- Manage the production of the required products;
- Direct and motivate the project team;
- Plan and monitor the project;
- Agree any delegation and use of Project Assurance roles required by the Project Board;
- Produce the project contract;
- Prepare Project, Stage and, if necessary, Exception Plans in conjunction with Team Managers, and appointed Project Assurance roles, and agree them with the Project Board;
- Manage business and project risks, including the development of contingency plans;
- Liaise with programme management if the project is part of a programme;
- Liaise with programme management or related projects to ensure that work is neither overlooked nor duplicated;
- Take responsibility for overall progress and use of resources, and initiate corrective action where necessary;
- Be responsible for change control and any required configuration management;

- Report to the Project Board through Highlight Reports and end stage assessments;
- Liaise with the Project Board or its appointed Project Assurance roles to assure the overall direction and assurance of the project;
- Agree technical and quality strategy with appropriate members of the Project Board;
- Prepare the Lessons Report;
- Prepare any follow-on action recommendations required;
- Prepare the End Project Report;
- Identify and obtain any support and advice required for the management, planning and control of the project;
- Be responsible for project administration;
- Liaise with any suppliers or account managers.

11.2.6 Team Manager

11.2.6.1 General

The allocation of this role to one or more people is optional. Where the project does not warrant the use of a Team Manager, the Project Manager takes the role.

The Project Manager may find that it is beneficial to delegate the authority and responsibility for planning the creation of certain products and managing a team of technicians to produce those products. There are many reasons why it may be decided to employ this role. Some of these are the size of the project, the particular specialist skills or knowledge needed for certain products, geographical location of some team members and the preferences of the Project Board.

The Team Manager's prime responsibility is to ensure production of those products defined by the Project Manager to an appropriate quality, in a time-scale and at a cost acceptable to the Project Board. The Team Manager reports to and takes direction from the Project Manager.

The use of this role should be discussed by the Project Manager with the Project Board and, if the role is required, planned at the outset of the project. This is discussed later in the pre-project preparation and kick-off processes.

11.2.6.2 Specific Responsibilities

- Prepare plans for the team's work and agree these with the Project Manager;
- Receive authorization from the Project Manager to create products (Work Package);
- Manage the team;
- Direct, motivate, plan and monitor the team work;
- Take responsibility for the progress of the team's work and use of team resources, and initiate corrective action where necessary within the constraints laid down by the Project Manager;

- Advise the Project Manager of any deviations from plan, recommend corrective action and help prepare any appropriate Exception Plans;
- Pass products which have been completed and approved in line with the agreed Work Package requirements back to the Project Manager;
- Ensure all issues are properly reported to the person maintaining the Issue Register;
- Ensure the evaluation of issues which arise within the team's work and recommend action to the Project Manager;
- Liaise with any Project Assurance roles;
- Attend any end stage assessments as directed by the Project Manager;
- Arrange and lead team checkpoints;
- Ensure that quality controls of the team's work are planned and performed correctly;
- Maintain, or ensure the maintenance of team files;
- Identify and advise the Project Manager of any risks associated with a Work Package;
- Ensure that such risks are entered on the Risk Register;
- Manage specific risks as directed by the Project Manager.

11.2.7 Project Assurance

11.2.7.1 General

The Project Board members do not work full time on the project, therefore they place a great deal of reliance on the Project Manager. Although they receive regular reports from the Project Manager, there may always be the questions at the back of their minds, 'Are things really going as well as we are being told?', 'Are any problems being hidden from us?', 'Is the solution going to be what we want?', 'Are we suddenly going to find that the project is over-budget or late?' There are other questions. The supplier may have a quality assurance function charged with the responsibility to check that all projects are adhering to their quality system.

All of these points mean that there is a need in the project organization for a monitoring of all aspects of the project's performance and products independent from the Project Manager. This is the Project Assurance function (Cartoon 11.4).

To cater for a small project, we start by identifying these Project Assurance functions as part of the role of each Project Board member. According to the needs and desires of the Project Board, any of these assurance responsibilities can be delegated, as long as the recipients are independent of the Project Manager and the rest of the project management team. Any appointed assurance jobs assure the project on behalf of one or more members of the Project Board.

It is not mandatory that all assurance roles be delegated. Each of the assurance roles which is delegated may be assigned to one individual or shared. The Project Board decides when an assurance role needs to be delegated. It may be for the entire project or only part of it. The person or persons filling an

CARTOON 11.4   Project Assurance.

assurance role may be changed during the project at the request of the Project Board. Any use of assurance roles needs to be planned at initiation stage, otherwise resource usage and costs for assurance could easily get out of control.

There is no stipulation on how many assurance roles there must be. Each Project Board role has assurance responsibilities. Again, each project should determine what support, if any, each Project Board role needs to achieve this assurance.

For example, an international standards group, such as ISO, may certify the supplier's work standards. A requirement of the certification is that there will be some form of quality assurance function that is required to monitor the supplier's work. Some of the Senior Supplier's assurance responsibilities may be delegated to this function. Note that they would only be delegated. The Project Board member retains accountability. Any delegation should be documented. The quality assurance could include verification by an external party that the Project Board is performing its functions correctly.

Assurance covers all interests of a project, including business, user and supplier.

Project Assurance has to be independent of the Project Manager; therefore, the Project Board cannot delegate any of its assurance responsibilities to the Project Manager.

11.2.7.2 Specific Responsibilities

The implementation of the assurance responsibilities needs to answer the question 'What is to be assured?' A list of possibilities would include:

- Maintenance of thorough liaison throughout the project between the supplier and the customer;
- Customer needs and expectations are being met or managed;
- Risks are being controlled;

- Adherence to the Business Case;
- Constant reassessment of the value-for-money solution;
- Fit with the overall programme or company strategy;
- The right people are involved;
- An acceptable solution is being developed;
- Project remains viable;
- The scope of the project is not 'creeping up' unnoticed;
- Focus on the business need is maintained;
- Internal and external communications are working;
- Applicable standards are being used;
- Any legislative constraints are being observed;
- The needs of specialist interests, e.g. security, are being observed;
- Adherence to quality assurance standards.

It is not enough to believe that standards will be obeyed. It is not enough to ensure that a project is well set up and justified at the outset. All the aspects listed above need to be checked throughout the project as part of ensuring that it remains consistent with and continues to meet a business need and that no change to the external environment affects the validity of the project.

11.2.8 Project Support

11.2.8.1 General

The provision of any Project Support on a formal basis is optional. It is driven by the needs of the individual project and Project Manager. Project Support could be in the form of advice on project management tools, administrative services such as filing and the collection of actual data to one or more related projects. Where set up as an official body, Project Support can act as a repository for lessons and a central source of expertise in specialist support tools.

One support function that must be considered is that of configuration management. Depending on the project size and environment, there may be a need to formalize this, and it quickly becomes a task with which the Project Manager cannot cope without support. See the Change theme for details of the work (Cartoon 11.5).

11.2.8.2 Specific Responsibilities

The following is a suggested list of tasks:

Administration

- Administer change control;
- Set up and maintain project files;
- Establish document control procedures;
- Compile, copy and distribute all project management products;
- Collect actual data and forecasts;

CARTOON 11.5   Project Support.

- Update plans;
- Administer the quality review process;
- Administer Project Board meetings;
- Assist with the compilation of reports;

    Advice

- Specialist knowledge (e.g. estimating, risk management);
- Specialist tool expertise (e.g. planning and control tools, risk analysis, investment appraisal);
- Specialist techniques, such as Product-based Planning;
- Standards.

11.2.9 Four Layers of Management

The PRINCE2 philosophy when designing what the project organization should be is to consider four layers of management. According to the size and importance of the project, you may not need all four to be represented, but that should be a decision you take when you understand the philosophy and can compare it to the needs of a specific project (Figure 11.2).

11.2.9.1 Layer One

A project may be part of a larger programme or it may be a major investment for a corporation, a key part of that company's strategy. What I am saying is that a project may be of concern to the very top level of management in the corporation. This would be the top layer in the diagram. This layer is concerned

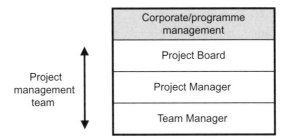

FIGURE 11.2   Four layers of management.

with the business strategy. This layer provides a vision of what the company should look like and what it should be doing in the future. It has to coordinate all the projects going on to change the company to the vision that they have for it. There will come a point when this layer says, 'Hang on, we have not enough time to handle all the detail, we need to delegate.' So for each project they appoint a Project Board to act on their behalf within certain constraints. I will address these constraints in the Progress theme.

11.2.9.2 Layer Two

Layer two in the diagram is a layer called the Project Board. This consists of those roles that are needed to take those decisions that are too big for the Project Manager's authority level. Examples of questions this Board would answer are:

- Does the Project Manager fully understand what we are looking for?
- Is this a good way of spending our money?
- Is the proposed solution in line with company strategy?
- The project is not sticking to its planned timeframe and/or budget. Should we continue or close the project?
- Do we want to pay for this major change request?
- Are we prepared to accept the product being offered by the Project Manager?
- Does it meet our requirements?

11.2.9.3 Layer Three

Layer three is the Project Manager role, the day-to-day planning, monitoring and control of the project. The work of this role is reasonably easy to understand. But very often the Project Manager is not the person providing the funds. The bigger the project, the more likely it is that the Project Manager will have to go to a higher level of management for decisions and commitments on money, the specification of what is needed, the resources required to do the job and acceptance of products developed by the project.

11.2.9.4 Layer Four

There are two simple examples of projects that might need layer four. One is where the skill sets needed are so varied and/or the numbers of resources are so large that no one person has the ability or time to manage the whole thing. Geography may be a factor in deciding whether you need Team Managers. If the developers are in groups some distance away from each other, it is very difficult to manage them all personally.

The other case is where the solution is to be provided by a third party. The external supplier will want to manage its own resources.

Depending on the project environment or the Project Manager's expertise, he or she might need some support. This might be purely administrative, such jobs as filing or note-taking, but it also includes specialist jobs such as configuration management or expertise in the planning and control software tool that is to be used on the project.

11.2.9.5 Changes to the Project Management Team

Ideally people appointed to a role on the project management team should stay in that role throughout the project life. In particular, the Executive and Project Manager should stay for the whole duration. This is not always possible. For example, the Armed Forces usually rotate their personnel every 3 years. If the project happens to be one that will take more years than that, there are often serious problems in losing the Executive who has been the driving force behind the project, bringing on new Senior Users who have different ideas or want changes to put their personal mark on the project, exchanging the Project Manager for someone who has not the same identification with the project.

There may be, however, good reasons for a change. A project moving out of a design phase into development may need different or additional Senior Suppliers; the skill set needed for Project Assurance may change as the project moves through its technical work; someone may leave the company. The PRINCE2 project management team structure and well-defined job descriptions should help to smooth out any personnel changes.

A stage boundary provides a useful opportunity for personnel changes. The end stage procedure checks for any changes, and the End Stage Report, current and next Stage Plans provide a useful batch of progress information for any newcomers.

11.3 THE THREE PROJECT INTERESTS

If we look at the decisions and commitments that a Project Board needs to make (budget commitment, resource commitment, specification of needs and alignment with company strategies) PRINCE2 says that the Project Board must represent the three bodies who contribute to the project: Business (money, company

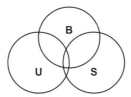

FIGURE 11.3 Business, user and supplier.

strategy), User (what are the requirements?) and Supplier (production of the specialist products) (Figure 11.3).

11.3.1 Business

The justification of any project depends upon its meeting a business need. The outcome of a project should match company strategy. A project should provide value for money. The business view should have a decision-making role in a project to ensure that these three prerequisites are present at the start of a project and are maintained throughout the project. The Executive looks after the business interests.

11.3.2 User

Users of the final products, on the other hand, are interested in getting as many of their requirements met as they can, which may clash at times with the need to get value for money. PRINCE2 therefore makes a distinction between the business interests and those who will use the project's outputs. The user role on the Project Board represents those who will:

- Specify the desired outputs;
- Use the project outputs to realize the benefits;
- Operate and maintain the project's outputs;
- Be affected by the outputs.

These interests are part of the Senior User role on the Project Board. Remember that you may need more than one person to represent different groups of users. Alternatively, a small project may be able to combine this role with that of the Executive.

11.3.3 Supplier

The Senior Supplier role on the Project Board represents those who will provide the project's outputs. There may be more than one supplier. You must be careful to appoint managers who can commit the required resources. There may be in-house and external suppliers. There may be one major supplier and many smaller suppliers. You do not want too many to share the Senior Supplier role. Can one major supplier commit the resources of smaller suppliers by means of contracts with them? If there are several suppliers who will not agree to have another supplier make commitments on their behalf, is it better to have the customer's Purchasing Manager take the Senior Supplier role and control all the suppliers through contracts?

If the selection of a supplier is an early part of the project, here again the Purchasing Manager may take the Senior Supplier role until a supplier is chosen.

The customer/supplier philosophy works for most projects. If a company has decided to create a product for a given market, then the customer and user role is normally taken by the marketing function to represent the perceived end users of the product.

Appendix B contains role descriptions for each member of the project management team.

11.4 LINKS

11.4.1 Controls

There are many links between the roles in the project management structure and the controls they exercise. The following are fully described in the Controls theme. This is just a summary.

11.4.1.1 Layer 1 – Corporate/Programme Management

Corporate/programme management control the Project Board. They exercise control in a number of ways.

They are responsible for the original terms of reference for the Project Board (the project mandate) and therefore control the statement of what the project is to deliver, the scope and any constraints.

They can define the overall targets of the project in terms of delivery dates and budget.

They provide the Project Board with the limits of cash and time (project tolerances) at a project level beyond which the Project Board must return to them for a decision on what to do.

They appoint the Executive (very often a member of corporate/programme management) to head the Project Board. They have the power to appoint other members of the Project Board, if they wish to do so.

They indicate what reports at what frequency they want from the Project Board.

11.4.1.2 Layer 2 – The Project Board

The Project Board has to approve that the project contract (Project Initiation Document) drawn up by the Project Manager is in line with the terms of reference handed down to them.

Within the project limits set by corporate/programme management the Project Board sets limits of time and budget deviation for each stage of the project (stage tolerances). The Project Manager cannot go beyond those limits without fresh authority from the Project Board.

The Project Board commits the budget and resources needed for each stage. This means that Project Board members need to be at managerial status in order to make these commitments. Their managerial level and authority will depend on the size and importance of the project. Having a Project Board member who has to go back to a line manager for the authority to commit to a plan simply delays the decision-making process and passes it to managers who may not have the same level of commitment to the project and interest in or knowledge of the project's objectives. (And if these line managers then want to pass the decision on to their line managers, heaven knows when a decision will be made.)

The Project Board has to approve the products of one stage before the Project Manager can move into the next stage.

The Project Board has to approve any change to the original specification. This is more fully discussed in the Change theme.

A project cannot close without the Project Board confirming that it is prepared to accept the results.

The Project Board stipulates what reports it wants from the Project Manager, their content and frequency.

The Project Board can appoint people to an independent Project Assurance role to monitor various aspects on its behalf.

11.4.1.3 Layer 3 – The Project Manager

The Project Manager agrees all work with Team Managers (or if that role is not used, with the individual team members).

The Project Manager can set tolerance limits for a team's work beyond which it cannot go without the Project Manager's approval. These limits are set within those handed down by the Project Board for the stage.

The Project Manager receives a regular report on each team's progress (Checkpoint Report).

The Project Manager can monitor the quality of work being produced by reference to the Quality Register.

The Project Manager is responsible for the Project and Stage Plans and monitors progress against these.

11.4.1.4 Layer 4 – The Team Manager

The Team Manager plans the team's work and agrees it with the Project Manager.

The Team Manager holds regular checkpoint meetings with the team.

11.4.2 Plans

The Project Manager creates and maintains the Project and Stage Plans.
    If there is a need for a recovery plan, the Project Manager creates this.
    Team Managers create Team Plans where required.

11.4.3 Risk

The Project Manager maintains a Risk Register.
    The Project Board and corporate/programme management are responsible for the identification of risks external to the project.
    The Project Manager is responsible for the identification of internal risks.
    An owner is appointed from the project management team to keep an eye on each risk.

11.4.4 Quality

The Executive is responsible for the quality of the Business Case, at the outset and as the project progresses.
    The Senior User role is responsible for defining the expected business benefits, the quality of the original specification, any user acceptance testing, and confirming that the solution's design and development continue to meet the user needs.
    The Senior Supplier role is responsible for the quality of the developed products.
    A company's independent quality assurance function may be represented on a project as part of the Project Assurance function.

11.4.5 Change Control

Having agreed at the end of initiation what the project will deliver, it is important that the Project Board agrees to any changes to this. However, there are projects where there may be large volumes of changes. During initiation the Project Board should decide if it will have the time to consider all the requests for change and off-specifications. If not (or it does not have the expertise to judge them) the Project Board can decide to appoint a Change Authority.

11.4.5.1 Change Authority

The Change Authority will consist of one or more people to whom consideration of changes is delegated. The Change Authority is normally given a change budget to pay for any approved changes with two restrictions:

1. The maximum amount to be spent on a single change before the issue should be referred to the Project Board.
2. The maximum amount to be spent in a single stage before referring to the Project Board.

The Project Board decides who should sit on the Change Authority. Common choices are the Project Manager, those with Project Assurance roles, a user committee or a combination of these.

The Configuration Management Strategy can be used to establish severity ratings for changes. Depending on the severity, the change could be directed to:

- Corporate/programme management;
- The Project Board;
- A Change Authority;
- The Project Manager.

These change authorities should be written into the appropriate job descriptions. For projects within a programme, programme management will define the authority level of the Project Board to approve changes.

11.5 DO'S AND DON'TS

Do not just use the generic structure slavishly. Use common sense and tailor it, when necessary, to the project.

Do not drop responsibilities. Do move them to another role if that makes more sense for the project in hand.

Do make sure that all responsibilities are given to an appropriate role.

11.6 IF IT IS A LARGE PROJECT

The larger the project the more likely it is that the project organization structure will need a person to fill each role. In fact the role of Senior User may have to be shared between two or three people in order to get a representative view of the user needs. It would be sensible to control the number of people filling this role. I have seen projects with 15 people clamoring to have a share of this role. The phrase that always comes to mind at such times is 'It will take us half an hour to get the coffee order'. If you are faced with lots of 'volunteers' for the role, make sure they are decision-makers, not opinion holders, organize them into a user committee, which meets and appoints a spokesperson to represent them all. The user committee can instruct the spokesperson on what they are to ask for, then get feedback from the spokesperson after any Project Board meetings.

Similarly a large project might have lots of suppliers. I do not recommend large numbers of them to share the Senior Supplier role. Two or three might be workable as a maximum, but it should not be allowed to get out of hand. If there are lots of external suppliers, organize the contracts so that there is a main supplier who is responsible for the minor suppliers. Another possibility here is to appoint the company's Purchasing Manager to the role and make that person accountable for obtaining the supplier resources. Before walking away from these ideas on how to restrict the numbers taking these two roles, let me emphasize that a key part of each role is their accountability for quality. The Senior

User role is accountable for the quality of the specification. The Senior Supplier role is accountable for the quality of the products supplied as part of the solution. Make sure that you have someone in the roles who picks up this accountability.

There will normally be only one person as Executive. Remember the Executive is the key decision-maker. The other roles advise and support the Executive. The Executive is always the person in charge of the purse strings. There may occasionally be projects where the supplier puts up some of the development cash. In such circumstances the supplier would quite correctly take a share of the Executive role. The division and balance of the decision-making would need to be carefully thought out in such cases.

Large projects are more likely to need to appoint people to the Team Manager role. This may be because the project is using external contractors, has people working in different geographical areas or is using a mix of skills beyond the Project Manager's scope.

11.7 IF IT IS A SMALL PROJECT

Let us take an example. Your boss wants you to organize the department's Christmas Lunch at one of six restaurants in town for, say, 100 people. Common sense says you do not want a huge number of people in the project management structure. Your boss is paying, so he or she is the Executive. The boss is also defining, or at least approving the arrangements, and so will also take the Senior User role. In terms of supplier, the major resource used is going to be you. Who can commit your time? Right, the boss again, so your Project Board consists of your boss. In terms of Project Assurance, no doubt your boss is capable of checking that personally, so no extra people needed there. You will probably do most, if not all of the work yourself, so no call for Team

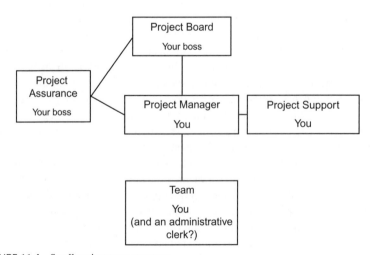

FIGURE 11.4 Small project team structure.

Managers. You might get someone to write to the restaurants or ask the staff what their choice of menu is, but that would be the extent of the 'team' that you would need. The remaining question is whether you need any support and in a small project such as this, the answer is likely to be 'No'. So although we began by considering the full project organization structure, we end up with a structure that looks like Figure 11.4.

All responsibilities are covered without unnecessary numbers or people being involved in their management.

There are two important things to remember:

1. Use your common sense. Remember that roles can be combined and ask yourself the question 'OK, who can make that commitment on behalf of the project?'
2. However small the project may be, you can not drop any of the roles or their responsibility and accountability. All you can do is move these to another role.

Chapter 12

Plans

12.1 PHILOSOPHY

A plan is the backbone of every project and is essential for a successful outcome. Good plans cover all aspects of the project, giving everyone involved a common understanding of the work ahead. My friends at Duhig Berry used the following picture to provide a formal definition of a plan (Cartoon 12.1).

A plan defines:

- The products to be developed or obtained in order to achieve a specified target;
- The steps required in order to produce those products;
- The sequence of those steps;
- Any interdependencies between the products or steps;
- How long each step is estimated to take;
- When the steps take place;
- Who will carry out the steps;
- Where controls are to be applied.

A plan:

- Shows in advance whether the target is likely to be achievable;
- Shows what resources are needed to accomplish the work;
- Shows how long the work will take;

'A plan is a document, framed in accordance with a predefined scheme or method, describing how, when and by whom a specific target or set of targets is to be achieved.'

CARTOON 12.1   Definition of a plan.

- Shows who is to do what and when;
- Provides a basis for assessing the risks involved in the work;
- Provides the base against which progress can be measured;
- Provides the information on the Project Manager's intentions to be communicated to those concerned;
- Can be used to gain the consent and commitment of those who have to contribute in some way.

A plan is, however, only a statement of intent. Because something is in our plan does not necessarily mean that it is cast in concrete. There will always be uncertainties.

It is commonly accepted that one of the most common causes of projects failing to deliver benefit is a neglect of the planning process.

There are many reasons advanced for this, one of the most common being that there is 'no time to plan'. What is really being said is that there is a strong desire to start the 'real' work, especially if there is a deadline to be met. The other side of this is where senior management does not recognize the importance of planning, and will not make the necessary time available.

The next excuse given for failure to plan is that there is 'no need'. This is perhaps where:

- The job has been done before;
- The project is expected to take only a short time;
- The Project Manager prefers to keep all the details 'in the head'.

There are, of course, dangers in these 'reasons' for not planning. Projects are always different, with different people, size, complexity and environments. Short projects can become very long when you realize that you have forgotten something vital. The human brain can retain only a very small number of linked events over a period of several days. When you start adding the details of what is actually happening to what you had planned, it does not take long for a required event to get lost somewhere in the brain cells. Project Managers who say that they keep all the details in their head are simply 'firefighters'. They lurch from one crisis to the next, always having to put fires out. Sometimes they are hailed as whiz kids because they solve (or waste everybody's time working around) a problem. Most of the problems that they go around solving would not have been there if they had planned properly in the first place! Undertaking a project without planning is just leaving things to chance.

Often people are expected to plan a project with no knowledge of how to go about it. Sadly it is often the case that people are promoted into project management (hence planning) positions without being given the necessary education and training to allow them to do the job effectively. Planning needs to be learned. It is not an inherent skill with which people are born. There are specific techniques (Critical Path Analysis, resource leveling, use of a planning tool, etc.) that need to be learned. Without expertise in these areas, planners are unlikely to do a good job.

The last excuse is that planning is *no fun*! What this means is that planning is hard work. There is a great desire to 'get going' with the stimulating business of the technical challenge.

12.2 HIERARCHY OF PLANS

Figure 12.1 introduces the PRINCE2 hierarchy of plans.

At the outset of a project, it is always difficult to plan in detail the activities and resource requirements for the production of all the products required. How accurately can you plan your own activities that you will be doing six months from now? Three months from now? Why should we think it would be an easy task to plan the work for one or more teams of people for the next year (or however long the project may take)? It is nevertheless necessary to provide overall estimates for the project in terms of duration and cost so that approval to proceed can be gained.

Differing levels of management within the project require different levels of detailed plan in order to discharge their responsibility. For instance the Project Board and the Project Manager need to assess the continuing viability of the project and therefore require a plan of the total project in overview.

The Project Manager needs to apply control on a day-to-day basis and therefore requires a detailed plan with activities broken down to a small handful of days covering the next period of, say, a few weeks. This is OK as long as there is a longer-term view available in less detail – i.e. the Project Plan.

Similarly, if our project uses several teams, the Team Manager will need a detailed plan for the work of the team members. Again it would be sensible to limit this to a short period of time.

We also need to create a new plan, and get it approved by the Project Board, if the original plan goes wrong.

These will now be examined in more detail.

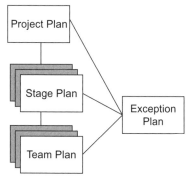

FIGURE 12.1 Plan hierarchy.

12.3 PROJECT PLAN

The highest level is the Project Plan, which is created at the start of the project and updated at the end of each stage. The initial Project Plan is a part of the Project Initiation Document. The Project Plan is a mandatory plan in a PRINCE2 project.

The Project Board does not want to know about every detailed activity in the project. It requires a high level view. This allows the Project Board to know:

- How long the project will take;
- What the major deliverables or products will be;
- Roughly when these will be delivered;
- What people and other resources will have to be committed in order to meet the plan;
- How control will be exerted;
- How quality will be maintained;
- What risks there are in the approach taken.

The Project Board will control the project using the Project Plan as a yard-stick of progress (Cartoon 12.2).

It is worth remembering the Business Case at this point. The Business Case details (amongst other things) the costs of development and operation of the completed product. The predicted development costs are taken from the Project Plan. This plan is therefore essential to the decision as to whether the proposed system is a viable proposition in business terms.

CARTOON 12.2   Authorize the project.

12.4 STAGE PLAN

Having specified the stages and major products in the Project Plan, each stage is then planned in a greater level of detail. Each Stage Plan is prepared, as I said, just before the end of the previous stage.

Stage Plans are required. Unless a project is very small it will be easier to plan in detail one stage at a time. Another part of the philosophy that makes stage planning easier is that a stage is planned shortly before it is due to start, so you have the latest information on actual progress so far available to you.

The procedure at stage planning time involves taking those major products in the Project Plan that are to be created during that stage, and breaking these down (typically) two or three additional levels of detail.

Given that each stage is planned at the end of the preceding one, the planner should now have a clearer view of:

- What has to be produced;
- How well the people perform;
- How accurate previous estimating has been;

than would have been the case earlier in the project.

Stage Plans have the same format as the Project Plan.

The Project Manager uses the Stage Plans to track progress on a daily basis through regular progress monitoring.

12.4.1 Plan Narrative

The Project and Stage Plans should have a narrative section. Suggested headings for the narrative are as follows:

- Plan description;
  - Project (and stage) identification;
  - The plan level, e.g. project or stage;
  - Summary of the plan and its background;
  - Intended implementation approach.

How do you intend to implement the plan? Is there anything in the Gantt chart that might need explaining? Some examples might be:

- You are not starting work on product X as soon as you could because you are waiting for the release of staff from another project;
- The construction work looks shorter than normal because we are taking current product Y and modifying it;
- The testing work looks longer than normal because we will be testing the product in a hazardous environment.
- Constraints or objectives that have affected the plan;
- Plan assumptions.

On what assumptions is the plan based? Examples are actual staff to be allocated, help or products from other sources at given times. It is essential to list your assumptions. If the Project Board accepts the plan, the Board is accepting your assumptions as reasonable. If your plan goes wrong because an assumption turns out to be incorrect, the Project Board cannot throw rocks at you because it agreed with the assumptions. It also gives the Project Board the chance to say if it knows anything about the assumptions that would make them invalid. An example here would be where you create a plan based on the assumption that good old Fred will be your senior technician. If the Senior Supplier knows that he or she has already committed Fred to another project, you can be told and replan. If no one knew of your assumption and you went ahead with the plan, fell behind and came up with the lame excuse, 'I would have been alright if you had given me Fred', no one is going to be too impressed.

- Plan prerequisites;
  Prerequisites are similar to assumptions but they must be in place on day one of the plan (and stay in place!) in order for the plan to succeed, e.g. trained staff, equipment and workplace arrangements.

- External dependencies;
- If the plan depends for its success on elements or products that are beyond the Project Manager's control, such as deliveries by suppliers or other projects, these would be identified here;
- Lessons incorporated;
  Details of any relevant lessons from other projects that have been used in the planning.

- Budgets;
  Time and cost budgets for the plan, including any change budget and risk management budget.

- Tolerances;
  What tolerance levels are agreed for the plan?

- Monitoring and control;
  Details of how the plan is to be monitored and controlled.

- Product Descriptions:
  Product Descriptions for the products to be created within the plan's scope. For a Team Plan, the relevant Product Descriptions will already be part of the Work Package.

- Schedule:
  This may include Product-based Planning Diagrams, a bar or Gantt chart, a planning network, tables of resource requirements by skill, plus the names of any specifically requested resources.

12.5 TEAM PLAN

Team Plans are optional. Their use or otherwise is dictated by the size, complexity and risks associated with the project.

Team Plans are the lowest level of detail and specify activities down to the level of a handful of days, say 10 at most. Team Plans may or may not contain the narrative sections associated with the higher levels.

Team Plans will be needed when internal or external teams are to do portions of the work. Part of the Project Manager's job is to cross-relate these plans to the Project and Stage Plans.

12.6 EXCEPTION PLAN

Finally, there is the Exception Plan. This is produced when a plan is predicted to exceed the time and cost tolerances agreed between the planner and the next higher level of authority. If a Team Plan is forecast to deviate beyond tolerances, the Team Manager may need to produce the Exception Plan and get approval for its introduction from the Project Manager. If a Stage Plan is forecast to deviate, the Project Manager will produce an Exception Report and the Project Board may require an Exception Plan to replace the current Stage Plan. If the Project Plan threatens to go beyond its tolerances, the Project Board must take the Exception Report to higher management, who might ask for a new Project Plan.

The Exception Plan takes over from the plan it is replacing and has the same format.

12.7 THE PRINCE2 APPROACH TO PLANNING

PRINCE2 offers a standard way in which to produce any level of plan. This means that all plans will have the same format and method of development. The process is based around the PRINCE2 technique of Product-based Planning, which is described in detail in Appendix C (Figure 12.2).

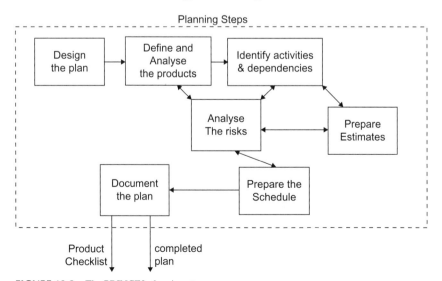

FIGURE 12.2   The PRINCE2 planning steps.

The PRINCE2 approach to planning:

- Defines the levels of plan needed for the project;
- Decides what planning tools and estimating methods will be used;
- Identifies the products whose delivery has to be planned;
- Identifies the activities needed to deliver those products and the dependencies between them;
- Estimates the effort needed for each activity;
- Allocates the activities to resources and schedules the activities against a timeframe;
- Analyzes the risks inherent in the plan;
- Adds explanatory text to the final plan.

12.7.1 Design the Plan

This process is carried out only once per project at the start. It defines the standards to be used in all future plans. The result should be a consistent set of plans. The activities in designing a plan are:

- Decide on what levels of plan are needed for the project, i.e. Project Plan, Stage Plans, Team Plans;
- Ascertain if the organization or programme uses a particular planning tool as standard;
- Identify the planning tool to be used in the initial Project Plan, part of the PID;
- Identify what estimating method(s) are available and suitable for the project;
- Ensure that the estimating method(s) chosen contain allowances for issue and risk analysis, telephone calls, ad hoc meetings, learning curves, experience, etc.;
- Discuss with the Project Board whether there should be a separate allowance for any anticipated contingency plans.

12.7.1.1 In Practice

Where the project is part of a programme, the programme will have made most of these decisions, and it is just a question of finding out what the standards are. Beware of allocating any resource, especially yourself, 100% of the time to an activity. No one is 100% efficient. There will inevitably be interruptions such as telephone calls, ad hoc meetings and nonproject work which demand your time. These should be allowed for in your estimate of how much time people can commit to the work in your plan. Even the most efficient of experienced workers are unlikely to devote more than 70% of their time to planned work. At least 50% of a Project Manager's time should be spent in managing. The Project Manager of a large project should not contemplate doing any of the specialist work at all.

12.7.1.2 For Small Projects

A really small project may not need a planning tool, but a little thought should be given to the other steps before diving in and assuming you can hold it all in your head. The comments about how efficient people are still holds true for the smallest project.

12.7.2 Define and Analyze the Products

The PRINCE2 approach to planning is product based. By defining the products and their quality requirements everyone can see and understand the required plan result. It means that whoever has to deliver a product knows in advance what its purpose is, to what quality it has to be built and what interfaces there are with other products.

The steps are:

- Identify the products required, using a Product Breakdown Structure;
- Write Product Descriptions for them;
- Draw a Product Flow Diagram showing the sequence of delivery and dependencies between the products;
- Optionally produce a Product Checklist.

The first three of these form the PRINCE2 Product-based Planning technique. This is described in detail with examples in Appendix C.

The planner is responsible for identifying the products. This will be either the Project Manager or a Team Manager, depending on the type of plan being produced. The users of any of the products to be delivered within the plan should be involved in writing the Product Descriptions, particularly in defining the quality criteria.

12.7.2.1 In Practice

This is a key point in PRINCE2. If you are not doing this step, then you are not really using PRINCE2. It is an ideal method of involving users, specialists and Project Assurance roles in the creation of a plan, without the normal problems of 'design by committee'.

12.7.2.2 For Small Projects

It is very tempting in small projects to assume that use of Product-based Planning is not needed. Experience has shown me that it is very easy to forget a product, realize that you have done things in the wrong order or fail to consider a quality requirement when you dive in and 'just do it.' It does not take much time to do this step and it will always pay dividends.

12.7.3 Identify Activities and Dependencies

For Stage and Team Plans the Product Flow Diagram may still be at too high a level for the purposes of estimation and control. This optional process allows a further breakdown into the activities to produce each product, based on the Product Flow Diagram until each activity will last only a handful of days.

The planner is responsible. This will be either the Project Manager or a Team Manager, depending on the type of plan being produced.

- Consider if a product in the Product Flow Diagram is too big to estimate or would need such a large effort that it would be difficult to control against that estimate.
- Where a product is too big, break it down into the activities needed to produce it. This should continue down to the level where an activity is less than 10 days effort, ideally no more than 5 days.
- Where a product has been broken down into several activities, put the activities into their correct sequence.
- Review the dependencies between products and refine them to give dependencies between the new activities. For example, where Product Flow Diagram dependencies went from the end of one product to the start of the next, is there now an opportunity to overlap or start some activities on a product before all the activities on its preceding product have been done.

12.7.3.1 In Practice

You may decide not to do this step, but simply extend the previous step down to the level where you have all the detail you need for your plan. This originally was included because all planning tools used Work Breakdown Structures and assumed you would be working with activities and tasks. This process was inserted as a bridge from PRINCE2's product approach. Other people found it convenient to use this process to draw a line below which Product Descriptions were not needed.

12.7.3.2 For Small Projects

Following the above comments this process will usually not be needed for a small plan.

12.7.4 Prepare Estimates

The objective is to identify the resources and effort required to complete each activity or product (Cartoon 12.3).

The Project Manager. Possibly there will be expert help available from Project Support.

- Examine each activity/product and identify what resource types it requires. Apart from human resources there may be other resources needed, such as equipment. With human resources, consider and document what level of skill you are basing the estimate on;
- Judge what level of efficiency you will base your estimates on and what allowance for nonproject time you will need to use;

CARTOON 12.3 Estimating.

- Estimate the effort needed for each activity/product;
- Understand whether that is an estimate of uninterrupted work, to which the allowances must be added, or whether the estimate already includes allowances;
- Document any assumptions you have made, e.g. the use of specific named resources, levels of skill and experience and the availability of user resources when you need them. Check the assumptions with those who have such knowledge, such as the Senior Supplier and Senior User.

12.7.4.1 In Practice

The organization may already have estimating guidelines for standard types of product. This should be particularly true for standard PRINCE2 management and quality products. For example, the amount of time to write an End Stage Report, Highlight Report, and to prepare and hold a quality review should be known.

12.7.4.2 For Small Projects

Beware of giving an estimate for the project before you have gone through this process. It seems easy to give a figure off the top of your head for a small project. But once given, the Project Board will hold you to this. It is amazing how many forgotten activities, unchecked assumptions and thoughts of people being 100% effective lie waiting to be discovered by this process in the smallest of projects.

12.7.5 Prepare the Schedule

A plan can only show whether it can meet its targets when the activities are put together in a schedule against a timeframe, showing when activities will be done and by what resources.

- Draw a planning network.
- Assess resource availability. This should include dates of availability as well as what the scale of that availability is. Any known information on holidays and training courses should be gathered.
- Allocate activities to resources and produce a draft schedule.
- Revise the draft to remove as many peaks and troughs in resource usage as possible.
- Negotiate a solution with the Project Board for problems such as too few resources, too many resources or inability to meet fixed target dates.
- Add in management and quality activities or products (Stage and Team Plans only).
- Define any milestones; points in the plan where attainment will show if we are on target to meet the plan. Another type of milestone might be a trigger for a payment to a supplier.
- Calculate resource utilization and costs (Cartoon 12.4).

12.7.5.1 In Practice

This may be the point when you transfer the plan to your planning tool.

12.7.5.2 For Small Projects

You may not need a planning tool. You should remember to add time and effort for any quality and management products.

12.7.6 Analyze the Risks

You should not commit to a plan without considering what risks are involved in it and what impact the plan might have on risks already known.

- Look for any external dependencies. These always represent one or more risks. They might not arrive on time. They might be of poor quality or be wrong in some other way;

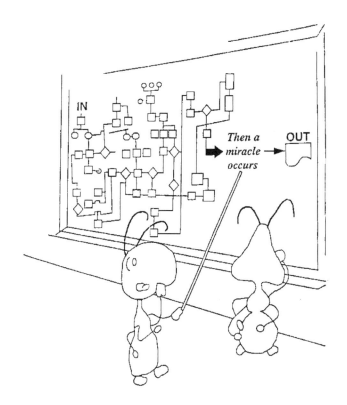

"Good work .... but I think we need

just a little more detail right here"

CARTOON 12.4   Scheduling.

- Look for any assumptions you have made in the plan, e.g. the resources available to you. Each assumption is a risk;
- Look at each resource in the plan. Is there a risk involved? For example, that a new resource does not perform at the expected level, or that a resource's availability is not achieved;
- Are the tools or technology unproven?
- Take the appropriate risk actions. Where appropriate, revise the plan. Make sure that any new or modified risks are shown in the Risk Register.

12.7.7 Document the Plan

A plan in diagrammatic form is not self-explanatory. It needs text.

- Agree tolerance levels for the plan;
- Document what the plan covers, the approach to the work and the checking of its quality, any external dependencies;

- Document any constraints and assumptions you have made;
- Add the planning dates to the Product Checklist (if used);
- Publish the plan.

12.7.7.1 In Practice

The majority of the material for the text will evolve from the previous planning steps. Some of it will already be known because of local standards.

12.7.7.2 For Small Projects

Even if you do not have to publish a plan, you should still document the assumptions.

12.8 LINKS

There is a link between the structure of plans and the controls described in the Progress theme. For example, at an end stage assessment the Project Board will examine the performance of the current Stage Plan and be asked to approve the next Stage Plan. The Team Manager will prepare a Team Plan and agree this with the Project Manager as part of accepting a Work Package.

12.9 DO'S AND DON'TS

By all means use a planning and control tool. It is much easier to modify a plan electronically rather than reach for the eraser. But do not let the tail wag the dog. I have known Project Managers shut themselves in their office for 2 or 3 days a week, adjusting the plan to reflect the last set of timesheets. By the time they emerge, things have changed (slightly) again and back they go to tune the plan again. By all means update the plan regularly with actuals. But then stand back and look at what the latest situation is telling you. If you have broken the plan down into sufficient detail, you should be getting warnings of slippage or faster progress than expected. Go out and have a word in the right ears. Can we recover? Can we take advantage of the progress? Is anyone struggling and in need of help? Project progress is often a case of swings and roundabouts. We have a good week followed by a bad week or vice versa. By all means update the plan with actuals every week, but the plan itself should only be modified every 2 or 3 weeks on the basis of definite corrective actions we need to take to put the plan back on an even keel. Naturally, if an event comes along that we know will require a major change, do not wait. But a lot of small hiccups will sort themselves out if the team knows that you know and have taken an interest in putting things right.

12.10 IF IT IS A LARGE PROJECT

You really will need to use a planning and control tool, a software package. There may already be a standard tool that you are expected to use. Think very carefully about whether you have the time to update it with actuals. In a large project it may well be worth delegating the maintenance of plans to Project Support. Do you have expertise in using the package? Can you afford the time to become an expert?

Many Project Managers struggle to create and update the plans themselves. Many of them have had to learn how to use the tool as they go along. In consequence they know about 10% of the tool's capabilities and are ignorant of many shortcuts and easier ways of doing things with the plan. The Project Manager's job is to generate the information to build the plan in the first place, use the updated plan as a guide to the status and look ahead for problems or risks.

12.11 IF IT IS A SMALL PROJECT

You may be prepared to put enough detail into the Project Plan to allow you to monitor and control the entire project. If so, no other plans are needed. But remember that in a small project you need to have broken down the creation of each product to a small handful of days, otherwise you will have insufficient detail against which to monitor progress. Weigh this need for detail against the Project Board's desire to be able to see the entire project on one page.

Chapter 13

Progress

13.1 INTRODUCTION

The purpose of the Progress theme is to describe the mechanisms that will monitor a project, compare actual progress against what was planned, forecast future events and control any deviations from plan.

The Progress theme supports the PRINCE2 principles of managing by stages, managing by exception and continued business justification.

Project control involves measuring actual progress against the planned targets. This covers the six tolerance areas of time, cost, scope, quality, benefits and risk.

There are two diagrammatic ways of looking at controls. A project needs a controlled start, a controlled progress and a controlled finish. This is represented in Figure 13.1.

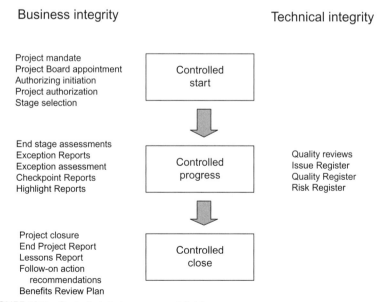

FIGURE 13.1 Controlled start, progress and finish.

13.1.1 Progress Philosophy

Good control does not happen by accident – The control needs of a project need to be assessed and appropriate mechanisms put in place.

Control needs planning – You cannot tell whether you are behind or ahead of schedule and above or below budget, unless you have a plan against which you can compare. Setting up project controls is part of the planning process. Failure to plan monitoring and control activities means that they probably will not get done.

Effective monitoring techniques support good control decisions – Without accurate, timely information, project management is blundering about in the dark and constantly reacting to problems rather than preventing or reducing them in advance.

Control needs to be appropriate to the project – As with all other aspects of project management, the level and formality of control should be appropriate for the project.

In setting up any practically based project control system we will need to put something in place that can, as the project is progressing, answer several fundamental questions.

What was expected to happen?	This is where plans are vital. Without them it is not possible to begin!
What *has* happened?	Accurate and timely status information is required if this question is to be answered.
What is the difference?	Comparison of plans against actuals gives us this.
How serious is it?	Without some benchmark which defines 'serious' this cannot be decided. (Tolerance is the key here. See the later explanation.)
What can be done about it?	Having got reliable information about all the preceding questions, sensible decisions at the proper level of authority can now be made.

Figure 13.2 looks at controls from the view of the management levels.

I shall take each one in turn and discuss it under the same headings used for other project management themes.

13.2 STAGES

13.2.1 Stages Philosophy

The Project Board only gives approval to the Project Manager to proceed one stage at a time. At the end of each stage the Project Board verifies that the project's continuation can still be justified by examining the status of:

● The Business Case;
● Risks;
● The Project Plan.

before it approves a detailed plan to produce the products of the next stage.

A PRINCE2 project must have at least two stages: initiation and the specialist work of the project. According to size and risk, the second stage may be broken down into more stages (Figure 13.3).

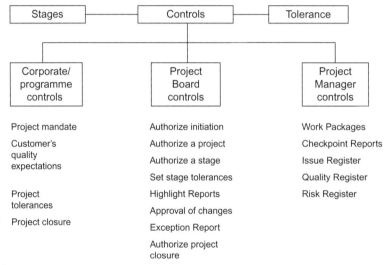

FIGURE 13.2 Controls.

Why plan in stages?

How can we make sure we stay in control?
How can we limit the risks?
How can we stop it if it goes wrong?
Where are the key decision points?
Alignment within a programme

Project Board

Too much time planning
How far ahead is it sensible to plan?
Too many unknowns
Too much guesswork

Project Manager

FIGURE 13.3 Why plan in stages?

13.2.2 Project Board Reasons for Stages

The Project Board wants to be in control without spending all its time on the project. It needs to feel it is making the big decisions guaranteeing that it will be warned of any major problems in advance, and does not want to feel that it has 'a tiger by the tail', in that once started, the project cannot be stopped if it turns sour.

With risky projects there is the need to pause and make sure that the risks are still controllable, so risky projects are likely to have more, smaller stages.

They key criterion for decision-making in business terms is the viability of the Business Case. Is the justification for what we are doing still valid? If not, the project should be in jeopardy. If it is, then it should go forward. These decisions are made in the light of the strategic or programme objectives.

Stages give the Project Board these opportunities at formal moments in the project to decide that the project is no longer viable and close it down.

Stage-limited commitment: At the end of each stage the Project Board only approves a detailed plan to produce the products of the next stage. The Project Plan is updated, but this is mainly for the guidance of the Project Board and will become more accurate as more stages are completed.

The stage-limited commitment, which is sometimes referred to as a 'creeping commitment', is especially important for large projects with a rapidly changing environment that makes it almost impossible to develop an accurate plan for the total project at the outset. However, this type of commitment requires that the provider of funds for the project must accept that the estimate for the completion of the system will inevitably change with time.

Sign-off of interim end-products: At the end of each stage, the interim end-products are reviewed by all affected organizational functions, particularly those that will use the end-products in order to develop the products of the next stage.

In theory, at the end of each stage, the Project Board can call for cancellation of the project because of the existence of one or more possibly critical situations. For example, the organization's business needs may have changed to the point at which the project is no longer cost-effective. A project may also be cancelled if the estimated cost to complete the project exceeds the available funds. In practice, however, cancellation of a project becomes progressively more difficult to justify as increasing amounts of resources are invested.

13.2.3 Project Manager Reasons for Stages

The Project Manager does not want to spend huge amounts of time at the outset trying to plan a long project in sufficient detail for day-to-day control. Trying to look ahead, say, 9 months and plan in detail what will happen and who will do what is almost certain to be wrong. How much easier it is to plan just the next few weeks in detail and have only a high-level plan of the whole project.

Stage ends are needed to obtain from the Project Board the required commitment of resources, money and equipment to move into the next stage.

13.2.4 Initiation Stage

However large or small the project, it is sensible to begin a project with an initiation stage. This is where the Project Board and Project Manager decide if there is agreement on:

- What the project is to achieve;
- Why it is being undertaken;
- Who is to be involved and in what role;
- How and when the required products will be delivered.

This information is documented in the Project Initiation Document (PID). The approved version of the PID is then 'frozen' and used by the Project Board as a benchmark throughout the project and at the end to check the progress and deliveries of the project.

13.2.5 Links

The concept of stages links to end stage assessments by the Project Board.

There is also a link to risks. As mentioned before, the riskier the project, the shorter and more frequent the stages may be to enable a formal risk review to be done by the Project Board as part of the decision whether to continue.

Another link is to the tolerance levels, described next in this chapter. It gives the Project Board tighter control to set exception limits for the next stage than simply to have exception limits for the entire project.

13.2.6 Do's and Don'ts

Always have an initiation stage, however short the project.

Do not split a project into more stages than Project Board control requires.

Do not have a stage that is longer than you can comfortably plan in detail. Remember, a Stage Plan is going to be the Project Manager's main basis for control. This means that you need to get each piece of work that you hand out down to a few days. This will allow you to monitor whether the work is slipping. A fact of life is that people only realize they will not finish on time when they get near the target date. If the pieces of work are 20 days or more in duration, then by the time the person tells you they will be late, it is usually too late to put any recovery actions in place.

13.2.7 If it is a Large Project

The stage-limited commitment is especially important for large projects with a rapidly changing environment that makes it almost impossible to develop an accurate plan for the total project at the outset.

13.2.8 If it is a Small Project

Even in a tiny project with a Project Board of one person it is sensible to begin with an initiation stage. In a small project it may only take half an hour or so to get this understanding, but many projects get into trouble because of misunderstandings at the outset. It is very easy to make assumptions on what you think is needed – and get it wrong. If you start the project by heading off in the wrong direction, then you only need to be slightly wrong to waste a lot of time, money and effort. It is also easy for a member of a Project Board to forget the original agreement and begin to think that something quite different was requested. Documenting the initial agreed objectives and scope and who was committed to do what can save the Project Manager from many arguments and headaches later on in the project.

13.3 TOLERANCE

13.3.1 Tolerance Philosophy

• Tolerances are the permissible deviation from a plan without having to refer the matter to the next higher level of authority.

No project has ever gone 100% to plan. There will be good days and bad days, good weeks and bad weeks. If the Project Board is going to 'manage by exception' it does not want the Project Manager running to it, saying, 'I have spent a pound more than I should today' or 'I have fallen half a day behind schedule this week'. But equally the Project Board does not want the project to overspend by a £million or slip 2 months behind schedule without being warned. So where is the dividing line? What size of deviation from the plan is OK without going back to the Board for a decision? These margins are the tolerances.

The second philosophical point about tolerances is that we do not wait for tolerances to be exceeded; we forecast this, so that the next higher level of authority has time to react and possibly prevent or reduce the deviation (Cartoon 13.1(a) and (b)).

13.3.2 Tolerance Overview

The elements of tolerance are time, cost, scope, risk, benefits and quality.
If we remember the four levels of project management:

• Corporate/programme management set the project tolerances within which the Project Board has to remain;
• The Project Board agrees stage tolerances with the Project Manager;
• The Project Manager agrees tolerances for a Work Package with a Team Manager.

Figure 13.4 will help to explain the concept.

CARTOON 13.1(A) and **(B)**   Tolerance.

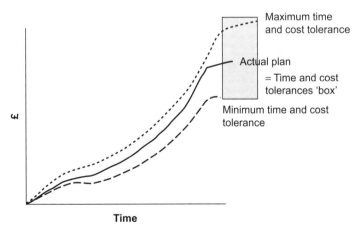

FIGURE 13.4   Example of time and cost tolerances.

As long as the plan's actual progress is within the tolerance margins, all is well. As soon as it can be *forecast* that progress will deviate outside the tolerance margins, the next higher level of authority needs to be advised.

13.3.3 Tolerance Detail

Project tolerances should be part of the project mandate handed down by corporate/programme management. If they are not there, it is the Executive's job during initiation to find out from corporate/programme management what they are.

The Project Board sets stage tolerances for the Project Manager within the overall project tolerances that they have received. The portion allocated to a stage should depend on the risk content of the work and the extent of the unknowns (such as technologies never used before, resources of unknown ability or tasks never attempted before) (Cartoon 13.2).

The Project Manager negotiates appropriate tolerances for each Work Package with the Team Manager. Again these will be tolerances within the stage tolerances set for the Project Manager.

13.3.4 Links

There is a link to the *Controlling a Stage* (CS) and *Managing Product Delivery* (MP) processes that will bring any forecast deviation to the notice of the appropriate level of authority.

13.3.5 Do's and Don'ts

What do we do if a project has such a tight deadline that our shortest plan can only just achieve that date, i.e. we are offered no time tolerance? We try

CARTOON 13.2   Cost tolerances.

to enlarge the cost tolerance. This would allow us to pay for overtime, extra resources, better equipment and better resources, anything that might save time if the target date was threatened.

If the converse was true and no cost tolerance was offered, we would ask for a greater time tolerance. This would allow us to not use overtime, drop some resources and use cheaper resources.

If both time and cost tolerances are tight, this is where we look at two other elements: scope and quality. For scope we list everything we have to deliver in order of priority. Then if the going gets tough, we take the list to the customer and say, 'You cannot have everything within the tolerances. What products can we drop?'

Quality is the dangerous aspect of tolerance. This is because quality reduction can happen without your knowing. If a team knows that it is under time and/or cost pressure, the easiest thing to do is relax on the quality checking, carry out fewer tests, let things slip through that you know are not exactly right. Occasionally there may be quality concessions that can be made in order to stay within other tolerances, such as 'You can have all the products, but you cannot have the colours you wanted.'

13.3.6 If it is a Large Project

It is very important to establish tolerances at all the levels described. The Project Manager should consider carefully any tolerances for scope and quality that may be called upon. Priorities for the various elements of the product need to be agreed at the beginning so that they can influence the sequence of design and development. There would be no point in trying to down-scope late in the project if all the minor 'nice-to-have's' have already been developed.

13.3.7 If it is a Small Project

There will probably be no Team Managers. In that case the Project Manager may still wish to allow a small tolerance for an individual's Work Package. The danger in telling an individual that they have a certain tolerance is that the tolerance becomes the expected target. For example, if you tell a person that they have until Thursday to do a job with a tolerance of one day, in their mind the target becomes Friday. Some managers prefer to set tolerances but keep these to themselves.

13.4 MANAGEMENT CONTROLS

Management controls work around the three areas of getting a project off to a controlled start, controlling progress and bringing the project to a controlled close. Let us take a look at the necessary management controls following our concept of up to four levels of management: corporate/programme management, Project Board, Project Manager and Team Manager.

13.5 CORPORATE/PROGRAMME MANAGEMENT CONTROLS

13.5.1 Philosophy

Corporate/programme management will have many things on their mind and will want to spend the minimum of time on any one project while still retaining control. This is the start of 'management by exception'. They agree the overall project objectives and time and cost objectives with the Executive of the Project Board and say 'Get on with it. As long as you are on course, just send us progress information. But come back to us if you forecast that you are moving outside the limits we have agreed with you.'

13.5.2 Executive Appointment

For the maximum amount of confidence in their Project Board, corporate/programme management should normally appoint one of their members to be the Executive. They can appoint people to other Project Board roles or leave the selection to the Executive.

13.5.3 Project Mandate

Corporate/programme management are responsible for the creation of the project mandate, which they will pass to the Executive of the Project Board. This gives them control over the project's objectives, scope and constraints.

13.5.4 Customer's Quality Expectations

As part of the project mandate, corporate/programme management should specify their quality expectations of the final product. This should cover such things as packaging or presentation, performance, reliability and maintainability.

13.5.5 Project Tolerances

Corporate/programme management sets tolerances for the whole project. It is the Executive's job to ensure this information is made available at the outset of a project as part of the project mandate or creation of the Project Brief.

13.5.6 Project Closure

The Executive must gain confirmation from corporate/programme management that the project mandate has been satisfied.

13.5.7 Links

Corporate/programme management set the project tolerances. This allows them to define the circumstances under which the Project Board must refer problems to them for a go/no go decision, rather than make the decision itself.

There will be entries in the Communication Management Strategy to describe how the Project Board, or at least the Executive, will keep corporate/programme management informed.

A higher-level architecture group may prescribe the project approach where the project is part of a programme. It will have to conform to the same architecture as the other parts of the programme. The Project Board, especially the Senior Supplier, has to check this.

13.5.8 Do's and Don'ts

Do keep reports and meetings to a sensible minimum. Try to avoid the monthly progress meetings where your project is one item on a crowded corporate/programme agenda.

Do avoid appointing the Project Board from below, i.e. without reference to corporate/programme management. This only leads to mistrust of the Project Board by corporate/programme management. If this happens, any so-called 'decision' by the Project Board will ping-pong between them and corporate/programme management for approval by the latter. What you are looking for is a Project Board that has the confidence of corporate/programme management, so that once the Project Board has taken a decision you can move on.

13.5.9 If it is a Large Project

The controls and reporting should be documented and copies kept in the project files.

13.5.10 If it is a Small Project

A small project may not interest corporate/programme management. In this case the Executive will assume their role.

13.6 PROJECT BOARD CONTROLS

13.6.1 Philosophy

The Project Board wants to 'manage by exception', i.e. agree a Stage Plan with the Project Manager and then let him/her get on with it without any interference or extra effort – unless the plan goes wrong.

13.6.2 Overview of Project Board Controls

The Project Board 'owns' the project. Its members are ultimately accountable for the success of the project, not the Project Manager. This is why the Project

Board members must have the requisite authority to commit resources and make decisions.

Project Board members will be busy with their other jobs, and therefore will want to spend the minimum amount of time controlling the project commensurate with making sure that the project meets its objectives within the defined constraints.

13.6.3 Controlled Start

13.6.3.1 Authorize Initiation

The Project Board examines the initiation Stage Plan to see if it reflects the work needed to initiate the project. This will be affected by any previous work done if the project is part of an overall programme.

The project mandate should contain the project objectives, customer quality expectations and project approach, among other things. One of the first tasks in PRINCE2 is to add any missing information, turning the project mandate into the Project Brief. It is therefore very important for the Project Board to examine this document and be satisfied with its contents before agreeing to initiate the project.

13.6.3.2 Authorize the Project

The PID is the internal 'contract' for the project, documenting what the project is to do, why it should be done (the Business Case), who is responsible for what and when and how products are to be delivered. There has to be agreement by customer and supplier on its contents before commitment to the project by the Project Board. If a viable Business Case does not exist, the Project Board should not proceed with the project.

13.6.4 Controlled Progress

13.6.4.1 Authorize a Stage

An end stage assessment happens (surprise, surprise!) at the end of each management stage, where the Project Board assesses the continued viability of the project and, if satisfied, gives the Project Manager approval to proceed with the next stage.

The Project Board defines the maximum deviations allowed from the Stage Plan without the Project Manager having to return to the Board for a decision on action to be taken. This is the key element of 'management by exception'.

The Project Board must be aware of the need to avoid technical or irrelevant discussions and to focus on the management aspects which, when taken as a whole, inform its decision on whether to proceed or not. As a rule of thumb, an end stage assessment should not last more than 2 hours. A sensible Project Manager will have been in touch with the Project Board, either verbally or through Highlight Reports, making sure that the members know what is coming and finding out what they think about the future of the project. 'No surprises' is the best way to ensure short end stage assessments.

The detail of the next Stage Plan may often cause modification of the Project Plan. The Project Board checks the figures against both the previous version of the Project Plan and the revised version to see what changes have been made. Any changes should be justified (e.g. against approved requests for change) before approval of the Stage Plan.

The 'bottom line' is whether the project is still predicted to deliver sufficient benefits to justify the investment, i.e. is the Business Case still sound?

The other aspects of the end stage assessment are:

- Current progress checked against the Project Plan;
- Current stage completed successfully (all products delivered and accepted);
- Confirmation that all delivered stage products have passed their predefined quality checks;
- Next Stage Plan examined against the Project Plan and authorized;
- I personally believe that an 'Approval to proceed' form should be signed by all Project Board members.

The Project Board must authorize its approval to proceed so that the project cannot drift without approval into the next stage.

13.6.4.2 Highlight Reports

The best way of characterizing *management by exception* is the expression 'no news is good news'. At a frequency defined by the Project Board in the PID, the Project Manager has to send a Highlight Report to the Project Board to confirm achievements toward meeting the Stage Plan (Cartoon 13.3).

CARTOON 13.3 Highlight Report.

The frequency of Highlight Reports is determined by the Project Board during initiation, and should relate to the commitment and level of risk in the stage.

The Project Manager prepares Highlight Reports, using progress information provided by the team members and analyzed at the checkpoints.

The principal focus of the Highlight Report is to identify:

- Products completed during the current reporting period;
- Products to be completed in the next period;
- Any real or potential problems.

Other limited narrative information, such as the budget and risk status, can be added (in my opinion, up to a total of one page of paper).

13.6.4.3 Change Request Approval

Having approved the objectives and products required in the project initiation, it is only right that the Project Board (or its delegated Change Authority) should have to approve any changes to them. Once requested changes have been estimated for the effort and cost of doing them, the customer has to decide on their priority, whether they should be done and whether the money to do them can be found. As for all the other decisions, it needs an assessment of the impact on the Project Plan, the Business Case and the risk situation.

13.6.4.4 Exception Report Review

If the Project Manager can forecast that the plan will end outside its tolerance margins, an Exception Report must be sent immediately to the Project Board, detailing the problem, options and a recommendation.

It should be stressed that if the project is not collecting reliable progress information, it will be difficult to know when that point has been reached.

13.6.4.5 Authorize an Exception Plan

If the Project Board, on reading the Exception Report, decides to accept a recommendation to proceed on the basis of a modified plan, it will ask the Project Manager to produce an Exception Plan, which replaces the remainder of the plan.

The Project Manager should prepare an Exception Plan and present it to the Project Board for approval at an exception assessment, identical to an end stage assessment. The less formal approach says that there may not be a meeting, but the Project Manager still needs to get his/her plan of remedial action approved by the Project Board.

13.6.5 Controlled Close

13.6.5.1 Authorize Project Closure

As part of its decision on whether to close the project the Project Board receives an End Project Report from the Project Manager, summing up the project's performance in meeting the requirements of the PID plus any changes that were approved.

The Project Board uses the original PID to confirm that the project has achieved its objectives, including the required quality. Any changes that were made after the PID was 'frozen' when the project was authorized are included, and their impact on Project Plan, Business Case and risks is assessed.

The report provides statistics on issues and their impact on the project, plus statistics on the quality of work carried out. It is created by the Project Manager and submitted to the Project Board.

13.6.5.2 Follow-on Action Recommendations

Follow-on action recommendations form part of the End Project Report. They describe any unfinished business at the end of the project.

The Project Board is presented with a list of all outstanding actions that are to be handed to the group that will support the product in its operational life. These may be change requests that the Project Board decided not to implement during the life of the current project or risks identified during the project that may affect the product in use. The Project Board has to confirm that all outstanding issues have been captured, and satisfy itself that nothing on the list should have been completed by the project.

13.6.5.3 Lessons Report

As another part of the End Project Report, the Project Manager has to present a report on what project management (and possibly technical) aspects of the project went well, and what went badly. The Project Board has the job of ensuring that this is passed to an appropriate body that will disseminate the report to other projects and possibly modify the relevant standards. It is important that an appropriate group is identified. There may be a project management support group or a quality assurance group.

(If any lessons are found earlier in the project, the Project Manager may decide to add a Lessons Report to an End Stage Report if this will benefit other projects earlier than waiting until the end of the project.)

13.6.5.4 Benefits Review Plan

Normally many products need time in use before the achievement of their expected benefits can be measured. This measurement after a period of use is an activity called a post-project review. Corporate/programme management will be responsible for ensuring that these measurements take place. The Project Manager has to provide a plan for how, when and by whom these measurements are to be done.

Post-project benefits reviews occur outside the project and, as such, are not part of the project.

Any corrective work identified by the post-project review would be done during product use and maintenance. A problem may not be with the product itself, but organizational ones, needing such solutions as retraining.

The post-project review can happen perhaps 6, 12 or 18 months after the project has finished (it depends on the nature of the product).

13.6.5.5 Customer Acceptance

The Project Manager should provide confirmation of customer acceptance of the end-product(s) before asking the Project Board to allow the project to close.

13.6.5.6 Operational and Maintenance Acceptance

The Project Manager must present evidence to the Project Board of the willingness of those who will operate and maintain the product in its operational life to accept the final product. This includes documentation and training.

13.6.6 Links

There is a link to the setting of tolerances, particularly stage tolerances.

Another link is to the change control mechanism, because the Project Board makes the decision on whether changes are to be implemented or not.

13.6.7 Do's and Don'ts

Do make sure that you get sign-off from the Project Board, confirming that the project *as defined in the PID* has been completed and the end-product accepted. However small the project has been, never assume that the end-product has been accepted.

Do not allow the Project Board to let the project drift on into modifying the end-product or creating extra products outside the scope of the initiation. Any such work thought up by the customer when you deliver what you believe to be the end-product should form part of another project and another PID. You will not be able to measure the success of the project fairly if you allow time and cost to be added for work that is not covered in the PID. Remember, project success is measured against the PID *plus any approved change requests*. It is your own Business Case that will suffer if you allow last minute 'wouldn't be nice if' tinkering to creep in.

13.6.8 If it is a Large Project

All of these controls should be used and documented.

13.6.9 If it is a Small Project

Many of these controls can be done informally, but the Project Board should always consider what documentation of its decisions is needed in case things turn sour later.

13.7 PROJECT MANAGER CONTROLS

13.7.1 Philosophy

A project is broken down into stages. The Project Manager is in day-to-day control of a stage based on a Stage Plan that the Project Board has approved. The Project Manager carries on with a stage until its end without needing another approval from the Project Board unless either:

- There is a forecast of an exception beyond tolerance limits or;
- Changes have been requested for which extra resources are needed.

13.7.2 Overview of Project Manager Controls

The basic idea is to:

- Agree with the Project Board what is to be done and the constraints within which the job has to be done;
- Get approval from the Project Board for a plan to do the work;
- Direct teams or individuals to do the necessary work;
- Confirm with the customer that the products meet requirements;
- Report back that the job has been done.

Breaking a project into stages, using tolerance levels and agreeing the need for any Highlight Reports with the Project Board complements this basic concept.

13.7.3 Controlled Progress

13.7.3.1 Quality Register

Details of all planned quality work are entered in the register. It is updated with actual results of the quality work. The Project Manager monitors the Quality Register on a regular basis.

13.7.3.2 Work Packages

A Work Package is an agreement between the Project Manager and either an individual or a Team Manager to undertake a piece of work. It describes the work, agreed dates, standards to be used, quality and reporting requirements. No work can start without the Project Manager's approval via a Work Package, so it is a powerful schedule, cost and quality control for the Project Manager.

13.7.3.3 Team Plans

As part of agreement on a Work Package, the Project Manager has to agree the Team Plan to produce the products involved. This is then reflected in the Stage Plan. The Project Manager can use this to confirm that the plan is reasonable, will fit within the stage tolerances given by the Project Board and that it contains adequate quality work.

13.7.3.4 Checkpoint Reports

This is a report from a team to the Project Manager. It is sent at a frequency agreed in the Work Package.

A specific aim of a Checkpoint Report is to check all aspects of the Work Package against the Team and Stage Plans to ensure that there are no nasty surprises hiding. Useful questions to answer are: 'What is not going to plan?' and 'What is likely not to go to plan?' The crucial question that underlies the objective of the meeting is 'Are we still likely to complete the work within the tolerances laid down by the Project Manager?'

Checkpoints should be taken as frequently as the Project Manager requires. They may coincide with the Project Manager's need to consider replanning. The checkpoint frequency is defined in the Work Package.

The information gathered at a checkpoint is used by the Project Manager to form the basis of the next Highlight Report.

13.7.3.5 Issue Register

The Issue Register is a key control document for the Project Manager, keeping track of all problems and change requests. It usually contains the answer to Project Board questions such as 'Why is the project going to cost more/take longer than you said in the PID?'

13.7.3.6 Risk Register

The status of risks should be monitored regularly. Risks are formally reviewed at each stage end, but should also be checked as part of the impact analysis of major change requests.

13.7.3.7 Stage Plan

The Stage Plan is the document against which the Project Manager is controlling a stage.

13.7.3.8 Configuration Management

Configuration management is the identification of the products to be created/used by the project, their tracking and control. This provides the Project Manager with the status of products.

13.7.3.9 Daily Log

Apart from the Stage Plan a Project Manager needs a diary to record significant events or remind him or her of informal issues or other tasks to deal with in the coming week.

The Project Manager keeps a Daily Log in which to record important events, decisions, happenings or statements. This is partly a defense mechanism in case some time later the other person forgets that they said something, but also to become part of the Project Manager's monitoring that what was said actually happens (Cartoon 13.4).

It is also useful for the Project Manager to set up a number of monitoring activities for the coming week.

Before the start of each week the Project Manager should take a look at the Stage Plan, the Risk Register, the Issue Register and the Quality Register. This should provide a number of monitoring points for action during the week, such as:

- What is on the critical path of my plan that is supposed to finish during the week? Is it going to finish on time? (Or else when?) Did it finish on time?
- Should the status of any risks be checked this week? Is it time to give a risk owner a nudge to follow-up on the risk's status?
- Are there any outstanding issues that I should be chasing which are out for impact analysis or for consideration by the customer?

Very nice, but not the kind of Daily Log I was looking for.

CARTOON 13.4 Daily Log.

13.7.4 Controlled Close

13.7.4.1 Acceptance Criteria

If all acceptance criteria can be ticked, this puts the Project Manager in a strong position to say that the project has achieved its objectives and can close.

13.7.4.2 Configuration Item Records

The Configuration Librarian does a check on all products produced and their status. This confirms that all products have been approved and is a necessary check before work to close the project can begin.

13.7.4.3 Issue Register

All issues should have either been dealt with or have Project Board agreement to being held over and passed to the operational support group. The Project Manager must check the status of all issues as part of closing the project.

The register is used together with the PID to check how the original objectives of the project were modified. It is also used to match against the follow-on action recommendations to ensure that there are no loose ends.

13.7.4.4 Quality Register

The Quality Register gives an assessment of whether the appropriate quality work was put into the project's products and whether there is an audit trail available.

13.7.5 Links

Progress links to the chapter on project organization as part of the 'who does what'.

There is a link to the work needed in *Starting up a Project* (SU).

There are links to the Change theme and configuration management.

There is a link to the Project Manager's Daily Log.

13.7.6 Do's and Don'ts

Do check the need for all these points against the environment of the project.

Do not be misled by the comfortable feeling at the start of a project that everybody is committed and behind you. This is the direction from which back-stabbing occurs! That 'togetherness' feeling can evaporate as problems and/or changes come along. I used to work for a very cynical Italian manager whose favorite phrase was, 'Do not plan for the honeymoon, plan for the divorce.' In other words, if everything in the project was to go sweetly, the 'honeymoon' feeling would last and there would be little need for controls and documentation of who agreed to do what and why. But life has a way of changing, people change their minds, forget things, unexpected events occur. Just in case things turn sour you need to have the controls mentioned in this chapter available to you and be able to lay your hands on documentation to support what happened and who decided what during the project.

13.7.7 If it is a Large Project

All of these items should be considered for use. Their documentation and safe filing should also be considered as they will form a key part of the Project Manager's audit trail of why things happened and who decided what.

13.7.8 If it is a Small Project

Many of the controls can be done informally. There may be no teams or only one reporting direct to the Project Manager with no Team Managers appointed. This shortens the checkpoint control. The Project Manager would hold the checkpoint meetings with the team and write up the Checkpoint Report personally. (Remember that it may have been agreed to give the Checkpoint Report orally.)

13.8 EVENT- AND TIME-DRIVEN CONTROLS

Some of the PRINCE2 controls described in this chapter are event-driven, others are time-driven. Below is a table, showing which controls are time-driven and which event-driven.

	Event-driven	Time-driven
Project initiation	✓	
Stages	✓	
Management by exception	✓	
End stage assessment	✓	
Highlight Report		✓
Exception Report	✓	
Work Package	✓	
Checkpoint Report		✓
Risk Register	✓	
Quality Register	✓	
Issue Register	✓	

Chapter 14

Quality

14.1 PHILOSOPHY

The ISO 9000 definition of quality is:

The totality of features and inherent or assigned characteristics of a product, person, process, service or system that bear on its ability to show that it meets expectations or satisfies stated needs, requirements or specification.

Many people get worried by some of the words in this definition, such as the word 'inherent'. What is hidden there? Basically, it means inbuilt or natural. An example might be a definition of the requirement for a lawn. The requirement would not have to say that the lawn should be green, because that is 'inherent'. The specification for a wheel might not need to specify that it should be round, because this is 'inherent' in a wheel.

The Quality theme supports the 'product focus' philosophy and addresses the quality methods and responsibilities not only for the technical products, but also for the management of the project. Only after establishing product quality criteria and quality control activities and resourcing can the full costs and timescales be estimated for the Project, Stage and Team Plans.

14.2 QUALITY OVERVIEW

It is likely that both the supplier and the customer will have quality standards already in place – a Quality Management System (QMS). Both may also have staff responsible for ensuring that these standards are used (quality assurance). Depending on the environment into which the final product will be delivered, there may be other legal or environmental standards to be reached. An example here would be a car's emission levels if we were building a new car. All of these need to be matched against the customer's quality expectations, the anticipated project timeframe, the cost and the solution method. Out of this comparison we should get a list of the development standards, the testing methods and the tools to be used.

These quality requirements need to be related to the various products that the project will create or use. We then need to get down to putting into our detailed plans the work necessary to ensure that quality is built in, who will do this and when.

After this we need to consider an audit trail of our quality work. How do we prove to the customer that the necessary quality work has been done?

14.3 THE QUALITY TRAIL

Step	Product	Process/Technique/Theme
Ascertain the customer's quality expectations	Project mandate or Project Brief	Starting up a Project (SU)
Define the project's acceptance criteria	Project Product Description	Starting up a Project (SU)
Write a Quality Management Strategy	Project Initiation Document	Initiating a Project (IP)
Add quality work and resources to a Stage Plan	Stage Plan	Managing a Stage Boundary
Identify planned quality check dates	Quality Register	Managing a Stage Boundary (SB)
Define a product's quality criteria	Product Descriptions	Product-based Planning
Explain the quality requirements for each piece of work	Work Package	Controlling a Stage (CS)
Report back on the quality work performed	Quality Register	Managing Product Delivery (MP)
Check that quality work is being done correctly	Quality Register	Controlling a Stage (CS)
Control changes	Issue	Change control
Keep track of changes to products	Configuration records	Configuration management

14.3.1 Customer's Quality Expectations

This is a definition in measurable terms of what must be done for the final product to be acceptable to the customer and staff who will be affected.

This will vary according to the type of final product. Suggestions are:

● Major functions;
● Appearance;

- Personnel level required to use/operate the product;
- Performance levels;
- Capacity;
- Accuracy;
- Availability;
- Reliability (mean/maximum time to repair, mean time between failures);
- Running costs;
- Security;
- Ease of use;
- Timings.

The customer's quality expectations should be made clear in the project mandate at the very outset of the project. If not sufficiently clear, the Project Manager should clarify the expectations when preparing the Project Brief (during *Starting up a Project* (SU)). The expectations should be measurable. 'Of good quality' may sound fine, but how can it be measured? Expectations of performance, reliability, flexibility, maintainability and capability can all be expressed in measurable terms.

Quality is one corner of a triangle as shown in Figure 14.1. The customer has to decide where, within the triangle, the project's main focus is to be. Does it incline more toward the cost, the time or the quality? This simple exercise shows that the three items are interlinked. If you want the product to be cheap, that may have an adverse effect on the quality, and so on.

It is dangerous to assume that the customer will always want a superb quality product that will last forever. Have a look at the products in your local cut-rate store and you will see what I mean. Let me quote you two different examples of customer quality thinking from projects in my past.

A telecommunications company had bid for a packet switching system in Australia. They had been told they were the favored supplier and their bid price looked good in relation to their competitors. Suddenly a bright young man employed by the Australian customer looked at the geography of the country and said to his bosses, 'Most of this system is going to be across the deserted middle of the country. It is going to be very expensive to fix any faults out there. Have we specified a high enough quality?' So the tender was recalled and when it reemerged it contained a quality requirement that said all components (hardware and software) supplied had to have a mean time between failure of 3 years.

FIGURE 14.1 The quality, cost and time triangle.

This was backed up by heavy penalty clauses in the event of failure. The bidding Telecommunications Company looked at its original bid, which had included testing work 'to a commercial level' and realized that this was not enough. So lots more testing to destruction was added to the price, plus duplicate equipment to take over in case of failure, and so on. The price of their bid became so high that they lost the contract (but probably saved themselves money in the long run).

The exploration arm of an oil company came to their data processing section with the results of a seismic survey carried out in the mountains of a South American country. They had a very short time in which to analyze the results and decide if there were oil or gas reservoirs there. Their exploration contract had to be renewed or they would lose their favoured position. Their quality need was for accuracy of analysis. Beyond that they needed a fast turnaround. They were not worried about the result layout being 'user-friendly'. The product was to be used once and then thrown away. There is a big difference in the approach to quality needed by these two projects.

14.3.2 Acceptance Criteria

Acceptance criteria are a definition in measurable terms of those aspects of the final product which it must demonstrate for the product to be acceptable to the customer and staff who will be affected by the product. However, some acceptance criteria, such as performance and mean time between failure, cannot be measured until the final product has been operational for some time. Such criteria must be added to the Benefits Review Plan.

Acceptance criteria should be suitable for the product, such as:

- Reference to meeting the customer's quality expectations;
- Target dates;
- Major functions;
- Capacity;
- Appearance;
- Availability;
- Development cost;
- Running costs;
- Maintenance;
- Ease of use;
- Timings;
- Personnel level required to use/operate the product.

Acceptance criteria may be split into 'time zones'. Some must be fully met before the project can be closed, but for others, such as performance, there may be a series of improving targets that must be met after periods of operational use.

Acceptance criteria should also be prioritized in case there comes a time when one criterion can only be fully met at the expense of another one. For example, delivery on time versus having a product that is 100% complete.

Expectations of performance, reliability, flexibility, maintainability and capability can all be expressed in measurable terms.

Acceptance criteria measurements defined when starting up the project may need refining. This can happen during initiation and at the end of each stage.

14.3.3 The Quality Management Strategy

The next step is to decide how the project is going to meet the customer's quality expectations for the product. The Quality Management Strategy is created during initiation. Other inputs to this should be the standards to be used to guide the development of the product and test its ability to meet the quality expectations. The supplier should have standards, but the customer may also have standards that it insists be used. Such standards have to be compared against the quality expectations to see which are to be used. There may be gaps where extra standards have to be obtained or created. The customer has the last say in what standards will be used to check the products. Regulatory standards may also need to be met.

The Quality Management Strategy identifies the standards to be used and the main quality responsibilities. The latter may be a reference to a quality assurance function (belonging to either the customer, the supplier or both). There is a cross-reference here to the Project Board roles. These roles contain Project Assurance responsibility, some of them affecting quality. If these have been delegated, there must be a match with the responsibility defined in the Quality Management Strategy.

The Quality Management Strategy refers to the establishment of the Quality Register and its purpose.

Product Descriptions are written for the key products shown in the Project Plan. These include specific quality criteria against which the products will be measured.

14.3.4 The Project Product Description

This is created in the *Starting up a Project* (SU) process as part of the Project Brief and is a prerequisite to selecting the project approach (Will the approach provide all the products at the required quality and meet the acceptance criteria?). It is reviewed during initiation and at each stage boundary. It is a summary of the project's final product. It defines what the project must deliver in order to be accepted by the customer, including:

- Purpose of the final product;
- Its set of products;
- Source products from which this product will be derived;
- The customer's quality expectations;
- Acceptance criteria;
- Project quality tolerances;
- Development skills required;

- The method(s) to be used when accepting the products;
- Who will be responsible for confirming acceptance.

It is officially the responsibility of the Senior User, but usually the Project Manager writes it in consultation with the Senior User and Executive. A full description of its contents can be found in Appendix A.

14.3.5 Adding Quality to Each Stage Plan

Each Stage Plan needs lower level detail than the Quality Management Strategy. This identifies the method of quality checking to be used for each product of the stage. The plan also identifies responsibility for each individual quality check. For example, for each quality review the chair and reviewers are identified. This gives an opportunity for those with Project Assurance roles to see each draft Stage Plan and input its needs for checking and the staff who should represent it at each check.

Any major products developed in the stage have Product Descriptions written for them, if they were not done as part of the Quality Management Strategy.

14.3.6 Product Descriptions

A Product Description should be written for each major product to be produced by the project. Among other information the description should contain:

- Title;
- Purpose;
- Composition (what are the themes of the product);
- Derivation (what is the source of the themes);
- Format (what does the product have to look like);
- Quality criteria (what quality does the product have to display);
- Quality tolerance;
- Quality method (how will the product be tested that it meets the quality criteria);
- The skills or resources required to check the quality.

The Product Description should be written as soon as possible after the need for it is recognized. Writing the description helps the planner understand what the product is and how long it is likely to take to build it.

The Product Description is also the first place where we start thinking about the quality of the product, how we will test the presence of its quality and who we might need in order to test that quality.

It is very sensible to get the customer to write as much of the Product Description as possible, particularly its purpose and quality criteria. This helps the customer define what is needed and is useful when delivering a product to be able to confirm that a product meets its criteria.

The Product Description is an important part of the information handed to a Team Manager or individual as part of a Work Package.

Any time that a product that has been approved by the Project Board has to be changed, the Product Description should also be checked to see if it needs an update.

14.3.7 Quality Tolerance

The quality tolerance of a product is defined as a range of values within which the quality criteria can vary and still be acceptable. For example, 'the white wine must be stored at 6°C, with a tolerance of 5°C–7°C', or 'time taken to process the order must be no more than 30 seconds, with a tolerance margin of −10 seconds, +0 seconds'.

14.3.8 Quality Register

The Quality Register is a summary of planned tests, personnel involved, tests carried out and test results. The initial entry is by the Project Manager when a Stage Plan is created. The Team Manager may wish to add the names of extra reviewers and the actual results as the quality checking is done. This information is normally passed to the Configuration Librarian to make the actual updates to the register, but this is defined in the Configuration Management Strategy (Cartoon 14.1).

14.3.9 Quality File

Although this is not mentioned in the official PRINCE2 manual, there should be one quality file for each project. It is the responsibility of the Project Manager. If a Configuration Librarian has been appointed to the project, it is important that the duties with regard to the quality file are clearly defined between this role and the Project Manager. Normally the Configuration Librarian will be allocated the duties of logging and filing all the documents.

CARTOON 14.1 The Quality Register.

The quality file should contain the Quality Register, the master copy of the Product Descriptions and the forms that are produced as part of the quality controls applied during the life of the project. It is an important part of the audit trail that can be followed by the user or an independent quality assurance body to assess what quality checking has been carried out and how effective it has been. As such, it is a deliverable product. The Project Manager is responsible for setting up the Quality Register and quality file and checking that either Team Managers or individuals are feeding information into the file.

Wherever possible, the originals of documents should be filed in the quality file. A copy can be filed if the original has to be circulated for signature or comments, but on its return the original should be replaced in the quality file.

The quality file should have sections for:

- Quality Register
  Each quality check should have a unique number to provide the basis for statistics on how many quality checks have been carried out.
- Quality review invitations
  On filing this document there should be a check that there is no unreported date slippage compared to the planned review date. If there is, the Project Manager should be notified.
- Quality review results
  When all corrective actions on the action list have been taken and the list signed off by the chair of the review, it is filed in the quality file. Review documents such as follow-up action list, annotated product copies and question lists should all be filed in the quality file.

14.4 QUALITY REVIEW

A quality review is a peer review of the quality of a product against its Product Description, including its quality criteria. It deserves a full description, so I have taken it out of this rather long chapter and put it in Appendix D.

14.5 LINKS

There is clearly a link to the project organization. If the customer or the supplier has an independent quality assurance function, how can they neatly fit into the project organization? The answer is via the Project Assurance role. Both customer and supplier could appoint someone from their quality assurance function to carry out part of their Project Assurance role. This gives them access to the detailed planning, when they can ensure that satisfactory testing with the correct participants has been planned. They can get feedback from these participants either directly or through the Quality Register about the results of quality work.

The Project Assurance function can do a valuable job by checking that the Product Descriptions are correct.

Clearly change control has an impact on quality. If uncontrolled changes are made, this is likely to destroy the quality of the project in terms of schedule and costs, as well as making it unclear what is being delivered. This means that there would be no connection between what was originally requested and what is finally delivered.

In the same way configuration management has links to quality. If you do not keep control over what version of a product you are using, the quality is likely to suffer.

14.6 DO'S AND DON'TS

Do treat the need for quality very seriously. The customer may, over time, forgive you for delivering late and may forgive you for coming in over budget. But the customer will never forgive you for delivering a poor quality product.

Do not miss out on any of the quality steps.

14.7 IF IT IS A LARGE PROJECT

Quality is like carpet underlay. It enhances the feel and life of the product, but it is very difficult to put it in afterward. In a large project, you cannot check everyone's work. Make full use of the Project Assurance role to check for you. Your job is to define the quality required, plan for it, monitor people who are checking for it and react quickly if there is a quality problem.

Where you have several teams working for you, ensure that the Project Assurance roles check the quality work intentions in the Team Plans and get customer people in there, checking that the supplier is delivering good quality. Finding out during acceptance testing that a poor quality solution has been delivered is far too late. All too often this leads to litigation and only the lawyers win there. Remember, the customer does not want large penalty payments. The customer wants a product that will meet the requirements.

14.8 IF IT IS A SMALL PROJECT

It is very easy to think that quality in a small project will look after itself. 'It is such a small project, we can check the quality when we have finished.' 'Delivering a quality product from a small project is easy', they will say. 'Only an idiot could get it wrong.' Well, if you do not go through the quality steps mentioned above, it could be 'welcome to the idiot's club.'

Chapter 15

Risk

15.1 PHILOSOPHY

Projects bring about change and change brings risks. Risks are inevitable in every project. Risk can be formally defined as:

the chance of exposure to the consequences of future events.

It is not uncommon to hear people say 'This is a high risk project.' This statement by itself is of limited interest or value. We need far more details. What are the actual risks? What are their causes? What is the probability of the risk occurring? How serious would the impact of that occurrence be? What can be done about it?

There are many methods of risk management on the market and quite a few software packages that will help you with a standard set of questions and 'forms' to come to a view of the risk situation of your project. To my mind, far more important than which method you choose is *when* should you carry out assessment of risk. Too many projects look at the risk situation at the beginning of a project, then forget about it for the rest of the project (or until a risk comes up and smacks them on the jaw!).

I suggest that you:

- Carry out risk assessment at the start of a project. Make proposals on what should be done about the risks. Get agreement on whether to start the project.
- Review the risks at the end of every stage. This includes existing risks that might have changed and new risks caused by the next Stage Plan. Get agreement on whether to continue into the next stage.
- Appoint an owner for every risk. Build into the Stage Plan the moments when the owners should be monitoring the risks. Check on the owners to see that they are doing the job and keeping the risk status up-to-date.
- Review every request for change for its impact on existing risks or the creation of a new risk. Build the time and cost of any risk avoidance or reduction into your recommendation on the action to be taken.
- Inspect the risks at the end of the project for any that might affect the product in its operational life. If there are any, make sure that you notify those charged with looking after the product. (Use the follow-on action recommendations for this.)

These points should be enough for you to keep control of the risk situation. If you have very long stages (which I do not recommend) and very few requests for change, you may decide to review risks on a monthly basis.

There is one other point of philosophy about risk. When considering actions, you have to consider the cost of taking action against the cost of not taking action.

15.2 RISK OVERVIEW

The management of risk is one of the most important ongoing parts of the Project Board's and Project Manager's jobs. We should remember that *occasionally* there may be the risk of something beneficial happening to a project. We need to be prepared to take advantage of such risks occurring. However, most risks to be considered are those that might bring bad news, and it is on these risks that we shall concentrate in this chapter.

So the focus of our risk attention is on the likelihood of something happening that we would wish to avoid. In a project, then, risk is anything that causes the project to end in such a way that it does not fully meet its identified targets and objectives.

Risks need to be:

- Identified;
- Assessed;
- Controlled.

The effect of failure to deliver a project on time, to an acceptable cost and level of quality can be disastrous. Although the cost of managing risk may appear significant, the cost of *not* managing risk effectively can be many times greater. As part of our assessment of what action to take about a risk, we have to balance the cost of taking action against the cost of not taking action.

Only by fully recognizing and understanding the risks that exist can potential problems and opportunities be understood and addressed. Both the likelihood of things happening and the consequences if they do occur must be understood by the project management team in order to have this true appreciation of the risk situation. The Project Board then needs to choose a course of action that can be taken to improve the situation.

It should be recognized that it may be desirable to accept some risks in order to obtain additional benefits to the project. *Note*: the option to take no action may sometimes be appropriate. This means that a decision is made that the perceived level of risk is acceptable.

How effectively a risk can be managed depends on the identification of its underlying causes and the amount of control that the project management team can exert over those causes. It is more effective to reduce the potential cause of a risk than to wait for that risk to materialize and then address its impact.

The impact of a risk that materializes should not be mistaken for the underlying cause of the risk. For example, *cost escalation* on a project is an ever-present risk impact. Expenditure should be monitored to determine the underlying causes of *why* costs are escalating.

It is important that the management of risk is considered as a continuous process throughout the life of a project. Once potential risks have been identified they need to be monitored until such time as either they cease to be material, or their effect has been reduced or mitigated as a result of management intervention. The potential for new risks being introduced with time, or in consequence of actions taken, also needs to be considered throughout the project life cycle. The obvious times for risk assessment and management are:

- Project initiation;
- End stage assessment;

and these should be considered the minimum number of times. Depending on the project's criticality and size, risks should be examined regularly, say, each month.

In broad terms, the Project Manager is responsible for seeing that risk analysis is done and the Project Board is responsible for the management of risk (the decisions on courses of action to take). In practice, the Project Manager may take decisions on certain risks where the consequences are within the tolerance margins, but even there it would be wise to advise the Project Board in the Highlight Report of any such decisions.

It is good practice to appoint one individual as responsible for monitoring each identified risk, the person best placed to observe the factors that affect that risk. According to the risk, this may be a member of the Project Board, someone with Project Assurance duties, the Project Manager, the Team Manager or a team member.

15.3 RISK MANAGEMENT STRATEGY

During initiation a Risk Management Strategy should be developed, describing how risk management is to be embedded in the various project management activities. The content of the strategy is identified in Appendix A, but it is worth a few extra words about some of its contents.

15.3.1 Risk Tolerance

Before deciding what to do about risks, the Project Board must consider its attitude towards risk taking. This is called its 'risk appetite'. This is then translated into measurable allowances. An example might be 'We want these two chemicals to be stored in separate buildings, but if this is not possible or economic, we are prepared to allow them in the same building, but with at least 110ft between them and chemical X must be in a concrete housing structure'. These risk margins form the risk tolerances. The view of how much the project is prepared to put at risk will depend on a number of variables. A project may be prepared to take comparatively large risks in some areas and none at all in others, such as risks to company survival, exceeding budgets or target date and fulfilling health and safety regulations.

Risk tolerance can be related to the five other tolerance parameters; risk to completion within *timescale* and/or *cost*, and to achieving product *quality*, project *scope* and the *benefits* within the boundaries of the Business Case.

Risk tolerances have to be considered carefully to obtain the optimum balance of the cost of a risk occurring against the cost of limiting or preventing that risk. The organization's overall risk tolerance must also be considered as well as that of the project.

15.3.2 Risk Categories

The manual says very little about risk categories. The 2005 manual offered a list of possible categories that can be used. I list these below.

Strategic/commercial risks

- Under-performance to specification;
- Management will under-perform against expectations;
- Collapse of contractors;
- Lack of availability of capital investment;
- Insolvency of promoter;
- Failure of suppliers to meet contractual commitments, this could be in terms of quality, quantity, timescales or their own exposure to risk;
- Market fluctuations;
- Fraud/theft;
- The situation being non-insurable (or cost of insurance outweighing the benefit).

Economic/financial/market

- Exchange rate fluctuation;
- Interest rate instability;
- Inflation;
- Failure to meet projected revenue targets.

Legal and regulatory

- New or changed legislation may invalidate assumptions upon which the project is based;
- Failure to obtain appropriate approval, e.g. planning consent;
- Loss of intellectual property rights;
- Unexpected regulatory controls or licensing requirements.

Organizational/management/human factors

- Management incompetence;
- Inadequate corporate policies;
- Poor leadership;
- Key personnel have inadequate authority to fulfill their roles;
- Lack of clarity over roles and responsibilities;
- Vested interests creating conflict and compromising the overall aims;

- Individual or group interests given unwarranted priority;
- Personality clashes;
- Lack of operational support;
- Health and safety constraints.

Political

- Change of government policy (national or international);
- Change of government;
- War.

Environmental

- Natural disasters;
- Transport problems, including aircraft/vehicle collisions.

Technical/operational/infrastructure

- Inadequate design;
- Human error/incompetence;
- Infrastructure failure;
- Operational life lower than expected;
- Residual value of assets lower than expected;
- Safety being compromised;
- Performance failure;
- Scope 'creep';
- Vague specification;
- Breaches in security/information security.

15.3.3 Risk Responsibilities

The Executive has the following risk responsibilities:

1. To ensure that a Risk Management Strategy is created and be accountable for all aspects of risk management;
2. To ensure that Business Case risks are identified, assessed and controlled;
3. To escalate risks to corporate or programme management when required.

The Senior User and Senior Supplier are responsible for the identification, assessment and control of risks that affect those whom they represent.

The Project Board makes the key decisions on risk management. Remember, the Project Board represents all the parties: the customer, the user and the supplier.

The Project Manager has the responsibility to ensure that any project risks are identified, recorded and regularly reviewed. The Project Manager is responsible for creating the Risk Management Strategy and Risk Register and ensuring that the appropriate level of information is gathered from all sources to enable a true assessment of a risk to be made. The customer and the supplier may each have a different set of risks to which they feel exposed, or will have a different view of a risk and the alternative actions. The customer will try to protect the achievement of its Business Case and get the supplier to take the risks (or bear the cost of any preventive or avoiding action). The supplier will try to protect the expected profit margin and therefore take the opposite view.

15.3.4 Early Warning Indicators

These are measurements of progress on which the Project Manager should keep an eye, because any deterioration could mean that one or more of the project's objectives are at risk. Suggested early warning indicators are:

- Number of Work Packages not completed to schedule;
- Number of product approvals not obtained;
- Number of issues raised per week/month/product;
- Number of issues remaining unresolved;
- Average length of time issues remain open;
- Number of defects found in a quality inspection;
- Adherence to budget;
- Adherence to schedule.

The last two would be spotted by use of the technique of Earned Value Analysis (not part of PRINCE2).

There may be external early warning indicators, such as the relationships with users and those who will operate the product after completion, adverse newspaper comments (remember Mrs. Thatcher's Poll Tax) and industry rumours about the suppliers.

15.4 RISK REGISTER

PRINCE2 uses a Risk Register to record and keep track of each identified risk. A Product Description of a Risk Register is provided in Appendix A. The Risk Register is created during initiation. If any risks are identified in *Starting up a Project* (SU), these are recorded in the Project Manager's Daily Log and transferred to the Risk Register when the latter is created.

Although the Project Manager's responsibility, the Project Manager will normally delegate its maintenance to Project Support. The procedures for registering risks and maintaining the Risk Register are defined in the Risk Management Strategy.

15.5 ILLUSTRATIVE LIST OF RISK ANALYSIS QUESTIONS

This section contains an illustrative list of questions that a Project Manager may require to have answered for a particular project. It is based on the (the Office of Government Commerce – owner of PRINCE2) OGC publication, 'Management of Project Risk' and can be related to the risk categories listed earlier.

15.5.1 Business/Strategic

1. Do the project objectives fit into the organization's overall business strategy?
2. When is the project due to deliver; how was the date determined?
3. What would be the result of late delivery?

4. What would be the result of limited success (functionality)?
5. What is the stability of the business area?

15.5.2 External Factors

1. Is this project exposed to requirements due to international interests (i.e. are there legal implications from overseas, or are foreign companies involved)?
2. Could there be 'political' implications of the project failing?
3. Is this project part of a programme? If so, what constraints are set for the project by that programme?

15.5.3 Procurement

1. Has the supplier a reputation for delivery of high quality goods?
2. Is the contract sufficiently detailed to show what the supplier is going to provide?
3. Are the acceptance criteria clear to both parties?
4. Is the contract legally binding/enforceable? (Consideration should be given to topics including ownership rights and liability.)

15.5.4 Organizational Factors

1. What consideration needs to be given to security for this project?
2. Does the project have wholehearted support from senior management?
3. What is the commitment of the user management?
4. Have training requirements been identified? Can these requirements be met?

15.5.5 Management

1. How clearly are the project objectives defined?
2. Will the project be run using a well-documented approach to project management?
3. Does this approach cover aspects of quality management, management of risk and development activities in sufficient depth?
4. How well do the project team understand the chosen methodology?
5. What is the current state of Project Plans?
6. Is completion of this project dependent on the completion of other projects?
7. Are the tasks in the Project Plan interdependent (and can the critical path through tasks be identified)?
8. What is the availability of appropriate resources? (What are the skills and experience of the project team? What is the make-up of the project team?)
9. Will people be available for training? (For IS projects this includes the project team, users and operations staff.)
10. How many separate user functions are involved?
11. How much change will there be to the users' operation or organization?

15.5.6 Technical

1. Is the specification clear, concise, accurate and feasible?
2. How have the technical options been evaluated?
3. What is the knowledge of the equipment? (For IT this is the hardware/software environment.)
4. Does the experience of the Project Manager cover a similar application?
5. Is this a new application?
6. What is the complexity of the system?
7. How many sites will the system be implemented in?
8. Is the proposed equipment new/leading edge? Is the proposed hardware/software environment in use already?
9. Who is responsible for defining system testing?
10. Who is responsible for defining acceptance testing?
11. On what basis is the implementation planned?
12. What access will the project team have to the development facilities?
13. Will the system be operated by the user or specialist staff?
14. Have requirements for long-term operations, maintenance and support been identified?

15.6 RISK MANAGEMENT PROCEDURE

15.6.1 Risk Identification

This should be a straightforward statement of the risk. PRINCE2 suggests these activities in risk identification (Figure 15.1):

- Record identified threats and opportunities in the Risk Register;
- Prepare early warning indicators to allow monitoring of these potential risks;
- Get stakeholder views on the identified risks.

People can sometimes get confused and identify the impact of a risk as the risk or as extra risks. For example, there may be a risk that bad weather will

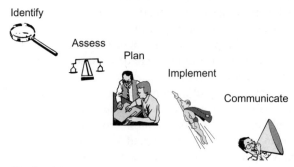

FIGURE 15.1 The five risk management steps.

delay the date for completion of an extra factory. Failure to meet the demands for products would be an impact of that risk, not the actual risk or an extra risk. In order to have a clear and unambiguous risk statement, consider the following risk aspects:

- Cause;
- Event;
- Effect.

15.6.1.1 Risk Cause

What is the source of the risk? What is the trigger or situation that would cause the risk?

15.6.1.2 Risk Event

What might happen as a result of the cause?

15.6.1.3 Risk Effect

What would be the impact of the event?

15.6.1.4 Example of Threat Identification

If we get heavy and prolonged rain (risk cause), the river might burst its banks (risk event), flooding the housing estate we are building (risk effect).

15.6.1.5 Example of Opportunity Identification

The forecast series of channel port blockades by French fishermen (risk cause) would cause cancellation of many car ferry crossings (risk event) increasing the attractiveness of the channel tunnel (risk effect).

15.6.2 Risk Assessment

Risk assessment breaks down into two steps: estimation and evaluation.

15.6.2.1 Risk Estimation

Risk estimation judges a risk by its:

- Probability;
- Impact;
- Proximity.

  Probability

- How likely is the threat or opportunity to occur?

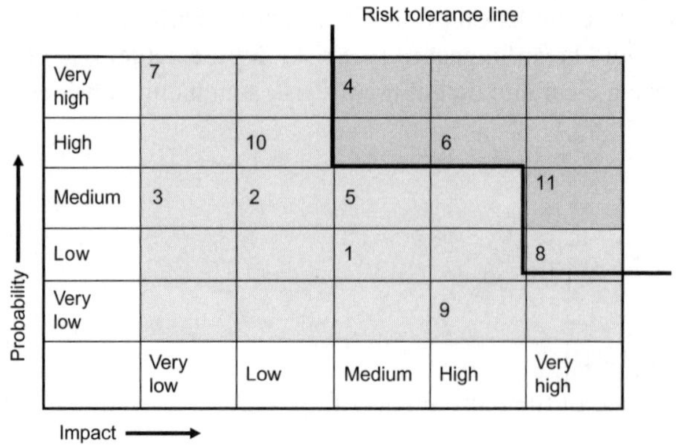

FIGURE 15.2   Risk profile.

Impact

It is not enough to simply say, 'the impact will be high.' Impact should be judged under the headings of:

- Time;
- Cost;
- Quality;
- Benefits;
- People/resources.

Many people also confuse the impact of the risk with the impact of risk responses. For example, 'bad weather causing a delay to factory completion will cost money for overtime to make up the lost time or payment to outsource production until the factory is completed' are not impacts of the risk. They are part of the assessment of responses to the risk.

Proximity

- How soon might the risk or opportunity occur? Something that might happen next week might get priority over a more important risk that might happen in 3 months time. The impact of a risk might vary according to when it is likely to happen.

15.6.2.2 Risk Evaluation

The aim here is to collate all the risks and assess the net effect of all identified risks and opportunities. This will allow comparison with the project risk tolerance set by the Project Board and may affect the continued business justification.

15.6.2.3 Risk Profile

A graphic way of viewing risks is in a summary risk profile. An example is shown in Figure 15.2. This puts risks, using their unique identifiers, in a table

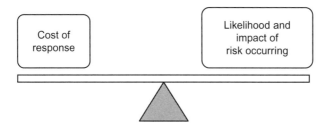

FIGURE 15.3 Risk balance.

of low to high probability and impact. In the example, the top right-hand corner contains risks with a high probability and high impact. The thick black line shows the risk tolerance level, so any risks to the right of that are beyond the risk tolerance levels. Such a table is a snapshot of known risks at a certain time and would need to be updated regularly. Updating it may show trends in known risks.

15.7 PLAN

This step identifies and evaluates a range of responses to the threats and opportunities.

The identification of suitable responses covers:

- Assessing the acceptable level of each risk;
- Generating alternative paths of action for risks which do not meet acceptability criteria;
- Assessing the reality of the countermeasures in the light of the project and company environment (Figure 15.3).

There is a standard list of types of alternative actions in the following order of preference:

15.7.1 Threats

Response	Definition	Example
Avoid	Change something in the project that either the threat can no longer occur or will have no impact if it does	Certain chemicals, if mixed, cause a fire, so store them in separate buildings
Reduce	Take action ahead of a risk occurring to reduce its probability	Operators may make errors because they have not read the instruction manual before using the product, so we will insist that they pass a test before being certified to use the product

(Continued)

Response	Definition	Example
	Take action ahead of a risk occurring to reduce its impact	There is a threat of a rail strike, so arrange to travel by taxi
Fallback	Create a fallback plan for what action to take to reduce the impact if the risk occurs	If the new style of exam is not ready on time, we will continue using the old style
Transfer	Responsibility for some or all of the financial impact of a risk is accepted by a third party	The Rembrandt picture is insured for £3million Put liquidated damage clauses in the supplier contract for any product failure
Accept	A conscious decision not to take action on a risk because the risk is so unlikely to occur or the cost of its occurring is so small or the cost of reduction actions is so great that it is not worth taking the preventative or reduction action	We accept the risk that unseasonal storms might wash out the national golf open championship in early summer

15.7.2 Opportunities

Response	Definition	Example
Share (Threat or opportunity)	The customer and the supplier agree to share the profits or losses of a joint venture, possibly within defined limits	You write a book for me and we agree to share the profits when they rise above the production costs
Exploit	Ensuring that an opportunity does occur and that the impact (benefits) will be realized	A large company has just had a major project failure. Create a marketing campaign to persuade it to take on your project management method
Enhance	This can be either enhancing the probability of an opportunity occurring or enhancing the impact if an opportunity should occur	We could offer a price reduction to swap old for new when the new model becomes available If our major competitor does stop offering its Dover-Calais service, we could increase the price of our service by 10%
Reject	A deliberate decision not to take an identified opportunity, perhaps because of the risk of diverting essential resources or insufficient financial incentive	We might increase early sales by beating a competitor to the launch of a product, but the shortening of timescales to do so would put our quality in jeopardy

Sometimes more than one risk response is required in order to completely respond to a risk. Sometimes the response to one risk can cause knock-on effects to other risks or create new ones.

15.8 IMPLEMENT

This step ensures that the planned actions are taken, their effectiveness monitored and, where necessary, any corrective action is taken.

In the implementation step of risk management the revised version of the PRINCE2 manual uses two role names 'risk owner' and 'risk actionee' (a name that I must admit to disliking).

15.8.1 Risk Owner

This is a named individual who is made responsible for the monitoring and control of an assigned risk, including the implementation of the agreed response actions.

15.8.2 Risk Actionee

The person assigned to carry out a risk response action is called a 'risk actionee', supporting and taking direction from the risk owner.

In many cases both roles may be given to the same person. The risk owner should be the person most capable of managing the risk. I worry that this can be confused with the Project Manager's management tasks, and prefer the old definition of a risk owner as the person best suited to keep an eye on the risk.

15.9 COMMUNICATE

This is a continuous process. It ensures that all relevant members of the project and stakeholders are kept aware of the situation of the risk. It is not normally necessary to create reports that are in addition to the regular PRINCE2 reports. Risk status should be conveyed in:

- Checkpoint Reports;
- Highlight Reports;
- End Stage Reports;
- End Project Reports;
- Lessons Reports.

The Communication Management Strategy will define the most appropriate method of communicating with stakeholders.

15.10 LINKS

There are many links to the PRINCE2 processes and activities.

Plan the Next Stage (SB process)
> When a draft plan has been produced, it should be examined for risks before being published.

Capture and Examine Issues and Risks (CS process)
> One aspect of examining new Project Issues is to see if they cause new risks or modify existing risks.

Review the Stage Status (CS process)
> Part of this process is to check if the status of any risks has changed since the last review.

Report Highlights (CS process)
> If a change in the risk situation is detected, the Project Manager should advise the Project Board of the change in the next Highlight Report.

Take Corrective Action (CS process)
> If a risk status becomes worse, the Project Manager may be able to take corrective action within the tolerance limits.

Escalate Issues and Risks (CS process)
> Where the event described in a risk either has happened or is about to happen, the Project Manager may forecast that the results will cause the stage to deviate beyond its tolerances. This would be escalated to the Project Board in an Exception Report.

Directing a Project (DP process)
> The Project Board should consider the risk situation before making all its decisions.

15.11 DO'S AND DON'TS

Do examine every plan for risks before publishing it.

Do appoint an owner for every risk.

Do try to delegate as many of these as possible. When writing up your Daily Log for actions to take next week, do look at the Risk Register to find owners who should be reporting on the status of risks.

Do not forget to warn the Project Board of any risk deterioration that might go beyond the tolerance margins.

Do not be shy about appointing a member of the Project Board as owner of a risk where it is appropriate.

15.12 IF IT IS A LARGE PROJECT

Some large organizations now employ a Risk Manager, an expert/consultant who advises all Project Managers on identifying and controlling risks.

It is sensible to set aside some time specifically to consider the risk situation. This will be a natural part of each stage boundary, but in a long project it is also worth setting this time aside, say, every 2 weeks.

15.13 IF IT IS A SMALL PROJECT

Risks are still an important factor.

Chapter 16

Change

16.1 PHILOSOPHY

Change consists of two closely linked activities: change control and configuration management. Neither can function effectively without the other. Change directly supports the principles of 'focus on products' and 'manage by exception' and indirectly supports the 'continued business justification' principle.

16.1.1 Change Control

No matter how well planned a project has been, if there is no control over changes, this will destroy any chance of bringing the project in on schedule and to budget. In any project there will be changes for many reasons:

- Government legislation has changed and this must be reflected in the product specification;
- The users change their mind on what is wanted;
- Because the development cycle is making the user think more and more about the product, extra features suggest themselves for inclusion;
- There is a merge of departments, change of responsibility, company merger or take-over which radically alters the project definition;
- The supplier finds that it will be impossible to deliver everything within the agreed schedule or cost;
- The supplier cannot meet an acceptance criterion, such as performance;
- A product delivered by an outside contractor or another project fails to meet its specification.

All of these need a procedure to control them and their effect on the project. This procedure must make sure they are not ignored, but that nothing is implemented of which the appropriate level of management is unaware. This includes the Project Board.

16.1.2 Configuration Management

No organization can be fully efficient or effective unless it manages its assets, particularly if the assets are vital to the running of the organization's business.

CARTOON 16.1   Configuration Librarian.

A project's assets likewise have to be managed. The assets of the project are the products that it develops. The name for the combined set of these assets is a configuration. The configuration of the final deliverable of a project is the sum total of its products.

In the foreword to its Product Configuration Management System (PCMS), SQL Software wrote 'If the product you develop has more than one version, more than a few component or more than one person working on it, you are doing configuration management. The only question is how well you are doing it.'

Configuration management is needed to manage the creation, safekeeping and controlled change to the project's products.

In PRINCE2 the procedures to control change and configuration are contained in the Configuration Management Strategy (Cartoon 16.1).

16.2 CONFIGURATION MANAGEMENT STRATEGY

The Configuration Management Strategy is created during the initiation of a project. There is a Product Description of its composition in Appendix A. It defines:

- The configuration management procedure;
- The issue and change control procedure;
- Roles and responsibilities for the two activities;
- Any tools and techniques to be used;
- A scale for prioritizing issues;

- A scale for rating the severity of issues, linking this to the management level required to handle each level;
- Use and membership of a Change Authority and its change budget.

The severity rating of issues brings up the question of whether to use a Change Authority.

16.2.1 Change Authority

It is part of the Project Board's responsibility to review and approve requests for change and off-specifications. If many of these are expected, the Project Board may decide to delegate the task, within limits, to a Change Authority. This can be an individual or a group. Examples would be those given Project Assurance roles, a group of users or the Project Manager.

16.2.2 Change Budget

There is no point in having a Change Authority if it has no money with which to pay for any approved work. This is the change budget, given by the Project Board. The Executive might have had to negotiate this with corporate/programme management during initiation. So the change budget is a sum of money to pay for the analysis and implementation of requests for change or off-specifications. The Project Board normally puts two limits on its use; the amount that can be spent on a single change, and the amount of the budget that can be spent in one stage. Anything outside these limits has to be referred to the Project Board.

The use of a Change Authority with its budget can greatly reduce the number of calls on the Project Board for decisions. The use of a Change Authority and what budget it is to have are documented as part of the Configuration Management Strategy.

16.3 OVERVIEW OF ISSUE AND CHANGE CONTROL

An issue is the formal way to record any inquiry, complaint or request (outside the scope of a quality review question list). It can be raised by anyone associated with the project. Issues fall into three groups:

1. A desired new or changed function;
2. A failure of a product in meeting some aspect of the user requirements. In such cases the report should be accompanied by evidence of the failure and, where appropriate, sufficient material to allow someone to recreate the failure for assessment purposes;
3. A problem or concern.

In other words, there is no limit to the content of an issue beyond the fact that it should be about the project (Cartoon 16.2).

CARTOON 16.2   Project Issue.

Any error found during a quality review normally goes on an action list. There are two exceptions to this:

1. Where an error is found during quality review which belongs to a different product than the one under review;
2. Where work to correct an error found during quality review cannot be done during the agreed follow-up period.

Such errors are put onto an issue as the way of getting them into the change control system.

When considering the procedures for handling issues, there is the possibility that the subject will be outside the scope of the project. An example might be a fault in a component that is used in many products across the department. Although it is being used in the project it clearly has a wider implication. There should be a procedure to close the issue off as far as the project is concerned and transfer it to a departmental level. The same approach applies if the project is part of a programme and an error is found in a quality review that affects other projects in the programme.

All possible changes should be handled by the same issue and change control procedure. Apart from controlling possible changes, this procedure should provide a formal entry point through which questions or suggestions also can be raised and answered.

16.4 ISSUE AND CHANGE CONTROL PROCEDURE

The procedure has five steps:

1. Capture;
2. Examine;

3. Propose;
4. Decide;
5. Implement.

16.4.1 Capture

The first step is to carry out a brief analysis, just enough to decide what type of issue it is, and whether it can be managed formally or informally. The outcome is normally one of the following:

- The issue is proposing a change to a baselined configuration item. The issue is a *request for change* and the decision can only be made by the Project Board (or Change Authority if one has been appointed);
- The issue requests a change to the agreed user specification, acceptance criterion or a Product Description. The issue is a *request for change* and the decision can only be made by the Project Board (or Change Authority if one has been appointed);
- A product does not meet its specification. The issue is an *off-specification*;
- The issue asks a question or voices a *concern*, but will not lead to a product change.

Informal
The latter type of issue can be immediately resolved and does not require further analysis, or decision from the Project Board/Change Authority. These issues can be logged by the Project Manager in the Daily Log and dealt with informally.

Formal
Issues needing more analysis and/or are considered more serious should be handled formally. An Issue Report should be raised, preferably by the originator, and this should be entered on the Issue Register by the Configuration Librarian, who will allocate a unique identifier to the issue and pass a copy back to the originator and another to the Project Manager. The issue is now classed as 'Open'.

16.4.2 Examine

The Project Manager allocates the issue to the person or team best suited to perform a full impact analysis on it. The issues are evaluated in terms of their impact on:

- Time;
- Cost;
- Quality;
- Scope;
- Benefits;
- Risks.

with the aim of making recommendations to the Project Manager on their resolution. The analysis should cover all aspects: business, user and supplier.

The Project Manager should review all open issues. He or she may do this alone, with a senior technical member of the team and/or with those carrying integrity responsibilities. The frequency of such meetings will depend on the volume of issues being received, but meetings should be held regularly and with sufficient frequency to ensure that no inordinate delay occurs in taking action.

All Issue Reports have to be closed by the end of the project or transferred to follow-on action recommendations, part of the End Project Report. The transfer of an issue to these recommendations can only be done with the approval of the Project Board.

16.4.2.1 Request for Change

A request for change records a proposed modification to the user requirements.

The request for change requires analysis to see how much work is involved. Senior team members with the appropriate skills and experience normally do this. This work is called impact analysis. The configuration library holds information that will help to identify what other products or configuration items will be affected.

It is particularly important that the librarian identifies any *baselined* configuration items that will need to change. This is because the Project Board has already been told of the completion of those items. The Project Board must therefore approve any change to such items.

16.4.2.2 Off-Specification

An off-specification is used to document any situation where the product is failing to meet its specification in some respect.

The Configuration Librarian allocates the next unique issue identifier from the register and sends a copy of the issue to its author. Senior team members carry out an impact analysis with the help of the Configuration Librarian to discover which products are affected by the off-specification and then assess the effort needed.

16.4.3 Propose

With the results of the impact analysis available, the next step is to look at alternative actions and propose the best response.

The alternatives are costed and the impact on the Stage Plan's budget and schedule assessed. Before making the decision the Project Manager will want to know the answer to two questions:

1. Can the work be done within the tolerance levels of the current plan? For this reason it is best that a batch of requests is studied, to give a wider view of the effect on the plans;
2. Does the advantage of taking action outweigh the costs of doing so?

In preparation for the decision, the requests for change should be awarded a priority rating. There are various ways of indicating the priority of an issue. One of these is the MoSCoW method, where this is an acronym for:

- Must have: essential for the product to work properly.
- Should have: important to have. Its absence could affect the level of benefits.
- Could have: a useful change, but its absence would not affect the Business Case.
- Won't have: not essential. This change can be delayed.

Severity can be indicated like this:

1. High/critical;
2. Medium/major;
3. Low/significant;
4. Cosmetic/minor.

The severity corresponds with the severity ranks in the change control procedure, indicating which level of management should make the decision about the issue.

16.4.4 Decide

16.4.4.1 Request for Change

In order for the request for change to be implemented, it must be approved by either the Project Manager or the Project Board. Whose decision it is will be documented in the Configuration Management Strategy, and depends on the following:

- If it is not a change to a configuration item that has already been *baselined* and the work can be done within the current plan's *tolerances*, the Project Manager *can* make the decision to implement it. Alternatively, it can be passed to the Project Board (or Change Authority if one has been appointed) for its decision. Since experience shows that there will be a lot of changes during the project, it is a good idea to make the Project Board decide on any changes other than trivialities. This keeps the Board aware of how many changes are being requested and their cumulative impact on the schedule and cost. If the Stage Plan runs into trouble later, it is usually too late for the Project Manager to get any sympathy about a claim that lots of requests have been actioned without asking for more time or money. The answer will usually be 'Why didn't you ask us? We could have cancelled or delayed some of them.' *It is important to note here that tolerances are not there to pay for small requests for change.* The Project Manager should only implement a small change without asking for extra time and money if work on the relevant product has not yet started and inclusion of the requested change will not cost extra.
- The decision must be made by the Project Board/Change Authority if the change is to one or more configuration items that the Project Board has already been told are complete (to any baseline, not necessarily the final

one). More than anything, this is to retain the confidence level of the Board. If it has been told that something is finished and later finds out that it has been changed without consultation, its sense of being in control evaporates.

- If the work to do the request for change cannot be done within the tolerance levels of the current Stage Plan, the decision on action *must* come from the Project Board. The Project Manager must submit an Exception Report with the request for change. This may lead to a request for an Exception Plan showing the new schedule and cost for the rest of the stage.

The Project Board's decision may be to:

- Implement the change. If the change required an Exception Plan, then this means approving the Exception Plan;
- Delay the change to an enhancement project after the current one is finished;
- Defer a decision until a later meeting;
- Ask for more information;
- Cancel the request.

If the Project Board has delegated the responsibility for decision on Issue Reports to a Change Authority, then the Change Authority will play the role described above. The decision should be documented on the Issue Report and in the Issue Register.

Whenever its status changes, a copy of the Issue Report should be sent to the originator.

16.4.4.2 Off-Specification

As with requests for change, the decision on action is taken by either the Project Manager or Project Board/Change Authority. If the error is because of a failure within the Project Manager's responsibility, the onus is on the Project Manager to correct the problem within tolerances. Similarly, if the error is from a Team Manager's failure to fulfill an agreed Work Package, the onus is on the Team Manager (or the supplier if the team is from an external company) to correct the error without asking the Project Manager for more time or money.

- If the off-specification does not involve a change to a configuration item that has already been baselined and the work can be done within the current plan's tolerances, the Project Manager should make the decision to implement it.
- If the off-specification requires changes to one or more configuration items which the Project Board has already been told are complete (to any baseline, not necessarily the final one), the Project Board/Change Authority must make the decision.
- If the work to do the off-specification cannot be done within the tolerance levels of the current Stage Plan, the decision on action must come from the Project Board. The Project Manager must submit an Exception Report with the off-specification. If the Project Board accepts the need for the extra work,

it will request an Exception Plan showing the new schedule and cost for the rest of the stage.

The Project Board's decision may be to:

- Correct the fault. If the work required an Exception Plan, then this means approving the Exception Plan;
- Delay correction of the fault to an enhancement project after the current one is finished;
- Defer a decision until a later meeting;
- Ask for more information.

The decision should be documented on the off-specification and the Issue Register, and an updated copy filed. Whenever its status changes, a copy should be sent to the originator.

16.4.5 Implement

The Project Manager is responsible for scheduling any approved changes. This work will possibly involve the issue of a new version of one or more products by the Configuration Librarian.

On receipt of a completed request for change or off-specification, the Configuration Librarian should ensure that any amended products have been re-submitted to the configuration library. The finalized request should be stored in the quality file, and the originator advised. The Issue Register should be updated with the final details and the originator advised.

16.5 CONFIGURATION MANAGEMENT

16.5.1 Configuration Management Overview

Within the context of project management the purpose of configuration management is to identify, track and protect the project's products as they are developed.

The objective of configuration management is to achieve a controlled and traceable product evolution through properly authorized specifications, design, development and testing.

This objective is met by defining and ensuring:

- The issue and control of properly authorized specifications;
- The issue and control of properly authorized design documents;
- The issue and control of properly authorized changes to the specification or design documents;
- The control of the various versions of a product and their relationship with its current state.

Configuration management is also the process of managing change to the elements that comprise a product. It implies that any version of the product and any revision of the themes that make up the product can be retrieved at any time, and that the resulting product will always be built in an identical manner. Product enhancements and special variants create the need to control multiple versions and releases of the product. All these have to be handled by configuration management.

Configuration management is a discipline which:

- Records what components or products are required in order to build a product;
- Provides identifiers and version numbers to all products;
- Controls access and change to components of a product once they have been declared complete by the developer;
- Provides information on the impact of possible changes;
- Keeps information on the links between the various parts of a product, e.g. what components comprise a product, where component X is used, of what does the 'full product' consist;
- Provides information on the status of products (Configuration Items) being developed, including who is responsible for the development;
- Is the sensible storage place for Product Descriptions;
- Gives project management the assurance that products are being developed in the correct sequence.

Configuration management holds a central position in project management. Product Breakdown Structures used in planning provide the identification information for the configuration items. The links allow the construction of the Product Flow Diagrams. They offer input and verification of the products required for a plan. You cannot adequately do change control without configuration management. It provides product copies and Product Descriptions for quality checks and keeps track of the status of the product. It provides the information to construct a release package, either a complete one or a partial one, and then records the issue of a release.

Configuration item records are valuable assets in themselves. Configuration management helps management know what its assets are supposed to be, who is responsible for their safekeeping and whether the actual inventory matches the official one.

Configuration management gives control over the versions of products in use, identifies products affected by any problems and makes it easier to assess the impact of changes.

Configuration management supports the production of information on problem trends, such as which products are being changed regularly or frequently, thereby assisting in the proactive prevention of problems.

Where the end product is to be used in more than one place, configuration management helps organizations to control the distribution of changes to these operational sites. Where there is any volume of changes, there will be the need to decide between putting together a 'release package' of several changes or issuing a complete new product. The latter may be a more controlled and cost-effective means of updating an operational product than sending out one changed product at a time. The decision and control mechanisms for this are part of configuration management.

Configuration management supports the maintenance of information on proven reliable releases to which products can revert in case of problems.

Because all products are under the control of configuration management once they have been developed, it makes it more difficult for them to be changed maliciously, thus improving security.

The data held in the configuration library helps to recreate a release after any disaster by identifying the products required and their storage place.

16.5.2 Configuration Management Detail

Configuration management covers all the technical products of a project. It should also be used to record and store management and quality products, such as plans, quality check details and approvals to proceed. Whether management products are included or not depends on a number of factors such as:

- Effort involved;
- Resource availability;
- Capability of any other current method for handling management and quality products;
- Project Manager's preference;
- Availability of configuration management software.

16.5.2.1 Costs

There are the expected costs of staffing and training Configuration Librarians. If a central office (say part of a project support office) has been set up to provide configuration management functions to a number of projects, there may be a need for a configuration manager.

If software is to be used to record and track the data, there will be the cost of its purchase or rental, any hardware bought to run it and the staff training. Having said that, it is very difficult to keep the comprehensive records required to do a complete job without a computer database and software. The costs here are far outweighed by the increase in speed, capacity and detail of information. The increase in speed of reaction by the Configuration Librarian probably reduces the number of librarians needed to cover all the site's products.

The need to go through the configuration management tasks may slow down slightly the handover of a finished item or the implementation of a change. But this penalty is very small when weighed against the risk and impact of operationally using a product that is from an incorrect release or has not been checked out. Without it there is also the risk of more than one person changing a product simultaneously, resulting in all but the final change being lost.

16.5.2.2 Possible Problems

If products are defined at too low a level, the Configuration Librarian may be overwhelmed by the amount of data to be fed into the library. This is particularly a problem where no configuration management software is being used.

If products are defined at too high a level, the information for impact analysis may be too vague and result in a larger than necessary product change being indicated, e.g. altering a whole set of products when only one product is affected.

Procedures must cater for emergency changes, where an emergency change is required in order to let the operational product continue.

Where configuration management is new, development staff may be tempted to view its controls as bottlenecks and bureaucracy. But it has been used in engineering for many years and is regarded in those circles as essential. It is also regarded as an essential part of any quality product, should you be looking for accreditation under such standards as ISO 9001. It is regarded as essential because of the control it gives and experience over many years, which has shown its value and the cost of problems arising when it is not used.

16.5.2.3 When Is it Done?

A Configuration Management Strategy is required as part of the PID. This should state:

- What method is to be used;
- Who has the responsibility for configuration management;
- What naming convention will be used to identify products of this project;
- What types of product are to be covered;
- What types of status are to be used (e.g. 'allocated', 'draft available', 'quality checked').

Once a product has been identified as required, it should receive an identifier from the configuration management method. Sensibly this should coincide with the creation of a draft Product Description.

Among the configuration management planning activities required are those to identify what *baselines* will be required (baselines are explained later in the chapter) and for what purpose, which baselines exist concurrently and which cannot and when baselines will be taken.

The status of a product should be tracked from the moment the Product Description is created.

16.5.2.4 Configuration Item Records

The detail to be kept about the products will depend to some extent on the complexity of the end product, the number of products, the resources available to keep the records and the information demanded by the maintenance and support groups. Below is a list of potential information about a product that should be considered against the needs of the project.

Project identifier	A unique identifier allocated by either the configuration management software or the Configuration Librarian to identify all products of the project
Item identifier	Unique identifier for a single product
Current version number	The number of this particular version of the product. This is usually linked to a baseline. You may wish to divide this into version and sub-version number, e.g. '3.1'
Variant	If required, covers the product in a different language, such as a user manual
Item title	Same as the name in the Product Breakdown Structure
Date of last status change	
Item attributes	You may wish to differentiate between management and specialist products, e.g. or separate the specialist products into groups, such as those provided from an external source
Stage	The management stage during which the product will be created or obtained and used
Owner	Who owns and is responsible for any decisions to alter it. This may be different to the person working on the product
Users	The person or group(s) who will use the product
Producer	The person or team responsible for creating or obtaining the product
Date allocated	Date allocated for work
Location	Where the product is kept
Source	Name of the supplier if from an external source
Links to related products	Products of which this product forms a part
Status	Current status of the configuration item as defined in the strategy – you might have your own ideas on the possible entries for this, but the following list may give you some extra ideas: • Product not defined; • Product Description in progress; • Product Description written; • Product Description approved; • Product ordered; • Product in progress; • Draft version available; • Product in test; • Product under review; • Product approved; • Product accepted; • Product delivered; • Product installed; • Product under change.

(Continued)

	(Not all of these need be used, just those which fit your status needs.)
Copy holders and potential users	Details of who holds a copy of the product plus who may require a copy when the product reaches a certain status
Project Issue cross-reference	If this version of the product has been caused by an issue, this should be cross-referenced as an audit trail
Correspondence cross-reference	A reference to any relevant correspondence that affects this product or version of it

16.5.2.5 Baselines

Baselines are moments in a product's evolution when it and all its components have reached an acceptable state, such that they can be 'frozen' and used as a base for the next step. The next step may be to release the product to the customer, or it may be that you have 'frozen' a design and will now construct the products.

Products constantly evolve and are subject to change as a project moves through its life cycle and, later on, in the operational life of the product. A Project Manager will need to know the answer to many questions, such as:

- What is the latest agreed level of specification to which we are working?
- What exact design are we implementing?
- What did we release to site X last January?

In other words, a baseline is a frozen picture of what products and what versions of them constituted a certain situation. A baseline may be defined as a set of known and agreed configuration items under change control from which further progress can be charted. This description indicates that you will baseline only products that represent either the entire product or at least a significant product.

A baseline is created for one of a number of reasons:

- To provide a sound base for future work;
- As a point to which you can retreat if development goes wrong;
- As an indication of the component and version numbers of a release;
- As a bill of material showing the variants released to a specific site;
- To copy the products and documentation at the current baseline to all remote sites;
- To represent a standard configuration (e.g. Product Description) against which supplies can be obtained (e.g. purchase of personal computers for a group);
- To indicate the state the product must reach before it can be released or upgraded;

- As a comparison of one baseline against another in terms of the products contained and their versions;
- To transfer configuration items to another library, e.g. from development to production, from the supplier to the customer at the end of the project;
- To obtain a report on what products of the baseline are not of status 'X'.

The baseline record itself should be a product, so that it can be controlled in the same way as other products. It is a baseline identifier, date, reason and list of all the products and their version numbers that comprise that baseline. Because of its different format it is often held in a separate file.

16.5.2.6 Product Status Account

Product status accounting provides a complete statement of the current status and history of the products generated within the project or within a stage. The purpose of this is to provide a report on:

- The status of one or all configuration items;
- All the events which have impacted those products.

This allows comparison with the plans and provides tracking of changes to products.

In order to provide this information it is necessary for the configuration management method to record all the transactions affecting each configuration item. At the simplest level this means that we can tell the status of each item and version. If we can afford to keep complete records, our library will have broken the specification down into parts, which are linked to design items, which in turn link to constructed components. All approved changes to any one of these will show the linkages and dates of any amendment, plus the baselines incorporating the changes. Our records will show who was responsible and possibly the costs.

For the purpose of status accounting the configuration management method should be able to produce reports on such things as:

- What is the history of development of a particular item?
- How many requests for change were approved last month?
- Who is responsible for this item?
- What items in the design baseline have been changed since it was approved?
- On what items have changes been approved but not yet implemented?

16.5.2.7 Configuration Auditing

Configuration auditing checks whether the recorded description of products matches their physical representation and whether items have been built to their specification. There are two purposes of configuration auditing. The first is to confirm that the configuration records match reality. In other words, if my configuration records show that we are developing version 3 of a product, I want to be sure that the developer has not moved on to version 5 without my knowing and without any linking documentation to say why versions 4 and 5 have been created. The second purpose is to account for any differences between a delivered product and its original agreed specification. In other words, can the configuration records trace a path from the original specification through any approved changes to what a product looks like now? These audits should verify that:

- All authorized versions of configuration items exist;
- Only authorized configuration items exist;
- All change records and release records have been properly authorized by project management;
- Implemented changes are as authorized.

This is defined as an inspection of the recorded configuration item description and the current representation of that item to ensure that the latter matches its current specification. The inspection also checks that the specification of each item is consistent with that of its parent in the structure. In a sense, it can be regarded as similar to stock control. Does the book description match with what we have on the shelf? In addition the audit should ensure that documentation is complete and that project standards have been met.

In engineering establishments, the aim of configuration auditing is to check that, in spite of changes that may have taken place in requirements and design, the items produced conform to the latest agreed specification and that quality review procedures have been performed satisfactorily. Verifying at successive baselines that the item produced at each baseline conforms to the specification produced for it in the previous baseline plus any approved changes does this.

Configuration audits should be done:

- Shortly after implementation of a new configuration management system;
- Before and after major changes to the structure of the project's end product;
- After disasters such as the loss of records;
- On detection of any 'rash' of unauthorized configuration items;
- Randomly.

16.5.2.8 Configuration Audit Checklist

Here is an example checklist for an audit. The following items should be examined:

- Do the configuration records match the physical items?
- Are (randomly tested) approved changes recorded in the Issue Register? Are they linked to the appropriate products? Is their implementation controlled by the configuration management method?
- Does the configuration library accurately reflect the inclusion of any random products? Are there links to relevant Project Issues?
- Are regular configuration audits carried out? Are the results recorded? Have follow-on actions been performed?

- Are (randomly tested) archived and back-up versions of products retained and recorded in the correct manner?
- Are the recorded versions of products used in multiple locations correct?
- Do product names and version numbers meet naming conventions?
- Is configuration library housekeeping carried out in accordance with defined procedures?
- Are staff adequately trained?
- Can baselines be easily and accurately created, recreated and used?

16.5.2.9 Building a Release Package

At the end of a project the product which has been developed is released into production. For many installations this may be a simple matter. The product will run operationally in the same environment used for its development, and 'release' is nothing more than 'cutting the tape'.

But there can be many problems concerned with the move of development work over to live operation:

- How do we release details of how to build the product to a sister company on another site?
- How do we ensure that we only release products that have been thoroughly tested as part of the whole product?
- How do we create innumerable copies of the product (like a software house or electrical component manufacturer) and guarantee that they will be identical?
- How can we change an operational product without the risk of it malfunctioning after the change?
- How can we keep a check on which of our customers or sites has what version of the product?
- How do we install a major enhancement of a product?
- If the people who developed the product are not to be the people who install the product, how do they know how to do it?
- Do we issue the complete product for every update or just the changed components?
- Do we issue a complete new operating manual or only the changed pages?

The answer is in release control, another important job for the Configuration Librarian. The tasks for the Configuration Librarian are:

- Identify the products to be included in the release;
- Ensure that all the required products have reached a status which allows them to be released into live operation;
- Report on any required products which do not have a current approved status;
- Build a release package;
- List the changes since the previous release and the error reports or requests for change solved by the release;

- Distribute the release;
- Be able to recreate any baseline (i.e. past release) if a site reports problems on a release;
- Know which site has what version and variant of the product.

16.5.2.10 Control of Releases

Each product release should have a release identifier of the same form as the version number described for a product (i.e. baseline number, issue number) which identifies:

- The level of functionality provide by the release – defined by the baseline number;
- The modification status of the release – defined by the issue number;
- The release configuration – by reference to the relevant baseline summary.

16.5.2.11 Revision of Release and Issue Number

The release identifier should be revised:

- When the new release of the product provides changed functionality – the baseline number is incremented up to the next whole number (e.g. 2.1 becomes 3.0);
- When the new release of the product provides fault fixes only – the issue number is incremented by one (e.g. 1.4 becomes 1.5);
- *Optionally* when the new release of the product consolidates many (e.g. 20) minor changes – the baseline number is incremented up to the next whole number.

16.5.2.12 Release Package Contents

A release should be accompanied by a release build summary. It should contain:

- The release name and identifier;
- The release date;
- The person/section/group with responsibility for the release. This will normally be the contact for any installation problems. If not then this information should be added;
- A brief description of the release, whether it is a complete or partial release, what has caused the release, what is its purpose and the major benefits over previous releases;
- A list of prerequisites for the installation of the release;
- A list of all the Project Issues answered by this release;
- A bill of material, listing what is contained in the release. This should cover documentation and any procedures;
- Assembly steps;
- Assembly test steps;

- Any customization steps. If the release can be tailored in any way, this describes the possibilities and lists the steps to be carried out;
- Notification of any dates when support for previous releases will cease;
- An acknowledgement to be completed and returned by the assembler on successful completion of the assembly.

While current, a baseline cannot be changed. It remains active until it is superseded by the next baseline.

16.6 LINKS

There is a very strong link between change control and configuration management. They are inseparable. You cannot have one without the other. It is sensible to give the same person or group responsibility for both elements.

Configuration management links to quality. If you lose control over which versions should be used, or release old versions of components or allow the release of an untested change, the quality of the product will suffer.

There is another link with organization and the *Initiating a Project* process. Before the project begins there should be a decision on how big the change control need is likely to be and what part of the project management team will administer change control. Will it be a member of the team, part time? Will an administrative clerk come in for half a day a week? Does it need a small group of specialist Configuration Librarians?

Another link is between *Starting up a Project* (SU), the organization, plans and change control. At the outset of a project a decision is needed on whether a Change Authority is needed and how changes will be funded.

16.7 DO's AND DON'Ts

Do relate the complexity of the configuration management method to the needs of the project.

Do not underestimate the importance of configuration management. As was said at the beginning of the chapter, if there is more than yourself working on the project, if there will be more than one version of a product, you need configuration management. Make sure that it is adequate for the job.

Do think about the stability of the customer's specification before you dive in to a project. The less stable it is, the more change control will be required and the higher the cost of authorized changes is likely to be.

Do not underestimate the importance of change control. There is no project control without it.

16.8 IF IT IS A LARGE PROJECT

There may be many changes, so many that the Project Board cannot find the time to consider them all. They can choose to appoint a Change Authority, a group of people representing the Project Board. The Change Authority will meet at a frequency based on the volume of changes coming through. In order for the change control board to operate, the Project Board will allocate it a change budget and provide certain restrictions. These may be the maximum amount of the budget to be spent in one stage and the maximum amount of the budget that can be spent on one change.

The Project Support Office should be handling configuration management, probably using one of the software tools available on the market. If the customer already has a configuration management method in place to look after all products in live operation, the project should use the same method.

16.9 IF IT IS A SMALL PROJECT

Members of the team can probably do configuration management. I looked at a feasibility study where one of the analysts performed the Configuration Librarian's job. It took about 2 hours of his time each week. There was a lockable filing cabinet in which the various versions of sections of the report were kept. Team members were responsible for telling the librarian when they wanted to move to a new version. The librarian checked the log and allocated the next version number, having first logged the reason for the change. These reasons had to be documented. Once a fortnight the analyst would take the configuration records round the office and check that there was a match between the records and the version numbers being used.

Change control will still be important.

Chapter 17

Tailoring PRINCE2 to the Project Environment

As I said in the introduction, PRINCE2 can be applied to any kind or size of project, i.e. the basic philosophy is always the same. The method should be tailored to suit the size, importance and environment of the project. Common sense PRINCE2 says, 'Do not use a sledgehammer to crack a walnut', but equally do not agree important things informally where there is any chance of a disagreement later over what was agreed.

A company may be reading about the PRINCE2 method and saying to itself, 'but we only have short, simple projects. How can we justify using everything in this method?' The answer is to tailor the method.

The 2009 manual uses two terms, embedding and tailoring, that we should understand and then move on. 'Embedding' refers to the adoption of PRINCE2 across an organization. A company may have an effective change control mechanism, tools and procedures and wish to use these instead of the change control part of PRINCE2. It may have its own configuration management tools and department. It may have a specific way of creating a Business Case. PRINCE2 should be modified to use these documents and procedures as part of this embedding. I have written several 'project management handbooks' for organizations, where they have modified terminology, combined processes, inserted their own documents, etc. Every project in the organization then used this embedded variation of PRINCE2.

Tailoring is done by a project management team to adapt the method to the context of a specific project.

17.1 GENERAL APPROACH TO TAILORING

Tailoring does not consist of dropping parts of the method. PRINCE2 is a series of interlinked themes, roles and processes. Simply dropping bits will leave gaps and create flaws. So what we want is a scaled version of the method that suits the needs of a project, not over-bureaucratic but offering the required level of control.

17.1.1 Tailoring Principles

The first point to recognize is that the basic principles of PRINCE2 must be preserved and form part of our tailored method. Just to remind ourselves of the seven principles, they are:

1. Continued business justification;
2. Learn from experience;
3. Defined roles and responsibilities;
4. Manage by stages;
5. Manage by exception;
6. Focus on products;
7. Tailor to suit the project environment.

By keeping these in mind, the method can be tailored without losing value.

17.1.2 Adapting the Themes

This is in line with what I said about 'embedding'. This incorporates any useful or mandatory terminology, standards, documents or procedures from the company or – in the case where you are a supplier – that the customer asks you to use. You may not have a local document, but senior management requires one or more specific points of information that are not in the PRINCE2 Product Descriptions. You can simply add these to form your version of a document. For example, your version of a Work Package may require additional information, such as contract number and terms and conditions.

If the project is part of a programme, the project may be required to use the programme's strategies, standards and procedures. This would affect:

- Quality;
- Plans;
- Risk;
- Change;
- Progress.

17.1.3 Adapting the Roles

PRINCE2 expects you to adapt the standard role descriptions to the needs of each specific project. In any given company, this may entail moving responsibilities from one role and adding them to another. That brings up a good rule to follow. Responsibilities can be moved, but they should not be dropped. Someone has to take each responsibility. In the spirit of PRINCE2, this does not mean moving all the Project Board's responsibilities to the Project Manager!

In small projects, it may be sensible to combine some of the roles, such as Executive and Senior User. The Project Manager may carry out the Project

Support and Configuration Librarian roles or get a team member to do them. There may be no need for Team Managers in many small projects.

In a programme environment, the programme board may choose to appoint one of its members as Executive for all or some of the projects in the programme. Possible candidates are the programme manager and business change managers. The programme's design authority may fulfill the role of Change Authority to ensure that changes are viewed for their impact across the programme. If you need more information on programme organization, the APMG bookshop has the MSP manual (Managing Successful Programmes) with full details.

17.1.4 Adapting the Processes

All the activities described in the processes have to be done or at least have to be deliberately reviewed to see if they are needed. This carries the danger of omitting some activities that later you regret, such as checking on risks, performing change control thoroughly, not updating the plans regularly, missing the odd quality check, etc. In small projects, some of the processes may take less than an hour, but they should still be done.

An easy mistake to make is to omit the start-up and initiation work because of management pressure to 'just get on with it'. Later when there are arguments about the scope of the project or whether the expenditure can be justified, it is either too late to go back or very expensive to correct – and it will always be the Project Manager's fault!

One company with whom I worked on tailoring the method decided to combine start-up and initiation. This was OK, but they had to realize that each project's initiation would have to be authorized by corporate/programme management, as there would not be a Project Board in existence.

Small projects may not need Team Managers, which removes the need for Checkpoint Reports, and the Project Manager can decide whether Work Packages are needed. If there is only one specialist stage, there may be no need for separate Stage Plans. All the necessary detail could be held in the Project Plan.

In small projects the Project Manager may decide to use the Daily Log instead of separate registers for risks, issues and quality and incorporate the Lessons Log. Capturing issues in the Daily Log may avoid the need for Issue Reports.

Reports and meetings are major ways of reducing the management effort in a small project. The Project Board and the Project Manager can decide that a number of reports can be given orally. An end stage assessment can be done without an actual meeting, simply an exchange of information by telephone or e-mail and the necessary decisions communicated, and a note made in the Daily Log.

How much of the Project Initiation Document does the Project Board wish to see? It has a number of sections where the only entry may be 'see the xyz folder for full details'. Examples here are the project management team structure, the

Project Plan, the Business Case and all the strategies. The 2009 manual suggests that a small project may run with only four sets of documentation:

- The Project Initiation Document;
- Highlight Reports (oral?);
- Daily Log;
- End Project Report.

Product Descriptions

The appendix contains suggested Product Description outlines for the PRINCE2 management products. Care should be taken to scrutinize them and tune them to any site or project's specific needs. Some headings have been omitted because they will be specific to the individual project, such as identifier, allocated to and quality check skills and people required, and these should be added in for 'real' Product Descriptions.

A.1 BENEFITS REVIEW PLAN

A.1.1 Purpose

The purpose of the post-project review is to find out:

- Whether the expected benefits of the product have been realized;
- If the product has caused any problems in use;
- What enhancement opportunities have been revealed by use of the product.

Each expected benefit is assessed for the level of its achievement so far and any additional time needed for the benefit to materialize.

Unexpected side effects, beneficial or adverse, which use of the product may have brought, are documented with explanations of why these were not foreseen.

Recommendations are made to realize or improve benefits, or counter problems.

A.1.2 Composition

- The benefits that are to be measured.
- Who is accountable for the expected benefits?
- How and when each benefit is to be measured?
- Required resources.
- The baseline measurements of each benefit taken at the start of the project against which the expected improvement is to be gauged.
- Questionnaire to judge the perception of the users.

General comments should be obtained about how the users feel about the product. The type of observation will depend on the type of product produced by the project, but examples might be its ease of use, performance, reliability, contribution it makes to their work and suitability for the work environment.

A.1.3 Format

Site reporting standards.

A.1.4 Derivation

- Business Case.
- Project Product Description.

A.1.5 Quality Criteria

- Covers all benefits mentioned in the Project Brief and Business Case.
- Covers all changes approved during the project life cycle.
- Includes discussions with representatives of all those affected by the end product.
- Describes each benefit in a tangible, measurable form.

A.1.6 Quality Method

Formal quality review against the Project Brief, Business Case and Issue Register.

A.2 BUSINESS CASE

A.2.1 Purpose

To document the reasons and justification for undertaking a project, based on the estimated cost of development and the anticipated business benefits to be gained. The Project Board will monitor the ongoing viability of the project against the Business Case.

The Business Case may include legal or legislative reasons why the project is needed.

A.2.2 Composition

- Business reasons for undertaking the project;
- Options considered;
- Reasons for choosing the selected option;
- Business benefits expected to be gained from development of the product;
- Negative consequences of the project;

- Benefits tolerance;
- Summary of the main risks;
- Development cost and timescale;
- Investment appraisal.

(These may refer to the programme Business Case if it is part of a programme.)

A.2.3 Format

The Business Case forms part of the Project Initiation Document (PID) to standard site practice with the composition shown above.

A.2.4 Derivation

Information for the Business Case is derived from:

- Project mandate/Project Brief (reasons);
- Project Plan (costs and timescale);
- The customer.

A.2.5 Quality Criteria

- Can the benefits be justified?
- Do the cost and timescale match those in the Project Plan?
- Are the reasons for the project consistent with corporate/programme strategy?

A.2.6 Quality Method

Quality review with the Executive and anyone appointed to the Executive's Project Assurance role.

A.3 CHECKPOINT REPORT

A.3.1 Purpose

To report at a frequency defined in the Work Package the progress and status of work for a team.

A.3.2 Composition

- Date of the checkpoint;
- Period covered by the report;
- Report on any follow-up action from previous reports;
- Products completed during the period;
- Quality work carried out during the period;

- Tolerance status;
- Products to be completed during the next period;
- Risk assessment;
- Other actual or potential problems or deviations from plan.

A.3.3 Format

According to the agreement between Project Manager and Team Manager, the report may be verbal or written. It should contain the information given above, plus any extra data requested by the Project Manager.

A.3.4 Derivation

- Team Plan actuals and forecasts;
- Risk Register;
- Team member reports.

A.3.5 Quality Criteria

- Every team member's work covered.
- Includes an update on any unresolved problems from the previous report.
- Does it reflect the Team Plan situation?
- Does it reflect any significant change to the Risk Register?
- Does it reflect any change in a team member's work which has an impact on others?

A.3.6 Quality Method

Informal check by Team Manager and those with Project Assurance responsibility.

A.4 COMMUNICATION MANAGEMENT STRATEGY

A.4.1 Purpose

The Communication Management Strategy identifies all parties who require information from the project and those from whom the project requires information. The plan defines what information is needed and when it should be supplied.

A.4.2 Composition

- Interested parties (such as user groups, suppliers, stakeholders, quality assurance and internal audit);
- Information required by each identified party;
- Identity of the information provider;

- Frequency of communication;
- Method of communication;
- Format.

A.4.3 Format

To the defined site standard for reports with the above content.

A.4.4 Derivation

- The Project Board;
- The Project Brief;
- The PID;
- The Quality Management Strategy;
- The project approach.

A.4.5 Quality Criteria

- Have all the listed derivation sources been checked?
- Has the timing, content and method been agreed?
- Has a common standard been agreed?
- Has time for the communications been allowed for in the Stage Plans?

A.4.6 Quality Method

Informal quality review between Project Manager and those identified in the Communication Management Strategy.

A.5 CONFIGURATION ITEM RECORD

A.5.1 Purpose

A record of the information required about a product's status.

A.5.2 Composition

- The project identifier;
- Item (product) identifier;
- Latest version number;
- Item title and description;
- Type of product;
- Status;
- Stage when created;
- 'Owner' of the product;
- Person working on the product;
- Date allocated;

- Library or location where the product is kept;
- Source – e.g. in-house, or purchased from a third-party company;
- Links to related products;
- Copyholders and potential users;
- Cross-reference to the issue(s) that caused the change to this product;
- Cross-references to relevant correspondence.

A.5.3 Format

Probably electronic, a database record.

A.5.4 Derivation

- Configuration Management Strategy;
- Product Breakdown Structure;
- Stage and Team Plans;
- Work Package;
- Quality Register;
- Issue Register.

A.5.5 Quality Criteria

- Does it accurately reflect the status of the product?
- Are all Configuration Item Records kept together in a secure location?
- Does the version number in the record match that of the actual product?
- Is the copyholder information correct?
- Do the copyholders have the latest version?

A.5.6 Quality Method

Audit by those with Project Assurance responsibility.

A.6 CONFIGURATION MANAGEMENT STRATEGY

A.6.1 Purpose

To identify how and by whom the project's products will be stored, controlled and protected. To describe how changes to products will be controlled.

A.6.2 Composition

This strategy consists of:

- An explanation of the purpose of configuration management;
- A description of (or reference to) the configuration management method to be used. Any variance from corporate/programme standards should be highlighted together with a justification for the variance;

- Reference to any configuration management systems, tools to be used or with which links will be necessary;
- How and where the products will be stored (e.g. project filing structure);
- What filing and retrieval security there will be;
- How the products and the various versions of these will be identified;
- Where responsibility for configuration management lies. This should include whether a Change Authority has been established and if there is a change budget;
- The issue and change control procedure;
- Reference to the Product Descriptions of the Product Status Account, Configuration Item Record and Issue Register;
- Scales for the priority and severity of issues.

A.6.3 Format

A word processor document containing headings as shown in the composition section of this Product Description.

A.6.4 Derivation

Details of the plan might come from:

- The customer's QMS;
- The supplier's QMS;
- Specific needs of the project's products and environment;
- The project organization structure;
- Any configuration management software in use or mandated by the customer.

A.6.5 Quality Criteria

- Responsibilities are clear and understood by both customer and supplier.
- The key identifier for project products is defined.
- The method and circumstances of version control are clear.
- The plan provides the Project Manager with all the product information required.

A.6.6 Quality Method

Formal quality review between Project Manager, configuration management specialists and those with Project Assurance responsibility.

A.7 DAILY LOG

A.7.1 Purpose

To record required actions or significant events not caught by other PRINCE2 documents. It acts as the Project Manager's or a Team Manager's diary. Before creation of the Risk and Issue Registers, it is used to record any early risks or issues.

A.7.2 Composition

(The following are only suggestions.)

- Date of entry;
- Action or comment;
- Person responsible;
- Target date;
- Result.

A.7.3 Format

This may be any form of notebook or electronic diary that is convenient for its user.

A.7.4 Derivation

- Risk Register;
- Stage Plan;
- Checkpoint Reports;
- Quality Register;
- Conversations and observations.

A.7.5 Quality Criteria

- Entries are understandable at a later date;
- Anything of a permanent nature is transferred to the appropriate record, e.g. Project Issue;
- Date, person responsible and target date are always filled in.

A.7.6 Quality Method

Informal check by the owner as the log is referenced, plus a more formal inspection against the quality criteria at each stage end.

A.8 END PROJECT REPORT

A.8.1 Purpose

The report is the Project Manager's report to the Project Board (which may pass it on to corporate/programme management) on how the project has performed against the objectives stated in its PID and revised during the project. It should cover comparisons with the original targets, planned cost, schedule and tolerances, the revised Business Case and final version of the Project Plan.

The End Project Report also includes any follow-on action recommendations and the final Lessons Report.

A.8.2 Composition

- Project Manager's report, summarizing the project's performance against its plans and tolerances;
- Benefits achieved to date;
- Expected net benefits;
- Deviations from the Business Case;
- A summary of quality activities and pointer to the quality records;
- Confirmation of product acceptance by the customer;
- Follow-on action recommendations (changes proposed but not carried out and risks that might affect the operational product);
- Lessons Report (see its own Product Description).

A.8.3 Format

To the defined site standard for reports with the above content plus any extra information requested by the Project Board.

A.8.4 Derivation

- The final Project Plan with actuals;
- The PID;
- Issue, Risk and Quality Registers.

A.8.5 Quality Criteria

- Does the report describe the impact of any approved changes on the original intentions stated in the PID?
- Does the report cover all the benefits which can be assessed at this time?
- Does the quality work done during the project meet the quality expectations of the Customer?

A.8.6 Quality Method

Formal quality review between Project Manager and those with Project Assurance responsibility.

A.9 END STAGE REPORT

A.9.1 Purpose

The purpose of the End Stage Report is to report on a stage that has just completed the overall project situation and sufficient information to ask for a Project Board decision on the next step to take with the project.

The Project Board uses the information in the End Stage Report to approve the next Stage Plan, amend the project scope, ask for a revised next Stage Plan or stop the project.

Normally the End Stage Report for the last stage of a project is combined with the End Project Report.

A.9.2 Composition

- Review of the stage performance against the plan and tolerances;
- Current Stage Plan with all the actuals;
- Project Plan performance to date and outlook;
- Business Case review;
- Risk review;
- Issue and risk situation;
- Quality checking statistics;
- Report on any internal or external events which have affected stage performance.
- Lessons Report (if appropriate at this time);
- Follow-on action recommendations (if required at this time);
- Products handed over (if relevant).

A.9.3 Format

Site reporting standards covering the information described above plus any extra requested by the Project Board.

A.9.4 Derivation

Information for the report is obtained from:

- The Stage Plan and actuals;
- The next Stage Plan (if appropriate);
- The updated Project Plan;
- The Lessons Log;
- Data from the Quality Register;
- Completed Work Package data.

A.9.5 Quality Criteria

- Does it clearly describe stage performance against the plan?
- Were any approved modifications described, together with their impact?
- Does it give an accurate picture of the quality testing work done in the stage?
- Does it give an accurate review of the revised risk situation?
- Does it give an accurate assessment of the ability of the project to meet its Business Case?

A.9.6 Quality Method

Informal quality review between Project Manager and those with Project Assurance responsibility.

A.10 EXCEPTION REPORT

A.10.1 Purpose

An Exception Report is produced when costs and/or time scales for an approved Stage Plan or the Project Plan are forecast to exceed the tolerance levels set. It is sent by the Project Manager in order to warn the Project Board of the adverse situation.

An Exception Report may result in the Project Board asking the Project Manager to produce an Exception Plan.

A.10.2 Composition

- A description of the cause of the deviation from the Stage Plan;
- The consequences of the deviation;
- The available options;
- The effect of each option on the Business Case, risks, project and stage tolerances;
- The Project Manager's recommendations;
- Lessons – what can be learned from the exception for future benefit.

A.10.3 Format

Site reporting standards containing the information shown above.

A.10.4 Derivation

The information for an Exception Report is drawn from:

- Current Stage Plan and actuals;
- Project plan and actuals;
- Deviation forecast;
- Issue Register;
- Risk Register;
- Quality Register;
- Checkpoint Reports;
- Project Board advice of an external event which affects the project.

A.10.5 Quality Criteria

- The Exception Report must accurately show the current status of stage and project budget and schedule, plus the forecast impact of the deviation on both;
- The reason(s) for the deviation must be stated;
- Options, including 'do nothing' must be put forward, together with their impact on objectives, plans, Business Case and risks;
- A recommendation must be made.

A.10.6 Quality Method

Informal review between Project Manager, any Team Managers and those with Project Assurance responsibility.

A.11 HIGHLIGHT REPORT

A.11.1 Purpose

For the Project Manager to provide the Project Board with a summary of the stage status at intervals defined by them in the PID.

A Highlight Report normally summarizes a series of Checkpoint Reports. The Project Board uses the report to monitor stage and project progress. The Project Manager also uses it to advise the Project Board of any potential problems or areas where the Project Board could help.

A.11.2 Composition

- Date;
- Project;
- Stage;
- Period covered;
- Budget status;
- Schedule status;
- Products completed during the period;
- Actual or potential problems;
- Products to be completed during the next period;
- Issue and risk status;
- Project and stage tolerance status;
- Budget and schedule impact of any changes approved so far in the stage.

A.11.3 Format

Site reporting standards containing the above information plus any extra data requested by the Project Board.

A.11.4 Derivation

Information for the Highlight Reports is derived from:

- Checkpoint Reports;
- Stage Plan;
- The Issue Register;
- The Risk Register.

A.11.5 Quality Criteria

- Accurate reflection of Checkpoint Reports;
- Accurate summary of the Issue Register status;
- Accurate summary of the Stage Plan status;
- Highlights any potential problem areas.

A.11.6 Quality Method

Informal review between the Project Manager and those with Project Assurance responsibility.

A.12 ISSUE REGISTER

A.12.1 Purpose

The purpose of the Issue Register is to:

- Allocate a unique number to each issue;
- Record the type of issue;
- Be a summary of the issues, their analysis and status.

A.12.2 Composition

- Issue number;
- Issue type (Issue, request for change, off-specification, problem or concern);
- Author;
- Date created;
- Date of last update;
- Issue description;
- Priority;
- Severity;
- Status.

A.12.3 Format

Standard department form with the headings shown under 'Composition'.

A.12.4 Derivation

Project Issues may be raised by anyone associated with the project at any time.

A.12.5 Quality Criteria

- Does the status indicate whether action has been taken?
- Are the Project Issues uniquely identified, including to which product they refer?
- Is access to the Issue Register controlled?
- Is the Issue Register kept in a safe place?

A.12.6 Quality Method

Regular inspection.

A.13 ISSUE REPORT

A.13.1 Purpose

To record any matter which has to be formally brought to the attention of the project, and requires an answer. An issue may be:

- Request for change;
- Off-specification;
- Question;
- Statement of concern.

A.13.2 Composition

- Author;
- Date;
- Issue number;
- Type (request for change, off-specification or question);
- Description of the issue;
- Priority;
- Impact analysis;
- Recommendation;
- Priority;
- Severity;
- Decision;
- Signature of decision-maker(s);
- Date of decision.

A.13.3 Format

Department style of form with the headings shown under 'Composition'.

A.13.4 Derivation

Anyone may submit an issue. Typical sources are users and specialists working on the project, the Project Manager and those with Project Assurance responsibility.

A.13.5 Quality Criteria

- Is the statement of the problem/requirement clear?
- Has all necessary information been made available?
- Have all the implications been considered?
- Has the Project Issue been correctly logged?

A.13.6 Quality Method

Check by the person responsible for the Issue Register.

A.14 LESSONS LOG

A.14.1 Purpose

The purpose of the Lessons Log is to be a repository of any lessons learned during the project that can be usefully applied to other projects. At the close of the project it is written up formally in the Lessons Learned Report. Minimally it should be updated at the end of a stage, but sensibly a note should be made in it of any good or bad point that arises in the use of the management and specialist products and tools at the time of the experience.

A.14.2 Composition

- Lesson detail:
  - Cause(s);
  - Event;
  - Effect;
  - Recommendations;
- Whether the lesson was previously identified as a risk;
- Logged by (person recording the lesson);
- Priority.

A.14.3 Format

Freeform, electronic or handwritten; the main concern is that the information can be recovered for use in the next End Stage Report and the Lessons Learned Report at the end of the project.

A.14.4 Derivation

Information for the records in the Lessons Log is derived from:

- Observation and experience of the processes;
- Quality Register;
- Completed Work Packages;
- Risk Register;
- Highlight Report(s);
- Checkpoint Reports;
- Stage Plans with actuals.

A.14.5 Quality Criteria

- Each management control has been considered;
- The reasons for all tolerance deviations and corrective actions have been recorded;
- Input to the log is being done, minimally, at the end of each stage;
- Project Assurance and Project Support have been asked for their input;
- Statistics of the success of quality reviews and other types of test used are included.

A.14.6 Quality Method

Informal review on a regular basis and at each stage end by the Project Manager and those with Project Assurance responsibilities.

A.15 LESSONS REPORT

A.15.1 Purpose

The purpose of the Lessons Learned Report is to pass on to other projects any useful lessons that can be learned from this project.

The data in the report should be used by an independent group, such as quality assurance, who are responsible for the site QMS, to refine, change and improve project management and technical standards. Statistics on how much effort was needed for products can help improve future estimating.

A.15.2 Composition

- Scope – stage or project:
- What management and quality processes;
  - went well;
  - went badly;
  - were lacking;
- An assessment of the efficacy of technical methods and tools used;
- Recommendations for future enhancement or modification of the project management method, including the reasons;

- Measurements on how much effort was required to create the various products;
- A description of any abnormal events causing deviations to targets or plans;
- An analysis of Project Issues raised, their causes and results;
- Statistics on how effective quality reviews and other tests were in error trapping (e.g. how many errors were found after products had passed a quality review or test).

A.15.3 Format

Site reporting standards containing at least the above information.

A.15.4 Derivation

Information for the report is derived from:

- Observation and experience of the processes and techniques used;
- Checkpoint Reports;
- Observations of quality checks;
- Performance against plans;
- End Stage Reports;
- Any exception situations.

A.15.5 Quality Criteria

- Input to the report is being done, minimally, at the end of each stage;
- Every management control has been examined;
- A review of every specialist technique is included;
- Statistics of the success of quality reviews and other types of quality check used are included;
- The accuracy of all estimates and plans is included;
- Details of the effort taken for each product are given;
- The success of change control is reviewed.

A.15.6 Quality Method

Informal review at each stage end by the Project Manager and those with Project Assurance responsibilities.

Formal quality review by this group before presentation.

A.16 PLAN

A.16.1 Purpose

A Plan shows how and when objectives are to be achieved. It identifies the products to be delivered, the activities to produce them and their timings and the resources required to undertake the activities.

Project, Stage and Exception Plans should have the following composition. It is optional whether Team Plans use this format.

A.16.2 Composition

- Plan description, giving a brief description of what the plan covers;
- Project prerequisites, containing any fundamental aspects which must be in place at the start of the planned work, and which must remain in place for the plan to succeed;
- External dependencies;
- Planning assumptions;
- Any lessons incorporated;
- Gantt or bar chart;
- Product Breakdown Structure;
- Product Flow Diagrams;
- Product Descriptions;
- Activity network;
- Tolerances for time, cost and scope;
- Table of resource requirements;
- Requested/assigned specific resources.

A.16.3 Format

Gantt or bar chart plus text.

A.16.4 Derivation

Project Brief.

A.16.5 Quality Criteria

- Is the plan achievable?
- Does it support the rest of the PID?

A.16.6 Quality Method

Formal quality review with Project Manager and those with Project Assurance responsibility.

A.17 PRODUCT BREAKDOWN STRUCTURE

A.17.1 Purpose

- To show all products to be developed and quality controlled within a plan.

A.17.2 Composition

- Top-to-bottom diagram showing a breakdown of all products to be developed during the life of the plan. External products must be included, clearly distinguished from those to be developed.

A.17.3 Format

- Display from a planning and control tool;
- Spreadsheet, diagrams, mindmap or table.

A.17.4 Derivation

- Higher level plan (if there is one);
- Product Descriptions;
- A statement of the final product(s) whose creation or procurement is to be planned.

A.17.5 Quality Criteria

- Are all external products and project products included?
- Is any product defined as external really the source of the product rather than the product (an error)?
- Is a product defined as external when, in fact, it is a project product provided by an external team (an error)?
- Is the PBS consistent with the Product Checklist?
- Are management and specialist products identified and distinguished?
- Can Product Descriptions for the bottom-level products be written without further decomposition?
- Have enough bottom-level products been identified to meet management planning and control requirements?
- Will the combination of all the products identified fulfill the business need?
- Have all quality products been identified that meet the needs of customer, audit and Project Assurance as described in the Quality Management Strategy?

A.17.6 Quality Method

Formal quality review against known required end product(s).

A.18 PRODUCT CHECKLIST

A.18.1 Purpose

Lists the products to be produced within a plan, together with key status dates.

Updated at agreed reporting intervals by the Project Manager and used by the Project Board to monitor progress.

A.18.2 Composition

- Plan identification;
- Product names (and identifiers where appropriate);
- Planned and actual dates for:

- Draft product ready;
- Quality check;
- Approval.

A.18.3 Format

Standard department form with the headings defined under 'Composition'.

A.18.4 Derivation

Extracted from the Stage Plan.

A.18.5 Quality Criteria

Do the details and dates match those in the Stage Plan?

A.18.6 Quality Method

Informal review against the Stage Plan.

A.19 PRODUCT DESCRIPTION

A.19.1 Purpose

To define the information needed to describe each product to be created by the project.

A.19.2 Composition

- Identifier;
- Title;
- Purpose:
  - An explanation of the purpose of the product;
- Composition:
  - A list of the various parts of the product, e.g. chapters of the document;
- Form or format:
  - What the product should look like. If it is a document, the name of the template to be used;
- Derivation:
  - The sources of information for the product;
- Development skills required (at least type and number);
- Quality Criteria:
  - What quality measurements the product must meet;
- Quality tolerance;

- Quality Method:
  - What method of checking the product's quality is to be used, and what type of skill is required;
- Quality checking skills required.

A.19.3 Format

Standard department form with the headings defined under 'Composition'.

A.19.4 Derivation

- Project Brief;
- PID;
- Quality Management Strategy;
- Ultimate recipient of the product.

A.19.5 Quality Criteria

- Does it contain information under all the headings?
- Is there more than one purpose?
- Has the end user been involved in its writing?

A.19.6 Quality Method

Formal quality review.

A.20 PRODUCT FLOW DIAGRAM

A.20.1 Purpose

To show the required sequence of delivery of a plan's products and identify dependencies between those products, including any external products.

A.20.2 Composition

A diagram showing the product delivery sequence from top to bottom (or left to right) plus the dependencies between those products. Arrows indicate dependencies between products. External products must be clearly distinguished from the products developed by the plan. The PRINCE2 convention is for project products to be shown as rectangles and external products as ellipses.

A.20.3 Format

A chart normally flowing from top to bottom (or left to right depending on the shape of the visual medium used) with arrows connecting the various products to show the sequence of delivery and any inter-product dependencies.

A.20.4 Derivation

- Product Descriptions (derivation field);
- Product Breakdown Structure (external products).

A.20.5 Quality Criteria

- Is the final product from the Product Breakdown Structure (PBS) shown as the end of the Product Flow Diagram (PFD)?
- Are all external products identified and the dependencies understood?
- Are all bottom-level products on the PBS identified on the diagram?
- Are all integration products identified on the PBS shown on the PFD?
- Are all products identified in the PFD identified as products on the PBS?
- Are the product names the same in both diagrams?
- Are there any products without dependencies?
- Have dependencies been identified at a level suitable to that of the plan of which the PFD is a part?
- Are the dependencies consistent with the derivation fields (from Product Description) of all the products?

A.20.6 Quality Method

- Quality review

A.21 PRODUCT STATUS ACCOUNT

A.21.1 Purpose

The Product Status Account provides information about the state of products. For example, the report could cover the entire project, a particular stage or a particular area of the project. It is particularly useful if the Project Manager wishes to confirm the version number of products or confirm that all products within a specific plan have reached a certain status, such as draft, tested or approved.

A.21.2 Composition

The composition will vary but will normally consist of the following information:

- Date and report scope (stage, project, product type, supplier etc);

For each product identified the following additional information may be provided:

- Product Type;
- Product Identifier;
- Version Number.
- Status;

- Date Product Description baselined;
- Date product baselined;
- List of related products;
- Date on which a copy of product was issued for change;
- Planned date for next baseline;
- Planned date of next release;
- Any relevant notes, e.g. change pending, under review.

A.21.3 Format

Normally a table with columns for product, status and date of last status change. The Project Manager may vary this and ask for any information held in the Configuration Item Record.

A.21.4 Derivation

- Configuration Item Records.

A.21.5 Quality Criteria

- Covers all item requested;
- Accurate.

A.21.6 Quality Method

Verification against sample Configuration Item Records and actual products.

A.22 PROJECT BRIEF

A.22.1 Purpose

To briefly explain the reasons for the project, the customer's expectations and any limitations which apply.

A.22.2 Composition

The following is a suggested list of contents which should be tailored to the requirements and environment of each project.

- Project Definition, explaining what the project needs to achieve:
  - Background;
  - Project objectives;
  - Project scope;
  - Outline project deliverables and/or desired outcomes;
  - Any exclusions;

- Constraints;
- Assumptions;
- Project tolerances;
- Users and stakeholders;
- Interfaces;
- Outline Business Case:
  - Reason for the project;
  - Description of how this project supports business strategy, plans or programmes;
- Project Product Description;
- Project approach:
  - Defines the type of solution to be developed or procured by the project. It should also identify the environment into which the product must be delivered;
  - Type of solution, e.g.:
    ○ Off-the-shelf;
    ○ Built from scratch;
    ○ Modifying an existing product;
    ○ Built by one or more external suppliers;
    ○ Adding to/modifying a product developed by another project;
    ○ Built by company staff;
    ○ Built by contract staff under the supervision of the Project Manager;
  - Reason for the selection of approach, e.g. part of a programme;
  - Implications on the project;
- Project management team structure;
- Role descriptions;
- References to associated documents or products.

If earlier work has been done, the Project Brief may refer to document(s), such as Outline Project Plan.

A.22.3 Format

Site project request standards containing at least the information shown above.

A.22.4 Derivation

- Project mandate;
- If the project is part of a programme, the programme should provide the Project Brief;
- If no project mandate is provided, the Project Manager has to generate the Project Brief in discussions with the customer and users;
- Any significant change to the material contained in the Project Brief will thus need to be referred to corporate/programme management.

A.22.5 Quality Criteria

- Does it accurately reflect the project mandate?
- Does it form a firm basis on which to initiate a project (Initiate the Project (IP))?
- Does it indicate how the customer will assess the acceptability of the finished product(s)?

A.22.6 Quality Method

Informal quality review between Project Manager and Project Board during the process '*Start Up the Project*' (SU).

A.23 PROJECT INITIATION DOCUMENT

A.23.1 Purpose

- To define the project;
- To form the basis for the ultimate assessment of the project's success and the project's management.

There are two primary uses of the document:

1. To ensure that the project has a sound basis before asking the Project Board to make any major commitment to the project;
2. To act as a base document against which the Project Board and Project Manager can assess progress, evaluate change issues and answer questions of the project's continuing viability.

A.23.2 Composition

The PID must answer the following fundamental questions:

- **what** the project is aiming to achieve;
- **why** it is important to achieve it;
- **who** is going to be involved in managing the project and what are their responsibilities;
- **how** and **when** it is all going to happen?

The following list should be seen as the information needed in order to make the initiation decisions.

- *Background*, explaining the context of the project, and steps taken to arrive at the current position of requiring a project.
- *Project Definition*, explaining what the project needs to achieve. Under this heading may be:
  - Project objectives;
  - Project deliverables and/or desired outcomes;

- Project scope;
- Constraints;
- Exclusions;
- Interfaces;
- Assumptions;
- *Project approach*;
- *Business Case*, explaining why the project is being undertaken;
- *Project Organization Structure*, defining the project management team and including job descriptions;
- *Quality Management Strategy*. (See the separate Quality Management Strategy Product Description)
- *Project Plan*, explaining how and when the activities of the project will occur. (For details of the Project Plan content see the separate Product Description.)
- *Project Tolerances*, showing tolerance levels for time, cost, quality, benefit risk and resources. Tolerances for quality should already be in the Quality Management Strategy and benefit tolerances in the Business Case, so a choice can be made to simply point to their presence in those documents rather than repeat them.
- *Project Controls*, stating how control is to be exercised within the project, and the reporting and monitoring mechanisms which will support this.
- *Communication Management Strategy*. (See separate Product Description.)
- *Risk Management Strategy* (See the separate Risk Management Strategy Product Description).
- Summary of any tailoring of PRINCE2 for the project.

A.23.3 Format

Site reporting standards.

A.23.4 Derivation

- Customer's or supplier's project management standards;
- Customer's specified control requirements.

(Much of the information should come from the project mandate, enhanced in the Project Brief.)

A.23.5 Quality Criteria

- Does the document correctly represent the project?
- Does it show a viable, achievable project which is in line with corporate strategy, or overall programme needs?
- Is the project organization structure complete, with names and titles?

- Does it clearly show a control, reporting and direction regime that can be implemented and is appropriate to the scale, business risk and importance of the project?
- Has everyone named in the organization structure received and accepted their job description?
- Does the project organization structure need to say to whom the Project Board reports?
- Are the internal and external relationships and lines of authority clear?
- Do the controls cover the needs of the Project Board, Project Manager and any Team Managers?
- Do the controls satisfy any delegated Project Assurance requirements?
- Is it clear who will administer each control?

A.23.6 Quality Method

Formal quality review between the Project Manager and those with Project Assurance responsibility.

A.24 PROJECT MANDATE

The 2009 version of the PRINCE2 manual does not recognize the project mandate as a PRINCE2 product, since it has no control over its creation. I believe that it is useful to be able to show anyone about to create a project mandate what information, in an ideal world should be in it.

A.24.1 Purpose

Project mandate is a term to describe an initial request for a project, which may require further work to turn it into a Project Brief.

A.24.2 Composition

The actual composition of a project mandate will vary according to the type and size of project and also the environment in which the mandate is generated.

The following is a list of contents which would make up an 'ideal' mandate, and should be tailored to suit the specific project. An actual mandate may have much less information. The ideal mandate contains:

- Authority responsible;
- The customer(s), user(s) and any other known interested parties;
- Background;
- Outline Business Case (reasons);
- Project objectives;
- Scope;
- Constraints;

- Interfaces;
- Quality expectations;
- An estimate of the project size and duration (if known);
- A view of the risks faced by the project;
- An indication of who should be the project Executive and Project Manager;
- Reference to any associated projects or products.

A.24.3 Format

May be in any format.

A.24.4 Derivation

A project mandate may come from anywhere, but it should come from a level of management that can authorize the cost and resource usage.

A.24.5 Quality Criteria

- Does the mandate describe what is required?
- Is the level of authority commensurate with the anticipated size, risk and cost of the project?
- Is there sufficient detail to allow the appointment of an appropriate Executive and Project Manager?
- Are all the known interested parties identified?

A.24.6 Quality Method

Informal review between Executive, Project Manager and the mandate author.

A.25 PROJECT PRODUCT DESCRIPTION

A.25.1 Purpose

The Project Product Description is a special form of Product Description that defines what the project must deliver in order to gain acceptance. It is used to:

- Gain agreement from the user on the project's scope and requirements;
- Define the customer's quality expectations;
- Define the acceptance criteria, method and responsibilities for the project.

The Product Description for the project product is created in the Starting up a Project process as part of the initial scoping activity, and is refined during the Initiating a Project process when creating the Project Plan. It is used by the Closing a Project process as part of the verification that the project has delivered what was expected of it, and that the acceptance criteria have been met.

A.25.2 Composition

- *Title*: Name by which the project is known.
- *Purpose*: This defines the purpose that the project product will fulfill and who will use it. It is helpful in understanding the product's functions, size, quality, complexity, robustness, etc.
- *Composition*: A description of the major products to be delivered by the project.
- *Derivation*: What are the source products from which this product is derived? Examples are:
  - Existing products to be modified;
  - Design specifications;
  - A feasibility report;
  - Project mandate.
- *Development skills required*: An indication of the skills required to develop the product, or a pointer to which area(s) should supply the development resources.
- *Customer's quality expectations*: A description of the quality expected of the project product and the standards and processes that will need to be applied to achieve that quality. They will impact on every part of the product development, thus time and cost. The quality expectations are captured in discussions with the customer (business and user stakeholders). Where possible, expectations should be prioritized.
- *Acceptance criteria*: A prioritized list of criteria that the project product must meet before the customer will accept it – i.e. measurable definitions of the attributes that must apply to the set of products to be acceptable to key stakeholders (and, in particular, the users and the operational and maintenance organizations). Examples are: ease of use, ease of support, ease of maintenance, appearance, major functions, development costs, running costs, capacity, availability, reliability, security, accuracy or performance.
- *Project level quality tolerances*: Specifying any tolerances that may apply for the acceptance criteria.
- *Acceptance method*: Stating the means by which acceptance will be confirmed. This may simply be a case of confirming that all the project's products have been approved or may involve describing complex handover arrangements for the project product, including any phased handover of the project's products.
- *Acceptance responsibilities*: Defining who will be responsible for confirming acceptance.

A.25.3 Derivation

- Project mandate;
- Discussions with the Senior User and Executive – possibly via scoping workshops;
- Request for proposal (if in a commercial customer/supplier environment).

A.25.4 Format

A Product Description for the project product can take a number of formats, including:

- Document, presentation slides or mindmap;
- Entry in a project management tool.

A.25.5 Quality Criteria

- The purpose is clear;
- The composition defines the complete scope of the project;
- The acceptance criteria form the complete list against which the project will be assessed;
- The acceptance criteria address the requirements of all the key stakeholders (e.g. operations and maintenance);
- It defines how the users and the operational and maintenance organizations will assess the acceptability of the finished product(s);
- All criteria are measurable;
- Each criterion is individually realistic;
- The criteria are realistic and consistent as a set. For example, high quality, early delivery and low cost may not go together;
- All criteria can be proven within the project life (e.g. the maximum throughput of a water pump), or by proxy measures that provide reasonable indicators as to whether acceptance criteria will be achieved post-project (e.g. a water pump that complies with reliability design and manufacturing standard);
  - The quality expectations have considered:
    - The characteristics of the key quality requirements (e.g. fast/slow, large/small, national/global);
    - The elements of the customer's QMS that should be used;
    - Any other standards that should be used;
    - The level of customer/staff satisfaction that should be achieved if surveyed.

A.25.6 Quality Method

Review between Project Manager and the Project Board.

A.26 QUALITY MANAGEMENT STRATEGY

A.26.1 Purpose

The purpose is to define how the supplier intends to deliver products that meet the customer's quality expectations and the agreed quality standards.

A.26.2 Composition

- Quality control and audit processes to be applied to project management;
- Quality control and audit process requirements for specialist work;
- Quality records to be kept and any reports to be produced;
- Quality responsibilities;
- Reference to any standards to be met;
- Any Quality Management systems, tools and techniques to be used to ensure quality.

A.26.3 Format

The Quality Management Strategy is part of the PID.

A.26.4 Derivation

- Customer's quality expectations (project mandate and/or Brief);
- Corporate/programme Quality Management Strategy.

A.26.5 Quality Criteria

- Does the plan clearly define ways to confirm that the customer's quality expectations will be met?
- Are the defined ways sufficient to achieve the required quality?
- Are responsibilities for quality defined up to a level which is independent of the project and Project Manager?
- Does the plan conform to corporate Quality Policy?

A.26.6 Quality Method

Review between Project Manager and whoever is assuring the project on behalf of the customer.

A.27 QUALITY REGISTER

A.27.1 Purpose

- To issue a unique reference for each quality check or test planned;
- To act as a pointer to the quality check and test documentation for a product;
- To act as a summary of the number and type of quality checks and tests held.

The log summarizes all the quality checks and tests which are planned/ have taken place, and provides information for the End Stage and End Project Reports, as well as the Lessons Learned Report.

A.27.2 Composition

For each entry in the log:

- Quality check reference number;
- Product checked or tested;
- Planned date of the check;
- Quality check method;
- Staff responsible; names and roles
- Actual date of the check;
- Result of the check;
- Number of action items found;
- Target sign-off date;
- Actual sign-off date.

A.27.3 Format

Standard departmental form with the headings shown in 'Composition'.

A.27.4 Derivation

The first entries are made when a quality check or test is entered on a Stage Plan. The remaining information comes from the actual performance of the check. The sign-off date is when all corrective action items have been signed off.

A.27.5 Quality Criteria

Is there a procedure in place which will ensure that every quality check is entered on the log?
    Has responsibility for the log been allocated?

A.27.6 Quality Method

Regular checking should be done by those with Project Assurance responsibility for the customer and provider. There may also be an inspection by an independent quality assurance function.

A.28 RISK MANAGEMENT STRATEGY
A.28.1 Purpose

The Risk Management Strategy describes the risk management procedure, techniques and standards to be applied and the responsibilities for risk management.

A.28.2 Composition

- *Introduction*: The purpose, objectives, scope and responsibility of the strategy.
- *The risk management procedure*: A description of (or reference to) the risk management procedure to be used. Any variance from corporate/ programme management standards should be described, together with its justification. The procedure should cover the risk activities of:
  - Identify;
  - Assess;
  - Plan;
  - Implement;
  - Communicate.
- *Risk tolerance*: The threshold levels of risk exposure, which, when exceeded, require the risk to be escalated to the next level of management. (For example, a project-level risk tolerance might be the threatened loss below a tolerance limit of certain workforce skills. Such risks would need to be escalated to corporate/programme management.) The risk tolerance should define the risk expectations of corporate/programme management and the Project Board.
- *Risk Budget*: Describing if a risk budget is to be established and, if so, how will it be used.
- *Tools and techniques*: Any risk management systems or tools to be used, and any preference for techniques which may be used for each step in the risk management procedure.
- *Records*: Definition of the composition and format of the Risk Register and any other risk records to be used by the project.
- *Reporting*: Any risk management reports to be produced, their recipients, purpose and timing.
- *Timing of risk management activities*: When risk management activities are to be undertaken, e.g. at end stage assessments and issue impact analysis.
- *Roles and responsibilities*: The roles and responsibilities for risk management activities.
- *Scales*: The scales to be used for estimating probability and impact of a risk, e.g. to ensure that the scales for cost and time are relevant to the cost and timeframe of the project.
- *Proximity*: How the proximity of a risk is to be assessed. Typical proximity categories will be: imminent, within a month, within the stage, within the project or beyond the project.
- *Risk categories*: The risk categories to be used (if at all).
- *Risk response categories*: Definition of the risk response categories to be used.
- *Early warning indicators*: Indicators to be used to track critical aspects of the project, so that if predefined levels are reached, corrective action will be triggered.

A.28.3 Format

A Risk Management Strategy might be:

- Stand-alone document or a section of the PID;
- Entry in a project management tool.

A.28.4 Derivation

- Any relevant corporate/programme management risk management process or strategy;
- Project Brief;
- Business Case.

A.28.5 Quality Criteria

- Responsibilities are clear and understood by both customer and supplier;
- The risk management procedure is clearly documented and can be understood by all parties;
- Scales, expected value and proximity definitions are clear and unambiguous;
- The chosen scales are appropriate for the level of control required;
- Risk reporting requirements are fully defined.

A.28.6 Quality Method

- Quality review

A.29 RISK REGISTER

A.29.1 Purpose

The purpose of the Risk Register is to:

- Allocate a unique number to each risk;
- Record the type of risk;
- Be a summary of the risks, their analysis and status.

A.29.2 Composition

- Risk number;
- Risk category (e.g. schedule, quality, legal);
- Author;
- Date risk identified;
- Date of last risk status update;
- Risk description;
- Likelihood;
- Severity;

- Countermeasure(s);
- Status;
- Risk owner;
- Risk actionee.

A.29.3 Format

Standard department form with the headings shown in 'Composition'.

A.29.4 Derivation

Business risks may have been identified in the Project Brief and should be sought during project initiation. There should be a check for any new risks every time the Risk Register is reviewed or a new plan made, minimally at each end stage assessment. The Project Board has the responsibility to constantly check external events for business risks.

A.29.5 Quality Criteria

- Does the status indicate whether action has been/is being taken or is in a contingency plan?
- Are the risks uniquely identified, including to which product they refer?
- Is access to the Risk Register controlled?
- Is the Risk Register kept in a safe place?
- Are activities to review the Risk Register in the Stage Plans?
- Has responsibility for monitoring the risk been identified and documented?

A.29.6 Quality Method

Regular review by the person who has business Project Assurance responsibility.

A.30 WORK PACKAGE

A.30.1 Purpose

A set of instructions to produce one or more required products given by the Project Manager to a Team Manager or team member.

A.30.2 Composition

Although the content may vary greatly according to the relationship between the Project Manager and the recipient of the Work Package, it should cover:

- Date of the agreement;
- Team Manager or person authorized;
- Work Package description;

- Techniques, processes and procedures to be used;
- Development interfaces;
- Operations and maintenance interfaces;
- Configuration management requirements;
- Joint agreements – effort, cost, start and end dates;
- Tolerances – for time and cost and, possibly, scope and risk;
- Constraints – people, timings, charges, rules to be followed;
- Reporting arrangements;
- Problem handling and escalation;
- Stage Plan extract;
- Copies of the relevant Product Descriptions;
- Approval method.

A.30.3 Format

This product will vary in content and in degree of formality, depending on circumstances. Where the work is being conducted by a single team working directly for the Project Manager, the Work Package may be a verbal instruction, although there are good reasons for putting it in writing, such as avoidance of misunderstanding and providing a link to performance assessment. Where a supplier under a contract is carrying out the work and the Project Manager is part of the customer organization, the Work Package should be a formal, written document.

A.30.4 Derivation

There could be many Work Packages authorized during each stage. The Project Manager creates a Work Package from the Stage Plan.

A.30.5 Quality Criteria

- Is the required Work Package clearly defined and understood by the assigned resource?
- Is there a Product Description for the required product(s) with clearly identified and acceptable quality criteria?
- Does the Product Description match up with the other Work Package documentation?
- Are standards for the work agreed?
- Are the defined standards in line with those applied to similar products?
- Have all necessary interfaces been defined?
- Do the reporting arrangements include the provision for exception reporting?

A.30.6 Quality Method

Agreement between Project Manager and recipient.

Project Management Team Roles

Here is a description for each role in the project management structure. These can be used as the basis for discussion of an individual's job and tailored to suit the project's circumstances. The tailored role description becomes that person's job description for the project. (Author's note: Two copies of an agreed job description should be signed by the individual, one for retention by the individual, the other to be filed in the project file.)

B.1 PROJECT BOARD

B.1.1 General

The Project Board is appointed to provide overall direction and management of the project. The Project Board is accountable for the success of the project, and has responsibility and authority for the project within the limits set by corporate/programme management.

The Project Board is the project's 'voice' to the outside world and is responsible for any publicity or other dissemination of information about the project.

B.1.2 Specific Responsibility

The Project Board approves all major plans and authorizes any major deviation from agreed Stage Plans. It is the authority that signs off the completion of each stage as well as authorizes the start of the next stage. It ensures that required resources are committed and arbitrates on any conflicts within the project or negotiates a solution to any problems between the project and the external bodies. In addition, it approves the appointment and responsibility of the Project Manager and any delegation of its Project Assurance responsibility.

The Project Board has the following responsibility. It is a general list and will need tailoring for a specific project.

At the beginning of the project:

- Assurance that the PID complies with relevant customer standards and policies, plus any associated contract with the supplier;

- Agreement with the Project Manager on that person's responsibility and objectives;
- Confirmation with corporate/programme management of project tolerances;
- Specification of external constraints on the project such as quality assurance;
- Approval of an accurate and satisfactory Project Initiation Document;
- Delegation of any Project Assurance roles;
- Commitment of project resources required by the next Stage Plan.

As the project progresses:

- Provision of overall guidance and direction to the project, ensuring it remains within any specified constraints;
- Review of each completed stage and approval of progress to the next;
- Review and approval of Stage Plans and any Exception Plans;
- 'Ownership' of one or more of the identified project risks as allocated at plan approval time, i.e. the responsibility to monitor the risk and advise the Project Manager of any change in its status and to take action, if appropriate, to ameliorate the risk;
- Approval of changes;
- Compliance with corporate/programme management directives.

At the end of the project:

- Assurance that all products have been delivered satisfactorily;
- Assurance that all acceptance criteria have been met;
- Approval of the End Project Report;
- Approval of the Lessons Report and the passage of this to the appropriate standards group to ensure action;
- Decisions on the recommendations for follow-on actions and the passage of these to the appropriate authorities;
- Arrangements, where appropriate, for a post-project review;
- Project closure notification to corporate/programme management.

The Project Board is ultimately responsible for the assurance of the project, that it remains on course to deliver the desired outcome of the required quality to meet the Business Case defined in the project contract. According to the size, complexity and risk of the project, the Project Board may decide to delegate some of this Project Assurance responsibility. Later in this chapter Project Assurance is defined in more detail.

One Project Board responsibility that should receive careful consideration is that of approving and funding changes. The chapter on Change Control should be read before finalizing this responsibility of approving and funding changes.

Responsibility of specific members of the Project Board is described in the respective sections below.

B.2 EXECUTIVE

B.2.1 General

The executive is ultimately responsible for the project, supported by the Senior User and Senior Supplier. The executive has to ensure that the project is value for money, ensuring a cost-conscious approach to the project, balancing the demands of business, user and supplier.

Throughout the project the executive 'owns' the Business Case.

B.2.2 Specific Responsibility

- Ensure that a tolerance is set for the project by corporate/programme management in the project mandate;
- Authorize customer expenditure and set stage tolerances;
- Approve the End Project Report and Lessons Report;
- Brief corporate/programme management about project progress;
- Organize and chair Project Board meetings;
- Recommend future action on the project to corporate/programme management if the project tolerance is exceeded;
- Approve the sending of the notification of project closure to corporate/programme management.

The Executive is responsible for overall business assurance of the project, i.e. it remains on target to deliver products that will achieve the expected business benefits, and the project will complete within its agreed tolerances for budget and schedule. Business Project Assurance covers:

- Validation and monitoring of the Business Case against external events and against project progress;
- Keeping the project in line with customer strategies;
- Monitoring project finance on behalf of the customer;
- Monitoring the business risks to ensure that these are kept under control;
- Monitoring any supplier and contractor payments;
- Monitoring changes to the Project Plan to see if there is any impact on the needs of the business or the project Business Case;
- Assessing the impact of potential changes on the Business Case and Project Plan;
- Constraining user and supplier excesses;
- Informing the project of any changes caused by a programme of which the project is part (this responsibility may be transferred if there is other programme representation on the project management team);
- Monitoring stage and project progress against the agreed tolerance.

If the project warrants it, the Executive may delegate some responsibility for the above business Project Assurance functions.

B.3 SENIOR USER

B.3.1 General

The Senior User is responsible for the specification of the needs of all those who will use the final product(s), user liaison with the project team and for monitoring that the solution will meet those needs within the constraints of the Business Case.

The role represents the interests of all those who will use the final product(s) of the project, those who will operate and maintain the final product(s), those for whom the product will achieve an objective, or those who will use the product to deliver benefits. The Senior User role commits user resources and monitors products against requirements. This role may require more than one person to cover all the user interests. For the sake of effectiveness the role should not be split between too many people.

B.3.2 Specific Responsibility

- Ensure the desired outcome of the project is specified;
- Make sure that progress towards the outcome required by the users remains consistent from the user perspective;
- Promote and maintain focus on the desired project outcome;
- Ensure that any user resources required for the project are made available;
- Approve Product Descriptions for those products which act as inputs or outputs (interim or final) from the supplier function, or will affect them directly and that the products are signed off once completed;
- Prioritize and contribute user opinions on Project Board decisions on whether to implement recommendations on proposed changes;
- Resolve user requirements and priority conflicts;
- Provide the user view on recommended follow-on actions;
- Brief and advise user management on all matters concerning the project.

The Project Assurance responsibilities of the Senior User are that:

- Specification of the user's needs is accurate, complete and unambiguous;
- Development of the solution at all stages is monitored to ensure that it will meet the user's needs and is progressing towards that target;
- Impact of potential changes is evaluated from the user point of view;
- Risks to the users are constantly monitored;
- Testing of the product at all stages has the appropriate user representation;
- Quality control procedures are used correctly to ensure products meet user requirements;
- User liaison is functioning effectively.

Where the project's size, complexity or importance warrants it, the Senior User may delegate the responsibility and authority for some of the Project Assurance responsibility.

B.4 SENIOR SUPPLIER

B.4.1 General

Represents the interests of those designing, developing, facilitating, procuring, and implementing the project products. The Senior Supplier role must have the authority to commit or acquire supplier resources required.

If necessary, more than one person may be required to represent the suppliers.

B.4.2 Specific Responsibility

- Agree objectives for specialist activities;
- Make sure that progress towards the outcome remains consistent from the supplier perspective;
- Promote and maintain focus on the desired project outcome from the point of view of supplier management;
- Ensure that the supplier resources required for the project are made available;
- Approve Product Descriptions for specialist products;
- Contribute supplier opinions on Project Board decisions on whether to implement recommendations on proposed changes;
- Resolve supplier requirements and priority conflicts;
- Arbitrate on, and ensure resolution of any specialist priority or resource conflicts;
- Brief non-technical management on specialist aspects of the project.

The Senior Supplier is responsible for the specialist Project Assurance of the project. The specialist Project Assurance role responsibilities are to:

- Advise on the selection of technical strategy, design and methods;
- Ensure that any specialist and operating standards defined for the project are met and used to good effect;
- Monitor potential changes and their impact on the correctness, completeness and assurance of products against their Product Description from a technical perspective;
- Monitor any risks in the specialist and production aspects of the project;
- Ensure quality control procedures are used correctly so that products adhere to technical requirements.

If warranted, some of this Project Assurance responsibility may be delegated. Depending on the particular customer/supplier environment of a project, the customer may also wish to appoint people to specialist Project Assurance roles.

B.5 PROJECT MANAGER

B.5.1 General

The Project Manager has the authority to run the project on a day-to-day basis on behalf of the Project Board within the constraints laid down by the board.

In a customer/supplier environment the Project Manager will normally come from the customer organization.

B.5.2 Responsibility

The Project Manager's prime responsibility is to ensure that the project produces the required products, to the required standard of quality and within the specified constraints of time and cost. The Project Manager is also responsible for the project producing a result that is capable of achieving the benefits defined in the Business Case.

B.5.3 Specific Responsibility

- Manage the production of the required products;
- Direct and motivate the project team;
- Plan and monitor the project;
- Agree any delegation and use of Project Assurance roles required by the Project Board;
- Produce the project contract;
- Prepare Project, Stage and, if necessary, Exception Plans in conjunction with Team Managers and appointed Project Assurance roles, and agree them with the Project Board;
- Manage business and project risks, including the development of contingency plans;
- Liaise with programme management if the project is part of a programme;
- Liaise with programme management or related projects to ensure that work is neither overlooked nor duplicated;
- Take responsibility for overall progress and use of resources, and initiate corrective action where necessary;
- Be responsible for change control and any required configuration management;
- Report to the Project Board through Highlight Reports and end stage assessments;
- Liaise with the Project Board or its appointed Project Assurance roles to assure the overall direction and Project Assurance of the project;
- Agree technical and quality strategy with appropriate members of the Project Board;
- Prepare the Lessons Report;
- Prepare any follow-on action recommendations required;
- Prepare the End Project Report;
- Identify and obtain any support and advice required for the management, planning and control of the project;
- Be responsible for project administration;
- Liaise with any suppliers or account managers.

B.6 TEAM MANAGER

B.6.1 General

The allocation of this role to one or more people is optional. Where the project does not warrant the use of a Team Manager, the Project Manager takes the role.

The Project Manager may find that it is beneficial to delegate the authority and responsibility for planning the creation of certain products and managing a team of technicians to produce those products. There are many reasons why it may be decided to employ this role. Some of these are the size of the project, the particular specialist skills or knowledge needed for certain products, geographical location of some team members and the preferences of the Project Board.

The Team Manager's prime responsibility is to ensure production of those products defined by the Project Manager to an appropriate quality, in a timescale and at a cost acceptable to the Project Board. The Team Manager reports to and takes direction from the Project Manager.

The use of this role should be discussed by the Project Manager with the Project Board and, if the role is required, planned at the outset of the project. This is discussed in the *Starting up a Project* (SU) and *Initiating a Project* (IP) processes.

B.6.2 Specific Goals

- Prepare plans for the team's work and agree these with the Project Manager;
- Receive authorization from the Project Manager to create products (Work Package);
- Manage the team;
- Direct, plan and monitor the team work;
- Take responsibility for the progress of the team's work and use of team resources, and initiate corrective action where necessary within the constraints laid down by the Project Manager;
- Advise the Project Manager of any deviations from plan, recommend corrective action, and help prepare any appropriate Exception Plans;
- Pass products which have been completed and approved in line with the agreed Work Package requirements back to the Project Manager;
- Ensure all issues are properly reported to the person maintaining the Issue Register;
- Ensure the evaluation of issues which arise within the team's work and recommend action to the Project Manager;
- Liaise with any Project Assurance roles;
- Attend any stage assessments as directed by the Project Manager;
- Arrange and lead team checkpoints;
- Ensure that quality controls of the team's work are planned and performed correctly;

- Maintain, or ensure the maintenance of team files;
- Identify and advise the Project Manager of any risks associated with a Work Package;
- Ensure that such risks are entered on the Risk Register;
- Manage specific risks as directed by the Project Manager.

B.7 PROJECT ASSURANCE

B.7.1 General

The Project Board members do not work full time on the project, therefore they place a great deal of reliance on the Project Manager. Although they receive regular reports from the Project Manager, there may always be the questions at the back of their minds, 'Are things really going as well as we are being told?', 'Are any problems being hidden from us?', 'Is the solution going to be what we want?', 'Are we suddenly going to find that the project is over-budget or late?' There are other questions. The supplier may have a quality assurance function charged with the responsibility to check that all projects are adhering to the quality system.

All of these points mean that there is a need in the project organization for an independent monitoring of all aspects of the project's performance and products. This is the Project Assurance function.

To cater for a small project, we start by identifying these Project Assurance functions as part of the role of each Project Board member. According to the needs and desires of the Project Board, any of these Project Assurance responsibilities can be delegated, as long as the recipients are independent of the Project Manager and the rest of the project management team. Any appointed Project Assurance jobs assure the project on behalf of one or more members of the Project Board.

It is not mandatory that all Project Assurance roles be delegated. Each of the Project Assurance roles which is delegated may be assigned to one individual or shared. The Project Board decides when a Project Assurance role needs to be delegated. It may be for the entire project or only part of it. The person or persons filling a Project Assurance role may be changed during the project at the request of the Project Board. Any use of Project Assurance roles needs to be planned at initiation stage, otherwise resource usage and costs for Project Assurance could easily get out of control.

There is no stipulation on how many Project Assurance roles there must be. Each Project Board role has Project Assurance responsibility. Again, each project should determine what support, if any, each Project Board role needs to achieve this Project Assurance.

For example, an international standards group, such as ISO, may certify the supplier's work standards. A requirement of the certification is that there will be some form of quality assurance function that is required to monitor the supplier's work. Some of the Senior Supplier's Project Assurance responsibility may be delegated to this function. Note that they would only be delegated. The Project Board member retains accountability. Any delegation should be documented. The customer's quality assurance could include verification by an external party that the Project Board is performing its functions correctly.

Assurance covers all interests of a project, including business, user and supplier.

Project Assurance has to be independent of the Project Manager; therefore, the Project Board cannot delegate any of its Project Assurance responsibility to the Project Manager.

B.7.2 Specific Responsibility

The implementation of the Project Assurance responsibility needs to answer the question 'What is to be assured?' A list of possibilities would include:

- Maintenance of thorough liaison throughout the project between the supplier and the customer;
- Customer needs and expectations are being met or managed;
- Risks are being controlled;
- Adherence to the Business Case;
- Constant reassessment of the value-for-money solution;
- Fit with the overall programme or company strategy;
- The right people being involved in writing Product Descriptions, especially the quality criteria;
- The right people being planned to be involved in quality checking at the correct points in the product's development;
- Ensuring that staff are properly trained in the quality checking procedures;
- Ensuring that quality checking follow-up actions are dealt with correctly;
- Ensuring that the quality checking procedures are being correctly followed;
- An acceptable solution is developed;
- Project remains viable;
- The scope of the project is not 'creeping up' unnoticed;
- Focus on the business need is maintained;
- Internal and external communications are working;
- Applicable standards are being used;
- Any legislative constraints are being observed;
- The needs of specialist interests, e.g. security, are being observed;
- Adherence to quality assurance standards.

It is not enough to believe that standards will be obeyed. It is not enough to ensure that a project is well set up and justified at the outset. All the aspects listed above need to be checked throughout the project as part of ensuring that it remains consistent with and continues to meet a business need and that no change to the external environment affects the validity of the project. This includes monitoring stage and team planning, Work Package and quality review preparation.

B.8 PROJECT SUPPORT

B.8.1 General

The provision of any project support on a formal basis is optional. It is driven by the needs of the individual project and Project Manager. Project Support could be in the form of advice on project management tools and administrative services, such as filing, the collection of actual data, to one or more related projects. Where set up as an official body, Project Support can act as a repository for lessons learned, and a central source of expertise in specialist support tools.

One support function that must be considered is that of configuration management. Depending on the project size and environment, there may be a need to formalize this, and it quickly becomes a task with which the Project Manager cannot cope without support. See the chapter on Configuration Management for details of the work.

B.8.2 Main Tasks

The following is a suggested list of tasks:

Administration
- Administer change control;
- Set up and maintain project files;
- Establish document control procedures;
- Compile, copy and distribute all project management products;
- Collect actual data and forecasts;
- Update plans;
- Administer the quality review process;
- Administer Project Board meetings;
- Assist with the compilation of reports;

Advice
- Specialist knowledge (e.g. estimating, management of risk);
- Specialist tool expertise (e.g. planning and control tools, risk analysis);
- Specialist techniques;
- Standards.

Product-based Planning

Product-based Planning is fundamental to PRINCE2 and I thoroughly recommend it. There are two reasons for this. First, a project delivers products, not activities, so why begin at a lower level? The second reason is about quality. We can measure the quality of a product. The quality of an activity can only be measured by the quality of its outcome (the product).

Product-based planning has three components:

1. Product Breakdown Structure (PBS);
2. Product Descriptions (PD);
3. Product Flow Diagram (PFD).

C.1 PRODUCT BREAKDOWN STRUCTURE

Most planning methods begin a plan by thinking of the activities to be undertaken, and listing these in a hierarchical structure called a Work Breakdown Structure (WBS). These activities, however, depend on what products are required to be produced by the project, so the correct start point for a plan is to list the products. In fact, by jumping straight to the lower level of detail of activities, it is possible to miss some vital products and hence vital activities from the plan.

A PBS is a hierarchy of the products whose creation is to be planned (apart from creating products, there might be some that you purchase or obtain from other sources). At the top or core of the hierarchy is the final end product, e.g. a computer system, a new yacht, a department relocated to a new building. This is then broken down into its major constituents at the next level. Each constituent is then broken down into its parts, and this process continues until the planner has reached the level of detail required for the plan.

There are three types of 'product' that might appear in a PBS: simple products, intermediate 'products' and external products. Let us explain these terms.

C.1.1 Simple Products

Products at the lowest level of any branch of the hierarchy are 'simple products', so called because they are not broken down into more detail. These require a PD to be written for each of them.

The lowest level on a PBS is not fixed. It depends on the level of detail required in the plan to allow the Project Board, Project Manager or Team Manager to exercise an appropriate level of control.

C.1.2 Intermediate Products

'Intermediate product' is a term used to describe a product that is broken down into further products, i.e. anything between the top level and the bottom level of the PBS is called 'intermediate'.

An intermediate product may be a product itself where one or more activities, such as assembly or testing, will need to be applied to that product after its sub-products have been produced. These products should appear in the PFD and require a PD to be written for them. As with simple products, they should be represented in the diagrams in a rectangle.

Another type of intermediate 'product' is not a 'product' itself. It may simply be used as a trigger to further thoughts by the planner of what actual products are required. An example of this type of intermediate product might be 'training' – this is not a product in itself, but is used as a starting point to think of real products, such as lecture notes, student notes, exercises and case studies. This style of intermediate product may be used in the PBS but should *not* be carried forward into the PFD.

Both types of intermediate product may appear in the PBS. Let us take an example of a project whose objective is to purchase new equipment. There are many complications that can occur in purchasing, but for the sake of an example we shall keep this simple.

C.1.3 External Products

The PBS should include not only the products to be delivered by the project, but also any products that already exist or are to be supplied from external sources. The Project Manager is not accountable for the creation of external products, but the project does need the product(s) in order to achieve its objectives. A plan must therefore include any external products required to achieve the plan's objectives, plus suitable dependencies on these external products.

A different symbol should be used to identify external products. An ellipse is used to indicate an external product in both the PBS and the PFD. It should be noted that it is the product that is shown, not the source of the product. For example, if a plan needs the local train timetable, 'rail timetable' would be the external product, not the relevant train company.

There are two products in our example that will come from outside the project. 'Purchasing process details' already exist in the company and the Project Manager has no control over whether the potential suppliers will actually submit a tender (Figure C.1).

A PBS can be shown as a hierarchical diagram, a mind map or an indented list. The example is shown in all three styles.

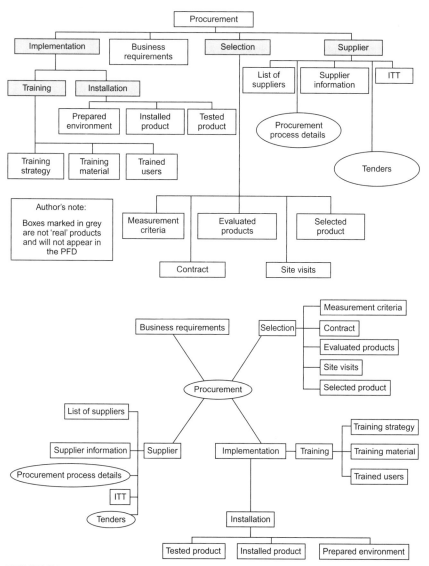

FIGURE C.1   Example Product Breakdown Structure for a purchasing project.

C.2 PRODUCT DESCRIPTION

For each identified product, a PD is produced. Its creation forces the planner to consider if sufficient information is known about the product in order to plan its production. It is also the first time that the quality of the product is considered. The quality criteria should be measurable statements on the expected quality of the product and what type of quality checking will be required. As an example, 'faster' and 'better' are not measurable and would therefore not be useful quality criteria. 'Able to bear a weight of 10 tons' and 'maximum response time of 3 seconds' are examples of measurable criteria.

The purposes of writing a PD are, therefore, to provide a guide:

- To the planner on how much effort will be required to create the product;
- To the author of the product on what is required;
- Against which the finished product can be measured.

These descriptions are a vital checklist to be used at a quality check of the related products.

The description should contain:

- The purpose of the product;
- The composition of the product;
- The products from which it is derived;
- Any standards for format and presentation;
- The quality criteria to be applied to the product;
- The quality verification method to be used.

The PD is given to both the product's creator and those who will verify its quality (Cartoon C.1(a) and (b)).

Garden Shed Product Description
Purpose: To house my garden tools

Hmmm, I see a nice cheap solution.

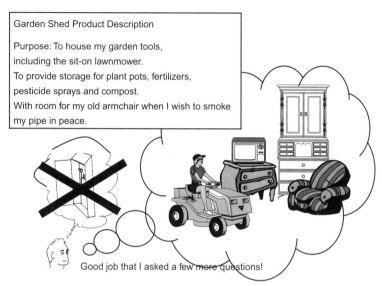

Garden Shed Product Description

Purpose: To house my garden tools,
including the sit-on lawnmower.
To provide storage for plant pots, fertilizers,
pesticide sprays and compost.
With room for my old armchair when I wish to smoke
my pipe in peace.

Good job that I asked a few more questions!

CARTOON C.1(A) AND (B)   Product Description.

C.2.1 Project Product Description

The first step in Product-based Planning is to actually to write a PD of the final product. This helps establish if the customer actually understands and can describe the required final product and helps establish the customer's quality expectations (and therefore needs to be done during the SU process).

C.3 PRODUCT FLOW DIAGRAM

The PFD is a diagram showing the sequence in which the products have to be produced and the dependencies between them. It is produced after the PBS. Figure C.2 is a PFD for the purchasing example.

A PFD normally needs only two symbols: a rectangle to contain the products, an ellipse to show any external products and arrows to show the dependencies.

Basic example of the use of external products, product groupings and simple products

'From the scenario provided by the lecturer draw a PBS and a PFD. When you have completed the PBS, the lecturer will give you an envelope containing the names of two products for which you then have to create PDs.'

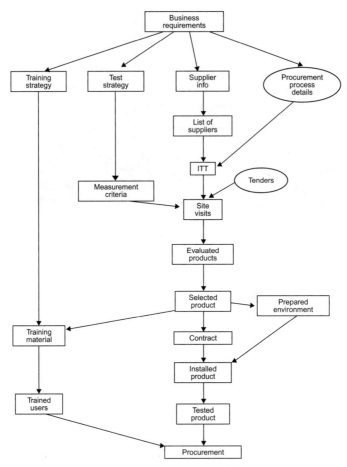

FIGURE C.2 Example Product Flow Diagram for a purchasing project.

The PBS and PFD for this statement (not for whatever is the subject in the scenario) would look like Figures C.3 and C.4 respectively.

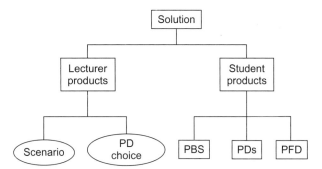

FIGURE C.3   Basic example Product Breakdown Structure.

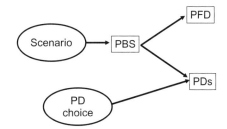

FIGURE C.4   Basic example Product Flow Diagram.

Quality Review

This is a team method of checking a document's quality by a review process. The purpose of a quality review is to inspect a document for errors in a planned, independent, controlled and documented manner and ensure that any errors found are fixed.

The quality review technique is a structured way of reviewing documents to ensure that all aspects are properly covered. It needs to be used with common sense to avoid the dangers of an over-bureaucratic approach but with the intent to follow the procedures laid down (to ensure nothing is missed).

The major aim is to improve product quality. There are several subordinate objectives. These are to:

- Trap errors as early as possible;
- Encourage the concept of documents as team property rather than belonging to an individual;
- Enhance product status data (i.e. not only has the creator declared it finished, but others have confirmed that it is of good quality);
- Monitor the use of standards;
- Spread knowledge of the document among those whose own products may interact with it (Cartoon D.1).

Quality review documentation, when filed in the quality file, provides, together with the Quality Register, a record that the document was inspected, that any errors found were corrected and that the corrections were themselves checked. Knowing that a document has been checked and declared error-free provides a more confident basis to move ahead and use that document as the basis of future work than simply taking the word of the creator.

D.1 ROLES AT THE QUALITY REVIEW

The roles involved in a quality review are:

- The presenter, who is normally the author of the document being reviewed. This role has to ensure that the reviewers have all the required information in order to perform their job. This means getting a copy of the document from

CARTOON D.1 Quality review.

the Configuration Librarian to them during the preparation phase, plus any documents needed to put it in context. Then the presenter has to answer questions about the document during the review until a decision can be reached on whether there is an error or not. Finally the presenter will be responsible for most, if not all, of the correcting work. The presenter must not be allowed to be defensive about the document.

- The chair. An open, objective attitude is needed. The chair has the following required attributes:
  - Sufficient authority to control the review;
  - Understands the quality review process thoroughly;
  - Chairmanship experience.

The chair is responsible for ensuring that the quality review is properly organized and that it runs smoothly during all of its phases.

For the preparation phase this includes checking that administrative procedures have been carried out and that the right people have been invited. This needs consultation with any appointed Project Assurance roles and reference to the Stage Plan.

- The reviewers, who must be competent to assess the product from their particular viewpoints.
- An administrator, someone who will note any required actions resulting from the review. This role may be taken by one of the other attendees, but if the review has several attendees it is sensible to give this role to someone other than the chair, so that the chair can concentrate on controlling the review.

It must be remembered that all these are roles. They must all be present at a quality review, but a person may take on more than one role.

D.1.2 People Involved

The interests of parties who should be considered when drawing up the list of attendees are:

- The product author;
- Those with Project Assurance responsibilities delegated by the Project Board;
- The customer;
- Staff who will use the document as a basis for further work;
- Other staff whose work will be affected by the product;
- Specialists in the relevant product area;
- Standards representatives.

D.2 PHASES

There are three distinct phases within the quality review procedure: preparation, review and follow-up.

D.2.1 Phase 1 – Preparation

The objective of this phase is to examine the document under review and to create a list of questions for the review.

The chair checks with the presenter that the document will be ready on time. If not, the Project Manager is advised. This will lead to an update of the Stage Plan and the Quality Register. The chair ensures that the team of reviewers is agreed, that they will all be available and that the venue has been arranged. Project Assurance may wish to be involved in confirming that the list of reviewers is satisfactory to them.

An invitation is sent out, giving the time and place for the review with copies of the document, the relevant Product Description and any checklist available. This should be done with sufficient time before the review to allow the reviewers time to examine the document and to provide a question list to the presenter.

Each reviewer will study the document and supporting documents (including the quality criteria in the Product Description), annotate the document with any spelling or grammatical errors and complete a question list.

A copy of the question lists will, wherever possible, be sent to the presenter before the review. The presenter and the chair should review these to allow the chair to set up an agenda, prioritize the questions and roughly allocate time to each point. To save time at the review, the presenter can acknowledge questions that identify agreed errors.

D.2.2 Phase 2 – Review

The objective of the review is to agree a list of any actions needed to correct or complete the document. The chair and the presenter do not have to reconcile these actions at the meeting – it is sufficient for the chair and reviewers to agree that a particular area needs correction or at least reexamination. Provided that the action is logged, the reviewers have an opportunity in the next phase to confirm that action has been taken.

The chair opens the meeting and introduces those present if necessary. Timing (suggested maximum of 2 hours) is announced.

The presenter then 'walks through' the questions in detail. This will be determined by the reviewers' question lists already sent to the presenter. If it is found that any part is understood and accepted, there is no point in walking through it.

The chair controls the discussion during the review, ensuring that no arguments or solutions are discussed (other than obvious and immediately accepted solutions!). The administrator notes actions on a follow-up action list. No other minutes are taken of the review.

At the conclusion of the walk-through, the chair asks the administrator to read back the actions and determines responsibility for correction of any points. A target date is set for each action and the initials of the reviewer(s) who will sign off each corrective action as it is completed and found acceptable are recorded on the follow-up action list by the administrator.

The chair, after seeking the reviewers' and presenter's opinions, will decide on the outcome of the review. There can be one of three outcomes:

1. The document is error-free;
2. The document will be acceptable on completion of the actions noted;
3. There is so much corrective work to be done that the entire document needs to be re-reviewed.

In the latter case, the chair will advise the Project Manager so that the Stage Plan can be updated. The Quality Register is updated. A result notification will be completed and the documents attached. These forms will be filed in the quality file.

The reviewers' question lists, copies of the document (probably containing the reviewer's annotations) and any other relevant documentation is collected by the chair and passed to the presenter to assist in the follow-up.

D.2.3 Phase 3 – Follow-Up

The objective of the follow-up phase is to ensure that all actions identified on the follow-up action list are dealt with.

The presenter takes the follow-up action list away from the review and evaluates, discusses and corrects, if necessary, all the errors.

When an error has been fixed, the presenter will obtain sign-off from whoever is nominated on the follow-up action list. This person may be the reviewer who raised the query initially, but other reviewers have the option of checking the correction.

When all the errors have been reconciled and sign-off obtained, the chair will confirm that the document is complete and sign off the follow-up action list. The documents will be filed in the Quality Register and the Stage Plan updated.

D.3 QUALITY REVIEW RESPONSIBILITIES

D.3.1 Chair's Responsibilities

D.3.1.1 Preparation

- Check with the presenter that the product is ready for review.
- If not, ensure that the Stage Plan is updated, e.g. a revised completion date.
- Consult with the presenter and those performing Project Assurance roles to confirm appropriate reviewers.
- Agree the amount of preparation time required with the presenter (and reviewers, if this is appropriate).
- Arrange a time, location and duration for the review in consultation with the presenter and the reviewers.
- Advise the Project Manager if there is to be any delay in holding the review.
- Arrange for copies of any relevant checklist or standard to be provided.
- Ensure the Configuration Librarian provides Product Descriptions and product copies for all reviewers.
- Send an invitation, Product Description, document copy, blank question list and product checklist (if there is one) to each reviewer.
- Send a copy of the invitation to the presenter.
- Decide if a short overview presentation of the document to the reviewers is required as part of the preparation, and arrange it if it is.
- Arrange with the reviewers for collection of their question lists prior to the review.
- In consulation with the presenter, create an agenda for the review from the question lists. Agree any obvious errors in the document with the presenter. Prioritize the questions and roughly allocate time.
- Confirm attendance with each reviewer shortly before the review. If a reviewer cannot attend, ensure that the reviewer's question list is made out and submitted. If too many reviewers cannot attend, reschedule the review and inform the Project Manager of the delay.
- If necessary, rehearse the review with the presenter.

D.3.1.2 Review

- Provide a copy of the agenda to all attendees.
- Open the review, stating objectives and apologizing for any non-attendees.

- Decide whether the reviewers present and the question lists from any unable to attend are adequate to review the document. If not, the review should be stopped, rescheduled and the Project Manager advised.
- Identify any errors in the document already agreed by the presenter and ensure that these are documented on the follow-up action list.
- Step through the agenda, with the appropriate reviewer enlarging where necessary on the question.
- Allow reasonable discussion on each question between presenter and reviewers to decide if action is required.
- Ensure that the administrator documents any agreed actions required on a follow-up action list.
- Prevent any discussion of possible solutions or matters of style.
- Ensure that reviewers are given a chance to voice their comments.
- Where agreement cannot be reached on a point in a reasonable time frame, declare it an action point and note the reviewer(s) concerned.
- Where necessary, decide on the premature close of the review in the light of the comments made.
- If faults are identified in documents not under review, ensure that an issue is raised and sent to the Configuration Librarian.
- Collect any annotated documents detailing minor or typographical errors.
- Read back the follow-up action list and obtain confirmation from the presenter and reviewers that it is complete and correct.
- Identify who is to be involved in working on each action item. Obtain a target date for completion of the work.
- Agree with the reviewers who is to approve the work done on each action item and note this on the follow-up action list.
- Pass the Action List and all copies of the annotated document to the presenter. Lodge a copy of the follow-up action list in the Quality Register.
- Decide with the reviewers what the status of the review is. It can be:
  - Complete with no errors discovered;
  - Complete with some rework required;
  - In need of rework and another review.
- If the review is incomplete, recommend a course of action to the Project Manager. There are five possible courses of action. The last two of these are not recommended:
  - The document should be reworked prior to another review;
  - The review should be reconvened to finish with no interim need for rework;
  - The review should be reconvened without rework with a different set of reviewers;
  - The review should be declared complete, the errors found so far corrected and the rest of the document accepted as is;
  - The review should be abandoned and the document used as is, i.e. none of the errors corrected, but noted in an issue.

D.3.1.3 Follow-Up

- Monitor the correction of errors and sign off the follow-up action list when all corrections have been approved.
- If an action cannot be taken within the time agreed, the chair and the presenter may decide to transfer it to an issue as a possible error. This requires the agreement of the Project Manager. The follow-up action list is updated with the Issue Register number and those waiting to sign off the action item informed.
- On completion and sign-off of all action items, sign off the follow-up action list as complete and file it in the Quality Register with copies to all reviewers. Update the Quality Register.
- Supervise the passage of the error-free document to the Configuration Librarian.

D.3.2 Producer's Responsibilities

D.3.2.1 Preparation

- Ask the Project Manager to nominate a chair if none is identified in the Stage Plan.
- Confirm with the chair that the document is ready for review. This should occur several days prior to the planned review date to allow for preparation time.
- Confirm the attendees with the chair and those holding Project Assurance responsibilities.
- Agree with the chair and reviewers the length of preparation time needed and review location.
- Assess the question lists from the reviewers, identifying any errors in the document that can be agreed without further discussion.
- Agree the agenda with the chair in light of the question lists.

D.3.2.2 Review

- Answer any questions about the document.
- Offer an opinion to the chair on whether a question has highlighted an error in the document.
- If the review is judged to be complete, collect from the chair the follow-up action list and any annotated copies of the document from the reviewers.

D.3.2.3 Follow-Up

- Resolve all allocated action items.
- Obtain sign-off for each action item from the nominated reviewers.
- If an action item cannot be resolved within a reasonable time frame, then decide with the chair to transfer it to an issue. An alternative is to agree new target dates.

- Pass the follow-up action list to the chair on resolution of all the action items.

D.3.3 Reviewer Responsibilities

D.3.3.1 Preparation

- Consult the Product Description and any pertinent checklists and standards against which the document should be judged.
- Allow sufficient time to prepare for the review.
- Consult any necessary source documents from which the document is derived.
- Annotate any spelling or typographical mistakes on the document copy, but do not add these to the question list.
- Check the document for completeness, defects, ambiguities, inconsistencies, lack of clarity or deviations from standards. Note any such items on the question list.
- Forward the question list to the chair in advance of the review. If possible, this should be done early enough to give the presenter time to digest the points and prepare an agenda with the chair.
- Forward a question list and the annotated document copy to the chair if unable to attend the review.

D.3.3.2 Review

- Ensure that the points noted on the question list are raised at the review.
- Restrict comments to faults in the document under review.
- Avoid attempting to redesign the document.
- Avoid 'improvement' comments if the document meets requirements and standards.
- Verify and approve the follow-up action list as complete and correct when read back by the chair.
- Agree to assist in the resolution of any action items if requested by the chair.
- Request to check and sign off any action items either raised personally or which impact the reviewer's area of expertise or interest.

D.3.3.3 Follow-Up

- Work with the presenter to resolve any allocated action item.
- Check and sign off those action items where allocated as reviewer.

Quality reviews can be either formal (i.e. a scheduled meeting conducted as described above) or informal (i.e. a 'get-together' between two people to informally walk through a document). A variation on a formal review is to have the reviewers forward their question lists, but only the chair and the presenter do the actual review.

Informal quality reviews will follow a similar format to the formal quality review – the paperwork emerging from both meetings is similar. The main difference will be the informality of the proceedings during the three phases and the overall time required.

For informal quality reviews two people can be given the task of checking each other's work on an ongoing basis. Alternatively, an experienced person can be asked to regularly hold reviews of an inexperienced person's work as it develops.

Factors in deciding whether a formal or informal review is needed are:

- The importance of the document;
- Whether it is a final deliverable;
- Whether it is the source for a number of other documents;
- The author's experience;
- Who the document's consumer is;
- Whether it is a review of a partial document.

Index